New European Baking

LAUREL KRATOCHVILA · PHOTOS BY **MAŁGOSIA MINTA**

New European Baking

99 Recipes for Breads, Brioches, and Pastries

PRESTEL

Munich · London · New York

Contents

Everyone has to start somewhere ...

Conjure up an image of Europe and you'll eventually land on bakeries. It may be after the grand monuments and terraced cafés, but you'll get there. Walk into a European bakery and you'll know at once, from the shape of the bread, whether you're in Riga or Paris, Rome or Warsaw, whether it's winter or summer. Bread can help you figure out where you are. At least, it did for me.

I didn't start my European life as a baker. I started as a bartender. I was 23 and smoking wouldn't be banned in Prague for another decade and a half, so I drafted heady Pilsners and ignored the possibility that I was a cliché. The Atlantic Ocean and half a continent seemed like enough distance to avoid the romantic entanglements and adult obligations on the horizon. Anything, so that I didn't have to go back to Boston.

There's a sweet spot when you work winter nights in Prague. Right around 4:30am. The public transport hasn't started up and the streetlamps won't turn off for another hour. There's a frigid fog everywhere and it's quieter than a forest. Bruce Chatwin wrote in his novel *Utz*: "Prague, after all, was a city where you heard the snowflakes falling." And indeed it is. So I would walk all the way home, clear across Prague, this big wedding cake I didn't have to share with anyone.

On those predawn walks towards my bed, the only other people I saw were bakers. The bakeries of the city — pekárny — were tucked into the ground floors of residential buildings, but they were largely semi-industrial and still recovering from the consolidation of communism. Through steamed up windows you could see piles of fluffy white rohlíky, sprinkled with caraway and salt, and

racks of šumava, stodgy rye loaves that never go stale. On the sweet side, there were simple koláčky, round Bohemian danishes with plum compote or poppy seeds and a smattering of streusel.

My favorite pekárna had a window that opened right onto the street. If the door wasn't open yet, you could knock on the window and a baker would hand you a rohlik for a few cents. The air smelled like clean yeast and the bakers wore all white. By contrast, I had beer on my shirt and my hair smelled like cigarettes. I should have felt solidarity with these men — after all, weren't we the only people awake? But I didn't. Their job looked like fun and I was jealous.

The bartending and early morning walks didn't last forever though. I took a day job selling books for a slow-to-smile Czech man and when I walked home during sensible afternoon hours, the bakers had already left. But I couldn't stop thinking about them. Bakery has a funny way of finding people.

I ended up marrying that Czech bookseller and we moved to Berlin, thinking it would be a good place to open another bookstore. Spoiler alert: It wasn't. The market was hard to read. Or rather: Did Berliners read? Maybe they just went to techno clubs? What was the mutual exclusivity of those two? We weren't sure, but regardless, the new store wasn't working. In the age of Amazon, cafés in bookstores had become de rigueur and it didn't seem like we had much of a choice. So we tiled a storage closet, threw in an Ikea oven and a coffee machine, and I started baking.

The failing bookstore compounded a homesickness I'd been feeling for a while, driving me to comfort-bake Yiddish classics in that tiny kitchen.

Mandel bread, rugelach, challah, and bagels. Lots of bagels. There was something tongue-in-cheek about baking these geriatric favorites. After all, hadn't my family left this part of the world a hundred years before, so that we didn't have to bake for a living? I wish I could say I gave more thought to opening a Jewish bakery in Berlin, but I didn't. I gave the storage closet bakery a family name — Fine — and Fine Bagels officially opened its doors in 2012.

In formerly divided Berlin, traditional bakeries are more rare than in other parts of Germany — even today. Still, Germany is a bread culture, with consumption rivaling France, and people were open to looking outside of their traditions if it meant enjoying an artisan product. The openness of my clientele and the unpolished Berlin food scene gave me space to learn and somehow the tiny bakery thrived.

There was one problem: I'd put the cart before the horse. In Europe, you need a piece of paper to do everything. "Everything-everything?" You ask. Yes. You want to work a cash register in a supermarket? There's a paper for that. You want to make bread? Better go get a certificate. If I was going to continue baking, I was going to have to become a registered artisan. This meant school, exams, and apprenticeships. There was no way around it.

I packed up my two-seater Citroën, drove fourteen hours to the Loire Valley, and for the next two years, I was part of the French system of boulangerie education. This meant formal trade schools mixed with apprenticeships that led me from rural country bakeries to traditional Parisian boulangeries. And, it turned out, all those years ago in Prague, I'd been right to be jealous. It's a wonderful profession.

Along the way, I got to know some of the most brilliant voices in the new wave of European bakery, people I'm not just proud to call friends and mentors, but whose stories I was inspired to tell — in part because they reflect my own. They are people who came into the craft through often unconventional and unusual means and who simultaneously challenge orthodoxy and reinvigorate what is good about the old ways. These bakers come from across the continent and across traditions but have more in common than it might seem.

The question, though, is why this book? And what makes an ancient profession in one of its most important strongholds new? Croissants have been around forever. So has a nice loaf of country bread. It's not like it's the most innovative profession, is it? To understand what's new, we need to look back to see what's been lost, but we don't have to go too far back. The twentieth century was generally a bad time for European bakeries. Put kindly, bakery went to shit. Two world wars and an Iron Curtain didn't help the situation, but industrialization, more than anything, was to blame. Technology changed everything about bakery. Commercial yeast meant bread that once rose overnight could now be made in less than an hour. Agricultural monocultures meant bakers could use flour from grains grown far away. Rapid transport meant factories could produce and ship pastries across countries. But with these seeming positives came a host of negatives. Regional specialties became endangered. Nutrition leaked away. Craftsmanship diminished. Traditions faded. Gluten became feared.

Despite all this, the independent bakery managed to survive — in form, if not quality. Select bakers carried the candles of tradition throughout it all, fighting the good fight for real food. They maintained

connections to grain growers, handcrafted their pastries, and nurtured sourdoughs. Through the legacy of these torchbearers and independent bakeries the movement has been finding a way back — as well as a way forward.

Now, a new generation of bakers is shaping and popularizing a better future for craftsmanship, while paying close attention to sourcing, community, and traditions both cultural and methodical. These new bakers are returning to traditional sourdough and slow fermentation. They're reinvigorating hand-crafted baker's pastries and putting lost bakery species back into circulation. They're reconnecting to their terroir and the communities they serve. And they're breaking free from the rigid gatekeeping system to create their own paths.

It's a cultural narrative as much as a social one. Until recently, most European bakeries were exceptionally male-dominated. Bakery is famously the last of the culinary fields to see real gender integration, but women are finally coming to the forefront of the profession. And, as we revive

enthusiasm for the local and the seasonal, it's uninhibited by the weight of history. Sometimes the most innovative work comes from those who have long been outsiders.

As we use our stories to inform our baking and our values, the Potemkin villages of last century's baking are rapidly falling out of favor. We're finally discovering the road back to quality and craftsmanship. Whether you read this book as a curious interloper, a seasoned baker, or as someone considering trading their day job for a turn in the boulangerie, this collection of recipes and stories is a look at the new European bakery — a movement that's at times contradictory but always delicious. You'll find the practical basics that inform the craft, as well as nods to history, but also the playful experimentation that only stepping away from tradition can bring.

For my part, it's been a privilege to work as a baker on a continent that respects bakers and an even bigger privilege to tell some of our stories. Every day I get to make something useful with my hands — I worry I might never have an existential crisis again.

Using this Book

This book is, above all, a practical book. Each chapter explores an area of bakery expertise — breads, enriched doughs, laminated pastries, and tarte doughs. There are several base recipes and technique tutorials to start each chapter and I suggest mastering the basics before moving on to more complicated recipes. Bakery is a craft that builds on itself, so think of these recipes as projects you can use to guide your home baking to bakery quality baking.

Read the Recipe

One of the most important aspects of baking is good organization and to really be organized, it's essential to read the recipe all the way through before starting your project. It will help you plan how your baking fits into your day, as well as anticipate any time-sensitive steps or necessary ingredients. Trust me on this. Recipes aren't like novels — no one wants a surprise ending!

A Note on Measures

If I can tell a home baker anything, it's this: Throw out your measuring cups and buy a kitchen scale. Volume measurements — as in American cups — will never give you the kind of accuracy and consistency of using a scale. And not only will you have better results, but you will also understand the logic of recipes better. Recipes are often based on proportions of ingredients by weight. Take, for example, a classic pound cake, which uses the same weight of butter, flour, and eggs. When you measure by weight, you see the 1-1-1 ratio easily. In cups and spoons, however, the measurements appear totally random!

The advantage of weighing ingredients is especially noticeable in bread and dough recipes in which the proportions are calculated in relation to the total quantity of flour — known as a baker's percentage. Using baker's percentages, the total amount of flour is always 100 percent, with all other ingredient quantities relative to that. So, if a recipe with 500g of flour calls for 10g of salt, we know the baker's percentage of salt is 2 percent. Looking at recipes with baker's percentages also makes for easy scaling, so you can make more or less of a recipe.

When using a kitchen scale, there are only a few things to remember: Always tare (zero) the scale before you weigh and always double check your units. You want to be sure you're measuring in grams rather than ounces, or vice versa. Use a kitchen scale that can weigh precisely to the gram and up to 2 kilos (4 ½ pounds).

Ingredients used in larger quantities, including liquid ingredients, are given in both metric weights and American cups. Ingredients like yeast and salt are given in grams and tablespoons or teaspoons, but less critical ingredients like spices are usually only given in tablespoons and teaspoons. I still encourage you to do yourself a favor and throw away your measuring cups!

A Note on Ovens and Temperatures

Everyone's oven is different! My home oven has a good 10 degree difference from my bakery oven — and it drives me up a wall. What's worse, is that I've spent half a lifetime in Europe and I still can't convert between Fahrenheit and Centigrade. I understand one, I understand the other, but the two systems in relation to each other? Not a chance. What I'm trying to get to is this: The nice round numbers in the Centigrade system — 170, 180, 200 — don't correspond with the nice round numbers in the Fahrenheit system. The problem with this is that many ovens don't allow for 1-degree precision and instead go by jumps of 5 degrees. To deal with that, I've converted the temperatures to the closest denomination of 5. A few degrees up or down won't make a big difference.

Now let's talk about airflow. For all the recipes in the book — except the bread recipes in Chapter 1 — I strongly recommend using convection or fan settings if you have the option. This will help you get an even bake and stave off burning.

Finally, stay in touch with your oven. Don't just walk away. A recipe may recommend a 15 minute bake, but your oven might run hot, or cold, or have no fan. That means 15 minutes probably won't work for you. Keep an eye on things and adjust bake times for your own oven.

A Note on Ingredients

Eggs: All eggs are presumed to be 50g eggs, which is closest in size to a large egg. The yolk is estimated to be 18g and the white 32g.
Milk: All milk is full-fat whole milk.
Butter: All butter, except for lamination butter (Chapter 3), is unsalted European or European-style butter with 82% fat content. If baking in the U.S., Kerrygold is a good option. Recipes will specify cold, melted, or room temperature.
Yeast: All yeast recipes call for instant yeast, not to be confused with active dry or fresh. You'll find more information on this in the introduction to Chapter 2 (p. 84).
Salt: Every salt is different! Recipes in this book call for table salt, fleur de sel, large grain gray sel de Guerande, and flaky Maldon salt. This isn't just me being fussy — it's for the sake of flavor and the sensation on your tongue! Measurements are given for the individual type of salt used in each recipe. If you wish to substitute one kind of salt for another, no problem! — just use the weight measurement rather than the teaspoon measurement. Otherwise, you could wind up with an over or underseasoned final product.

A Baker's Tools

· Dough hook (1)
· Dough scraper (2)
· Banneton/basket (3)
· Straight edge knife (4)
· Pie crimper or pizza cutter (5)
· Rolling pin (6)
· Scale (7)
· Bench knife (8)
· Flour brush (9)
· Bread knife (10)
· Pastry brush (11)
· Whisk (12)
· Thermometer (not pictured)

CHAPTER 1

Breads

A Slow Rise: Working with Sourdough

If you read the introduction to this book, you know the twentieth century was a bad time for bakeries. But a big part of why it was a bad time is because the world essentially turned its back on sourdough. It was no match for the speed and strength of newly available commercial yeast — or the industrialization that accompanied it. Commercial yeast makes bread that's beautiful but lacks flavor and aroma and easily becomes so hard by the end of the day that it's inedible. In the name of progress, we set aside flavor, aroma, and even longevity. But really, it was because speed equals "cheap." And so, hurried fermentations with commercial yeast became the bakery norm in Europe and worldwide.

Fortunately for breadmaking, the return to tradition and craftsmanship has gained enormous momentum, with a new generation of bakers rediscovering sourdough and learning skills from the purists who maintained the practice all along. It turns out that time — the element that was cut out with the switch to commercial yeast — is exactly the ingredient bread needs to be tasty, digestible, and long-lasting.

These days, old methods and forgotten grains are positively trendy — if one can call centuries-old craftsmanship trendy — and we're all the better for it. As a result, European shelves are surging with naturally flavorful breads, featuring tastes that were on the verge of being forgotten. And fortunately for us, natural leaven suits the home baker well. The long resting time means bread requires only small bursts of attention, while the long shelf life means you can bake once and eat bread all week.

Of course, there are the grumbles: "I don't like sourdough. How can you put peanut butter and jelly on that? It's sour." Well, if the English term sourdough turns you off, don't let it. It's something of a misnomer. In French, sourdough is called levain, which translates to "leaven" — there's no mention of sour. It's simply the agent that lifts your bread. And, as you'll learn in these pages, with a well-maintained starter and careful fermentation, your bread will be only as sour as you wish. If you are willing to put in the time to care for your starter, you'll make a tasty, mild loaf that goes as well with jam and butter as it does with cheese and mustard. In the end, there are no great mysteries to sourdough, just some tricks, and there are ways for even an infrequent baker to keep a starter and bake with sourdough.

What is Sourdough?

Sourdough is a naturally occurring leaven that's been around as long as there's been bread. It's a living culture of wild yeasts and lactic bacteria whose primary function is to make bread rise through the process of fermentation. Its secondary purpose is to add a pleasant scent and flavor to dough, as a by-product of fermentation. How does this fermentation happen? Well, those yeasts and bacteria don't know it's their job to make beautiful loaves of bread. They just want to eat, and if you feed them, they'll grow strong, proliferate, and do your bidding.

To get a bit scientific, let's start with the bacteria. Those folks nourish themselves on the sugars from the carbohydrates in flour and in exchange give off useful by-products: lactic acid, acetic acid, carbon dioxide, and aromas. Under good conditions — for our new buddies, that means water, food, and a moderate temperature — the fermentation is primarily lactic, which produces bread that has a gentle, creamy odor and is easy for everyone to eat. Sounds good, right? But when the conditions change — that means lower hydration, a cold temperature, and less food — acetic fermentation takes over. Too acetic, and you'll wind up with a sour loaf that has a whiff of vinegar, which is obviously less than ideal. Thankfully, your nose is one of the best ways to tell if your culture is happy — that is, properly fed, hydrated, and fermented. So if it hits you like a strong salad dressing mixed with a shot of bad grain alcohol, it probably isn't happy.

That's what the bacteria in your culture are up to, so what about the wild yeasts? The yeasts are also after the sugars from the flour. When they feed, they release their own by-products: gas (carbon dioxide) and alcohol. The alcohol isn't much to think about, as it evaporates in the oven, but the carbon dioxide is absolutely essential. It makes your bread rise!

Now that we've met our key players, there's one tiny detail you'll have to sort out. Before you can start feeding those yeasts and bacteria, you're going to have to find some. The good news — and this is very good news, since they're invisible — is that they're all around. They live in the air, and they live on flour. So, to build your own sourdough starter (also called just "a sour" or "a starter") from scratch, just add water, and they'll do the rest.

How to Build a Sourdough Starter

To avoid any confusion with terminology, the young starter that we're building into a fully active, mature sourdough starter will be called your "sourdough build." Only once it is fully active will we call it a "starter."

When making your sourdough build, always use organic flour. The pesticides, preservatives, and bleaching of conventional flours can diminish the presence and power of the yeasts. Even organic flours vary in their ability to nourish sourdough, depending on the type of grain. Some, like rye, are superfoods for a starter, and if it's whole-grain flour, that's even better.

The first four days as you build your starter, you'll feed it once a day. This involves mixing a portion of your starter build with fresh flour and water and tossing away the remaining starter build. From day five onwards, your starter will become more active, and the yeasts and bacteria will multiply, so you'll feed it twice a day.

To feed your starter, all you do is mix your ingredients (flour and water) well by hand or with a spoon, then put the mixture in a clear glass jar and cover it with a cloth or loose lid until the next feeding. The advantage of the glass jar is that you can watch the starter over time as it begins to bubble and rise — this is how you know it's coming to life. Each day you should notice bubbles forming and a mildly sour smell developing. When the starter is ready, usually at the end of day eight, it will be strong enough to double in size several hours after feeding.

Day 1: 40g (⅓ cup) light stone-ground wheat bread flour, 10g (1 tbsp plus 1 tsp) medium or dark rye flour, 50g (3 tablespoon plus 1 teaspoon) lukewarm water

Day 2: 50g (¼ cup) starter build (the mix from day 1; discard the rest), 40g (⅓ cup) light stone-ground wheat bread flour, 10g (1 tbsp plus 1 tsp) medium or dark rye flour, 50g (3 tablespoon plus 1 teaspoon) lukewarm water

Day 3: 50g (¼ cup) starter build (the mix from day 2; discard the rest), 40g (⅓ cup) light stone-ground wheat bread flour, 10g (1 tbsp plus 1 tsp) medium or dark rye flour, 50g water (3 tablespoon plus 1 teaspoon) lukewarm water

Day 4: 50g (¼ cup) starter build (the mix from day 3; discard the rest), 40g (⅓ cup) light stone-ground wheat bread flour, 10g (1 tbsp plus 1 tsp) medium or dark rye flour, 50g water (3 tablespoon plus 1 teaspoon) lukewarm water

Day 5, morning: 50g (¼ cup) starter build (the mix from day 4; discard the rest), 40g (⅓ cup) light stone-ground wheat bread flour, 10g (1 tbsp plus 1 tsp) medium or dark rye flour, 50g (3 tablespoon plus 1 teaspoon) lukewarm water

Day 5, evening: 50g (¼ cup) starter build (the mix from day 5 morning; discard the rest), 40g (⅓ cup) light stone-ground wheat bread flour, 10g (1 tbsp plus 1 tsp) medium or dark rye flour, 50g (3 tablespoon plus 1 teaspoon) lukewarm water

Day 6, morning: 50g (¼ cup) starter build (the mix from day 5 evening; discard the rest), 40g (⅓ cup) light stone-ground wheat bread flour, 10g (1 tbsp plus 1 tsp) medium or dark rye flour, 50g (3 tablespoon plus 1 teaspoon) lukewarm water

Day 6, evening: 50g (¼ tsp) starter build (the mix from day 6 morning; discard the rest), 40g (⅓ cup) light stone-ground wheat bread flour, 10g (1 tbsp plus 1 tsp) medium or dark rye flour, 50g (3 tablespoon plus 1 teaspoon) lukewarm water

Day 7, morning: 20g (1 tbsp plus 1 tsp) starter build (the mix from day 6 evening; discard the rest), 40g (⅓ cup) light stone-ground wheat bread flour, 10g (1 tbsp plus 1 tsp) medium or dark rye flour, 50g (3 tablespoon plus 1 teaspoon) lukewarm water

Day 7, evening: 20g (1 tbsp plus 1 tsp) starter build (the mix from day 7 morning; discard the rest), 40g (⅓ cup) light stone-ground wheat bread flour, 10g (1 tbsp plus 1 tsp) medium or dark rye flour, 50g (3 tablespoon plus 1 teaspoon) lukewarm tap water

Day 8, morning: 20g (1 tbsp plus 1 tsp) starter build (the mix from day 7 evening; discard the rest), 40g (⅓ cup) light stone-ground wheat bread flour, 10g (1 tbsp plus 1 tsp) medium or dark rye flour, 50g (3 tablespoon plus 1 teaspoon) lukewarm water

Day 8, evening: 20g (1 tbsp plus 1 tsp) starter build (the mix from day 8 morning; discard the rest), 40g (⅓ cup) light stone-ground wheat bread flour, 10g (1 tbsp plus 1 tsp) medium or dark rye flour, 50g (3 tablespoon plus 1 teaspoon) lukewarm water

By the evening of Day 8, you should have a strong starter that you can either begin using to make bread or continue maintaining on a refreshment schedule until you're ready to use it.

Refreshing and Maintaining Your Sourdough Starter

Once you build your starter, you have to refresh it regularly. All those invisible yeasts and bacteria are living things, and as we've already established, all they want to do is eat. That's what a refresh is: a feeding.

Want another way to think about it? There's this old math problem. You have ten guinea pigs. Don't like guinea pigs? Let's call them rabbits. The rabbits, they get a certain amount of food every day, but they're rabbits, so it's one big orgy — and not a suburban '70s swinger party but some real Roman debauchery. And now they're reproducing like mad. One week there's twenty rabbits, by the next there's 400. The colony is getting stronger, and the party is raging, but the amount of food all those rabbits require doesn't change. So, the question is, how long does it take before they've run out of food and start dying off, sending the rabbit population downhill and putting an end to the party?

That's a little like how a starter works. When it's well-fed, all those yeasts and bacteria are eating, dancing, breathing, schtupping, and getting louder and more raucous. They're high on all the sugars in the starter and giving back big perfumy exhales of gas, all of which will make a great loaf of bread once added to a dough. The yeasts and bacteria are getting stronger and stronger and things are looking good, until suddenly, they start running out of food. That's when their power drops off, and the flavor gets funky, which is no good for making bread.

All this is why, for the best possible results, you want to refresh or use your starter when it's ripe. What does it mean for a starter to be ripe? It means it's at the peak of its activity. In rabbit terms, the party is raging, they've got lots of carrots, and they're having tons of babies. The strongest starters are well-fed. The more love you give your starter, the more it will give back.

But how do you know when your starter is ripe? In practical terms, it will have doubled in size since its last refreshment (feeding) and have a domed top (photo 2), not a collapsed one. It will also have a creamy smell rather than an acidic one. As a final test, pinch off a tiny bit and toss it in water; it should float. All of these qualities combined mean your starter is ripe.

If all this sounds complicated, stay with me. There's good news, too. Once you build your starter, there are ways around some of the maintenance.

Refreshment Schedule for Frequent Bakers

If you want to always have your starter at peak activity for spontaneous bakes and don't mind a bit of babysitting, this method is for you. Using no refrigeration, you'll refresh your starter twice a day, each morning and evening, and store it in a cool corner of your kitchen just like the professionals do.

Morning: 5g (1 tsp) starter (discard the rest) 30g (¼ cup) light stone-ground wheat bread flour, 30g (2 tbsp) lukewarm water
Evening: 5g (1 tsp) starter (discard the rest), 30g (¼ cup) light stone-ground wheat bread flour, 30g (2 tbsp) lukewarm water

Refreshment Schedule for Weekend Bakers

If you like a fresh loaf of bread on Sunday mornings, follow this schedule. It involves chilling your starter all week — the cold slows down the activity — and then reactivating it through several refreshments before building your leaven. Time spent in the fridge will render your starter unpleasantly sour, but the refreshments will mellow that out.

Sunday evening: 5g (1 tsp) starter (discard the rest), 30g (¼ cup) light stone-ground wheat bread flour, 30g (2 tbsp) lukewarm water — refrigerate, covered, for up to two weeks

One to two weeks later, morning: 5g (1 tsp) starter (discard the rest), 20g (2 ½ tbsp) light stone-ground wheat bread flour, 10g (1 tbsp plus 1 tsp) medium or dark rye flour, 30g (2 tbsp) lukewarm water
Same day, evening: 5g (1 tsp) starter (discard the rest), 20g (2 ½ tbsp) light stone-ground wheat bread flour, 10g (1 tbsp plus 1 tsp) medium or dark rye flour, 30g (2 tbsp) lukewarm water
Next day, morning: 5g (1 tsp) starter (discard the rest), 20g (2 ½ tbsp) light stone-ground wheat bread flour, 10g (1 tbsp plus 1 tsp) medium or dark rye flour, 30g (2 tbsp) lukewarm water

At this point, the starter should be back to healthy activity and have a mild odor.

Refreshment Schedule for People Who Kill Sourdough Starters

There are two kinds of people in the world: those who keep houseplants alive and those who don't. Generally,

SOURDOUGH STARTERS BEFORE & AFTER FEEDING

those two types of people fall on the same sides of sourdough maintenance. The good thing is that keeping a sourdough culture going is easier than keeping most houseplants alive — though harder than caring for a cactus.

But c'mon. You aren't someone who really kills your starter. Contrary to popular belief, a sourdough starter is really hard to kill. Once you build your starter, you can keep it in the fridge for up to a month before you've reached the point of no return. All this means is that when you want to use it again, you'll have to devote several days to restoring its activity and reducing its acidity — both achieved by simply giving it regular refreshments. Follow the same pattern as the Refreshment Schedule for Weekend Bakers (p. 14), but instead of three refreshments, give it as many as eight, twice a day for four days, until it's back to activity and health.

Freezing Sourdough: For People Who Really Do Kill Sourdough Starters

Ok, I lied: Some people really do kill sourdough starters. This one's for them. When your starter is almost at peak activity, spread it in a thin, even layer on a sheet of parchment paper and let it dry at room temperature. Once it's dry, crumple up the paper, so the starter comes off in large flakes, then put them in an airtight container and freeze indefinitely. When you want to revive your starter, dissolve the flakes in twice as much warm water by volume, then add an equal amount of flour by weight. Don't worry if this first step isn't down-to-the-gram precise — we're just waking it up. Refresh twice a day according to the Refreshment Schedule for Frequent Bakers (p. 14) until strong and active, which should take four to five days.

A Note on Temperature

The thing about our little yeast colony is that it likes heat. The warmer it is, the faster it moves. And the faster it moves, the sooner it needs to eat. Of course, the opposite is also true: Cold will slow it down.

So, if you're a Sunday baker, you don't have to babysit your sourdough starter all week, feeding it every time it cries out. Keep that thing in the fridge and put it to sleep. When you take it out on Friday morning, it'll be a little slow and a bit too sour than is nice, but it doesn't matter. With three to four feedings over the next few days, it'll be back to speed.

Leaven

Every bread recipe starts with a leaven, which is just an extension of your starter, a preferment that will be added to your dough as the rising agent. We call it a leaven to differentiate it from the starter, but it's really just your final starter refreshment before baking — built into a larger quantity and used at its peak activity. If you're used to yeast baking, think of this as your yeast, because it is — it's just a living, breathing version. All you need to build your leaven is an active starter on the verge of a refresh, plus flour and water.

There are different kinds of leaven, all of which give different aromas and qualities to bread. Most of the recipes in this book use a liquid leaven, made with either whole wheat or light stone-ground wheat bread flour. Liquid starters have high hydration, ferment more slowly, and tend to produce bread with a creamier taste, but they have a short window of optimal use. Several recipes use a stiff leaven, which typically have more oomph and often a tangier, more acidic taste. In addition to being high power, they also have a longer peak activity window and are great for raising denser loaves, like rye breads.

Building Your Leaven

You can build your leaven, the final build of your starter before baking, just like you refresh your starter — by hand mixing a small portion of your ripe starter with flour and water; keep the remaining starter and continue refreshing according to your chosen schedule. The flour source and water quantity change the type and qualities of the leaven. The sourdough-based recipes in this

book are designed for a rest of eight to nine hours between building your leaven and using it, and provide approximate timings, but between building your leaven and using it, use your eyes and your nose first — with experience, you'll start to know the optimal time to use your leaven to make bread. And be flexible! Since everyone's home climate and sour culture are a little different, this means your timing may be different.

Your leaven has a peak of activity when it is at its strongest and makes the best bread. But how do you know when that is? Your ripe leaven will have the same qualities as your ripe starter. Use the timing provided in the recipes as an approximate guide but apply your senses just as you did for your starter. Your leaven will have doubled in size and be nicely domed rather than collapsed. It will float in water and won't smell very sour at all. Pull the domed top apart with your fingers, and it will smell creamy and a bit eggy, like a salt marsh. You're good to go!

Some people keep several different starters active at the same time. I like to keep one liquid starter and adapt it to my recipe when I build the leaven. After all, the starter will eat up whatever you feed it.

Bread Making Ingredients

Flour

Most recipes in this chapter call for an organic light stone-ground wheat bread flour, a stone-ground wheat flour with little or no bran (hence "light"). Stone-ground means that the flour was milled between two large stones, keeping the flour cool during the grinding process. The result is a subtly rustic flavor and aroma. Source your organic flours as locally as possible — the flavor and fermentation power will come through.

Think of the recipes in this chapter as foundations. You can play with other flours, swapping wheat for spelt, or replacing some of your flour with whole meals, but remember that every flour behaves differently, particularly when it comes to hydration. As a general rule, whole grain flours can absorb more water than lighter flours where most or all of the bran and germ are removed. Use your eyes and hands as you mix to achieve the right texture for the flour you're using.

Gluten

Let's just briefly address this taboo. Gluten is a protein that exists naturally in most flours. It's what gives dough its stretch, and allows big, beautiful holes to form in the crumb of your bread. Most gluten sensitivity has little to do with gluten itself and everything to do with poorly fermented bread. A proper fermentation means your flour and the proteins in it have arrived at a point where they're good for you to eat and digest.

Think of it like this: You wouldn't eat an unripe green apple straight off the tree, would you? That's a one-way ticket to a tummy ache. You need to wait until autumn and pick that apple when it's red and sweet and ready. The same goes for flour products. Our stomachs aren't made to eat that stuff raw, but fermentation starts the digestion process for us. If we do a wham-bam-oven-ma'am dough with a heap of commercial yeast, it's not going to sit well in our stomachs, which is why a lot of folks think they're allergic to bread. However, when we ferment flour organically, using natural leaven or tiny quantities of commercial yeast, the subsequent bread will be good to eat — and easy to digest — like a nice ripe apple in October.

Salt

Salt is an important agent in dough and not just for flavor. It also inhibits yeast activity and helps tighten dough, while the acid in the sour loosens it. Salt is the push to the pull of the leaven and a necessary part of any bread. But what's the most important thing to know about salt? Salt kills yeasts. At least, it kills yeasts when directly applied to them. So, when mixing your dough, be sure to keep the yeast and the leaven separate.

Not all salt is created equal — each brings its own flavor to the table. For bread, I like to use sel de Guérande, a rough and damp large grain unrefined gray sea salt from Western France that's loaded with minerals — it's a habit I picked up from rural boulanger Franck Perrault (p. 252). It dissolves easily in water and is relatively inexpensive. If you can't find this particular salt, use what you have in the house, but measure by the weight provided in the recipe, not the volume! The different sizes of salt crystals mean you can't simply substitute spoon for spoon. You could wind up with a painfully salty bread if you do!

Water

When first mixing dough by hand, you want to hit an ideal final dough temperature around 26°C (79°F) for vigorous and healthy fermentation. To do this, the easiest temperature factor to manipulate is your water temperature. And to calculate your water temperature, there's a formula that takes into account the temperature of your environment, the temperature of your flour, and the ideal final temperature of your dough. Use a small digital instant-read thermometer to find your temperatures. For an approximate room temperature situation where all your materials were stored at room temperature, you'll want your water to be between about 28–35°C (84-95°F). If you have an especially cold or warm room, read on and do some math:

4 × (Desired Final Dough Temperature) - (Room Temperature) - (Flour Temperature) - (Starter Temperature) = Water Temperature

For example, if your room is about 27°C (80°F), your flour is 25°C (77°F), your starter is 24°C (75°F), and your ideal final dough temperature is 26°C (79°F), here is the calculation:

(4 × 26°C / 79°F) - (27°C / 80°F) - (25°C / 77°F) - (24°C / 75°F) = (28°C / 84°F)

Adjust the input temperatures for your own weather and you'll see your dough temperature after mixing comes out to about 26°C (79°F). Really! Try it! Not up for all that math? Between us, you'll be fine with lukewarm water from the tap. People have been baking bread far longer than handy little battery-operated kitchen thermometers have been around. *Note: for doughs mixed in a stand mixer, you'll want slightly cooler water as the machine heats dough.*

The Stages of Bread Making

Once you've built a starter, it's time to bake bread! For all the kinds of risen bread in the world, different as they may be, there's always a pattern. A series of mixes, rises, shapes, and waits that end up, with any luck, exactly where you want to be when it's time to bake. While different grains and shapes behave differently, as do natural leavens and commercial yeasts, every bread undergoes stages of dough development that include a mix, a bulk fermentation, a shape, a final rise, and a bake.

Mixing

Most of the naturally leavened breads in this book are gently mixed by hand. A gentle mix, combined with the sourdough's slow development gives bread a more open crumb (bubble pattern). This is especially true when using more delicate grains that prefer gentler handling. The initial mixing of bread is similar to the initial mixing of cake, as there's been no chance for the gluten network to develop yet. Combine flour and leaven in a bowl (1-2). Dissolve the salt in the water (3) and add to the bowl (4). Move your hand around the bowl, squeezing any pockets of dry flour to create a uniform dough (5-6). Clean your hands with a dough scraper (7). In the early stages, most doughs will feel more like a sticky batter. As the dough develops, its texture will change, and you'll give your dough what are called turns (p. 18), sets of stretches and folds.

Autolyse

Most recipes in this chapter don't use an autolyse, but if your dough is too elastic and tight, this is an easy extra step to add extensibility (stretch) in future bakes. An autolyse is an initial mix and rest of the flour and water, with no addition of salt or leaven. It allows gluten development to happen away from the presence of natural yeasts, whose acidity can act counter to gluten development. The formation of a good gluten network

MIXING

before fermentation even begins helps create more extensible doughs.

Adding Leaven and Salt

This bears repeating! When giving your dough its initial mix, always keep in mind that salt kills yeast, especially the nice natural yeast culture you just spent weeks building. So, never, ever, put salt directly on your leaven; always dilute the salt in water or mix it into the flour first.

Bassinage

Bassinage is the withholding of a portion of the total liquid in your dough to incorporate at a later stage in the kneading process. It can be done with any liquid in your dough — water, oil, or other — and helps build dough strength and create a good gluten network. You'll see this in machine-mixed doughs like Neapolitan-Style Pizza (p. 56) and Fougasse (p. 60).

Bulk Fermentation

Coming directly after the mix, bulk fermentation, otherwise known as bulk proofing or bulk rising — or if you're James Dean–level cool, "the bulk," — is the first long rest for your dough and how you begin building the chemical skeleton for your bread. This is the point when the gluten — the protein that makes dough stretch — develops further, and when the yeasts multiply and begin releasing gasses, adding volume to your dough. For those new to bread making, bulk fermentation can be one of the more difficult stages to judge. A loaf that has undergone a just right bulk fermentation will be pillowy with nice bubbles, while a bread with too short of a bulk proof, will be underdeveloped and dense, and bread with a bulk proof that's too long, may find its all-important gluten network degraded and bake up flat.

The recipes in this book provide outlines of fermentation times, but all kinds of factors can make your dough move faster or slower. Weather, temperature, and the health of a starter can change your fermentation rates. What am I getting at? Take the provided fermentation times as a general outline but use your senses to help you decide when bulk fermentation is complete.

Here are a few clues you can use to help judge your dough's fermentation:

Feel: Touch your dough. It should feel markedly lighter and softer from when you started.

Smell: When properly fermented, the dough will take on a mild, creamy odor — a low-key version of a nice, lactic leaven, but not nearly as strong. Be aware of strong acidic odors like vinegar or alcohol, which can mean you've proofed your dough too long.

Float Test: Pull off a bit of dough and drop it in water. If properly bulked (shorthand for bulk proofed), it will pass a float test just like your leaven.

Scaling Up Recipes and Bulk Fermentation

The bread recipes in this book are portioned to make one loaf, but they can all be doubled, tripled, or scaled however you like. Keep in mind that the more dough there is, the faster it will ferment, so if you're going to scale up these recipes to produce a lot of bread, mind your dough and watch the clock.

Turns

Most doughs require turns while they're in their bulk fermentation stage. Turns are just a gentle way of stretching and mixing your dough at intervals to continue developing the gluten network that will give shape and strength to your final product, so it can hold expansion and air. As dough ferments, it relaxes, but giving it turns will bring the tension back. Turns can be done in a bowl (advisable for wetter doughs) or on a damp work surface. I keep a spray bottle on hand to mist my hands, bowl, or work surface.

As the bulk proof progresses, the dough should resist these turns more and more, and hold its shape for longer without spreading completely flat. If your dough never starts holding its shape, it may not be proofed enough, while if it starts falling apart late in the proof, that's a sign of over-proofing.

You can give your dough turns in two different ways:

The Stretch and Fold Method: Here, the dough is pulled as far upward as it will go with one hand, then turned back onto itself. This process is repeated, with the dough being stretched from different sides as you go, until it's tight and resists being pulled. As your fermentation progresses, it should take fewer and fewer turns for the dough to resist. You can give your dough turns in a mixing bowl (1A-3A), turning the bowl as you go, or on a damp work surface (1B-2B), returning the dough to a bowl to rest after turning.

The Gravity Method: The other option is to use gravity. With wet or lightly floured hands, use both hands to pull up your dough from the middle (1). Allow the hanging dough to fold under itself (2), then repeat from a different angle (3-5) until your dough is smooth and tight. This method works well for larger quantities of dough and dough at the final stages of its bulk proof.

For home baking, I like to give my dough several stretches and folds, then use the gravity method as a final touch to form a smooth ball for the subsequent rest. Whichever method you prefer, turning your dough every 30 to 45 minutes is a great way to feel your dough and understand how it's changing during the bulk ferment — through the process, you'll feel the dough become lighter as the yeasts release gasses.

But My Hands are Sticky

There are a few ways to deal with sticky dough while mixing. Most bakers make mixing and turning a one-handed affair, leaving the other hand free if they need to do anything else. In the early stages of dough mixing, there's no way out for a messy, dough-covered hand. Use your free hand and a bench knife to scrape the dough off the messy hand. In the later stages, water is your friend. Wet your hand up to the wrist before you give the dough folds. It won't stick — magic!

THE STRETCH AND FOLD METHOD IN A BOWL

THE STRETCH AND FOLD METHOD ON A TABLE

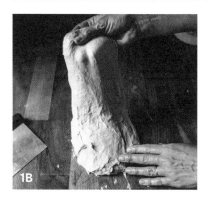 

THE GRAVITY METHOD

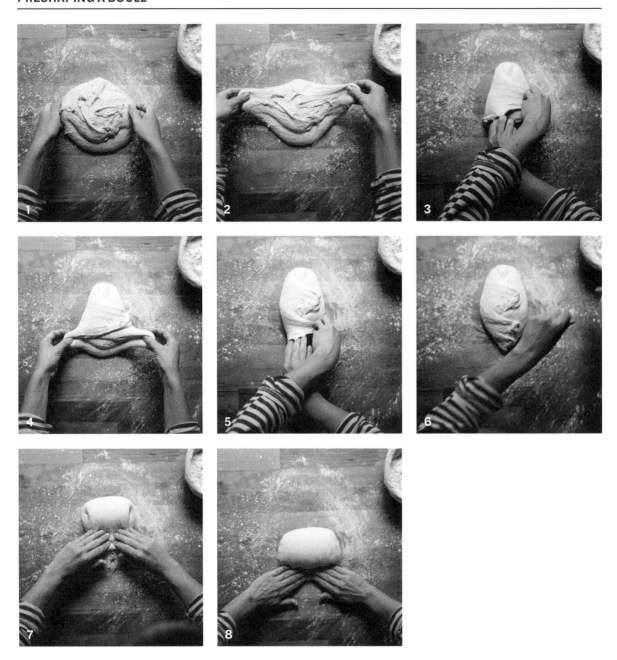

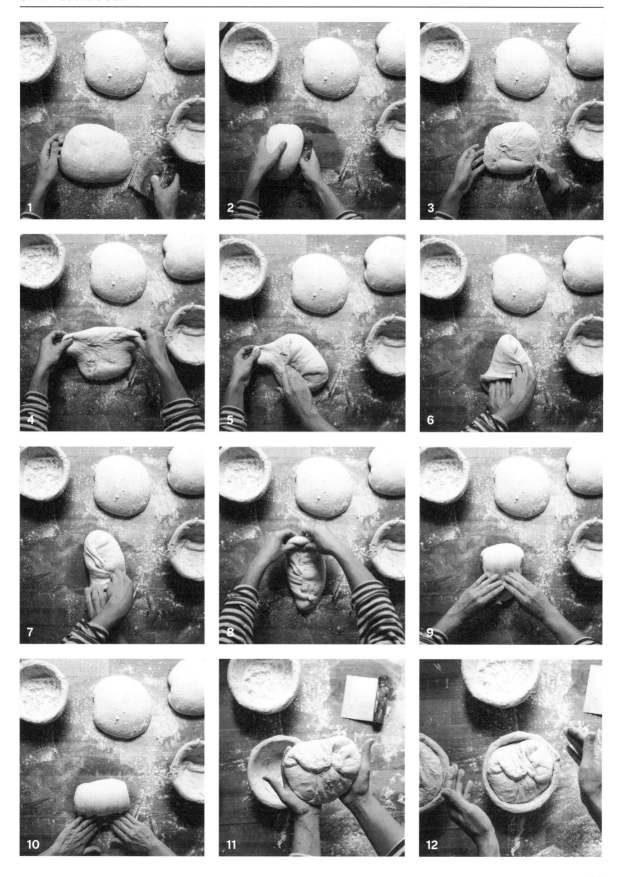

Shaping

To give a nice final shape to your dough, the shaping process is divided into a preshape and a shape. The preshape gets your dough ready for its final form. The most important element is doing this step deftly and with speed, two skills that come with practice. If you work too slowly, you may end up with messy, sticky dough that's difficult to manipulate.

Boule, which means "ball" in French, is a traditional bread shape and resembles a flat ball. Learning to preshape and shape a boule is a good starting point to learn how to shape different loaf styles.

Preshaping a Boule (photos p. 20):
Turn the dough out onto a floured work surface (1). Stretch opposing sides outward in opposite directions (2) then fold these into the middle, overlapping each side like an envelope (3). Continue stretching and overlapping the sides all the way down the length of the dough (4–6). Fold all this over itself (7–8), and leave to relax, smooth side up, for 20 minutes before the final shape. This rest is called the bench rest.

Shaping a Boule (photos p. 21):
Using your bench knife, flip the preshaped dough so that it is smooth side down (1–3). Stretch opposing sides outward in opposite directions (4), then fold these into the middle, overlapping each side like an envelope (5–6). Fold all along this seam (7) so it looks "stitched." Fold the top over about two-thirds of the way and press (8–9), then fold what is now the top all the way down to meet the bottom. Press to seal (10). Quickly scoop up the shaped loaf and put it, smooth-side down, in a floured proofing basket (11–12).

While that's how I like to shape a loaf, not everyone shapes the same. Here are instructions for another method: Using your bench knife, flip the preshaped dough so that it is smooth side down. Stretch and fold the top of the preshape to meet the very bottom and press. Then rotate your dough about 30 degrees and fold the top of the preshape to meet the bottom and press again. Continue rotating and folding your dough until the loaf resists continual folding and

you have a rounded shape. Scoop up the loaf and put it, smooth-side down, in a floured proofing basket.

But My Dough Is Too Sticky to Shape

Often, during the shaping stage, inexperienced bakers find themselves sticking to their dough. When giving dough a final shaping, you can use either water or flour (pick one or the other, not both!) on both your hands and the work surface, but lightly floured hands and a lightly floured work surface are much simpler for a beginner. However, the materials aren't usually the main reason why someone is sticking to their dough during shaping — it's speed. The slower you shape, the more likely the dough will stick to you and make a mess of both you and your loaf. Working quickly and handling the dough as little as possible will help prevent sticking. Trick: If you're still struggling to shape a sticky dough, use a wet bench knife, held at a 45-degree angle to an unfloured work surface, to push the dough in circles. The dough will form into a tight ball you can use as your preshape or final shape, and you won't stick.

The Final Proof

The proof is the final rise of your shaped bread. It's when your loaf gains the final internal structure that will inflate during the bake. The best way to tell when the proof is done is to gently tap the dough with a finger and see if it slowly springs back. If the dough springs back too fast, it's likely under-proofed, which will produce a dense and gummy loaf. If there's no spring back at all and your finger indent remains, your dough is probably over-proofed and will bake up a bit flat. This touch is something you'll develop as a baker over time — experience and comparison are the greatest teachers. Just as with the bulk proof stage, the timing provided in the recipes for the final proof are guidelines. For more consistent results and loaves that are easier to score, I recommend refrigerated overnight final proofs for all the recipes in this book.

Scoring Your Loaf

The beautiful cut marks on finished loaves aren't purely decorative. We cut or score loaves to create vents for the dough to expand and release steam. Unscored bread will explode unappealingly from the sides. Score your bread just before it goes into the oven. For the recipes in this book, that means when it's already in your cast-iron pot or on a pizza stone or steel. To score your bread, take a baker's lame (a razor mounted on a handle; I stick a razor blade on a coffee stirrer when I'm out of options) or a small, sharp, serrated knife and slice, at an angle, firmly and quickly across the surface of the dough in the pattern of your choosing (see photo). Speed and firmness will give you a clean cut with no drag marks. Keep your cuts 1–2cm (⅓–¾ inch deep — cuts that are too deep could lead to a flat, spread out loaf.

The Bake

This is the moment of glory, when your patience and fussing come together in an explosively risen loaf and a spectacularly caramelized crust! We hope. There are two elements we need to make it all work: heat and steam.

Bread is baked at very high temperatures. This helps the loaf to spring up, the crust to caramelize, and the interior to stay moist. Maybe heat is obvious, but why do we need steam? Because our bread is about to almost double in size! And to do so, it needs to have a supple crust. Putting a loaf into a dry, hot environment means a hard crust will form immediately, impeding the rise and causing cracks and unsightly explosions. But when you put your loaf in a humid baking environment, the crust stays soft, and the dough can gently expand and release steam along your score-lines or cuts.

Steam is an important tool, but we only want it at the beginning of our bake. For the same reason that steam allows the loaf to expand, it inhibits the formation and caramelization of a good crust! For the final portion of the bake, we want a dry environment, so the bread forms a crunchy, deep brown crust.

Most professional bakers use either an electric deck oven or a wood-fired oven. Either way, they have a very hot, stone base on which the bread is baked directly, and mechanisms for allowing steam into the oven. But the average person doesn't have this in their home kitchen — I sure don't. Thankfully, there are a few ways to mimic the bake of a professional bread oven at home.

The Cast-Iron Method: The most popular approach is the cast-iron method, which works in even the shoddiest of home ovens, as it helps evenly distribute heat to your bread and locks in steam. Start by putting a covered cast-iron pot in your oven as it preheats for the bake. Once the oven is preheated, carefully remove the pot and uncover it, then reverse your loaf into the pot, score, and cover the pot. Bake your bread, uncovering the pot halfway through. The cast iron mimics the solid heat of the stone floor of a professional oven, while the sealed top creates a steamy environment that allows the scored loaf to rise and expand. Once uncovered, the crust can dry out and get a good tan.

The Stone Method: The pizza stone method is good for pizza, but also longer oblong breads that might not fit in a cast-iron pot. Pizza stones — or steels — mimic the floor of a real bread oven but need to be properly heated. To do this, put the pizza stone or steel in the oven as it preheats for the bake, then allow it to continue heating for another half hour or so — the stone or steel heats more slowly than your oven. If you bake before the stone or steel is hot, you'll end up with a soft and pale bottom crust. A few minutes before you're ready to bake, set an old metal muffin tin or rimmed baking pan next to the pizza stone or steel and allow it to heat up. Once the stone or steel is warm, invert your bread onto the stone or steel and score it. As quickly as you can, toss some ice cubes into the heated metal tin or pan next to the stone or steel, and close the oven door. The ice cubes will release steam. Be careful not to toss the ice cubes on the oven floor or pizza stone or steel, which can damage your oven and break the stone or steel.

Is it Ready Yet?

There are a few ways to tell if your bread is properly baked. First, check the color: Is it a deep golden brown and crusty? Good sign! Now lift the loaf out of the cast iron pot. Yes, you need asbestos hands — do you want to be a baker or what? Make a fist and rap on the bottom of the loaf. If it makes a hollow knocking sound, that loaf is ready! If the bottom bends inward or gives way under your knocking and makes a dull sound, keep baking.

Cooling

This is the worst. You just spent a whole day making this loaf of bread and now you're supposed to wait even longer? But please, bear with me. Even after you remove your loaf from the oven, it's still baking and drying itself out. If you cut into it too soon, you halt this final stage and can end up with a gummy loaf. So please. Just wait until it's cool to the touch.

Storing

Rule number one: Do not put your cooling bread in a plastic bag. This is a one-way ticket to a rubbery crust. If you must bag your bread, do so in paper, at least until it cools. Once your loaf is fully cooled, wrap it in a clean dishcloth and store it at room temperature for up to a week. Toast to refresh.

Base Recipe: Daily Bread

Daily bread doesn't mean the same thing to everyone — it doesn't have to. It can be anything from a dense rye to a soft flatbread to crusty white rolls. Just as every table has its daily bread, every baker has theirs — a good, foundational loaf. A daily bread is rarely the fussiest loaf, nor the most creative, but it's a good place to start. This particular loaf is pretty honest — humble enough that it won't overpower a good meal yet elegant enough to provide good texture and chew. It's something you'll want to eat hot from the oven or toasted and slathered with butter five days later. Based on the classic country loaves made by rural French bakers, this sourdough style rose to prominence in the last two decades in large part thanks to San Francisco's Tartine Bakery and has since made a large-scale return to bakeries both in Europe and around the world.

These days, it can feel like you'll find the same loaf in Paris, as you'll find in Copenhagen, as you'll find in Berlin, and some complain that this bread and its ilk represent little more than a trendy monoculture. But that's wrong. People have made bread like this for hundreds of years; its process and proportions are rooted in tradition. Even if bakers vary their methods — some incorporate salt at different stages, some add an autolyse or hold back water, while others prefer a stiff leaven — these are minor tweaks. No one is reinventing the wheel. There are no secret ingredients — just one's own hands and flour. These are just tried and true methods passed down through the years. But in a world of seeming sameness, take comfort in the fact that the sameness is often superficial. Good bakers differentiate and give their bread a sense of place with locally grown and milled flours, as well as by using their own hands, their unique touch and specific gestures. Remember this as you make your own.

This daily bread recipe keeps it simple and uses light stone-ground wheat bread flour with whole wheat flour added through the leaven. The incorporation of rough sel de Guérande, large grain French gray sea salt, naturally adds minerals, but this is optional and you can use whatever salt you have on hand, just be sure to measure any substitutions by weight, not volume

Use this recipe and its method as an outline for the other wheat loaves in the book. Once you're comfortable, swap out some of the light stone-ground wheat bread flour for spelt flour, which tends to be a bit more extensible. Then get creative, mixing in seeds and porridges — any hydrated whole grain, such as oats, rye, or spelt. The recipes that follow this base will give you some ideas, but the more you play around, the more you'll understand.

Base Recipe: Daily Bread

Note: The process of making this loaf, from leaven to bake, is 24 hours, so always build your leaven with that in mind — that is, start 24 hours before your ideal bake time. The leaven takes 8–9 hours to ripen before you can use it to mix your dough, which is perfect timing for it to sit overnight or for the duration of a workday.

To summarize: If you want to do an evening bake, build your leaven the previous evening. For a morning bake, build your leaven in the morning. The relatively low percentage of starter in the leaven slows its maturation, so that you wake up to a creamy, ripe starter, and not one that's super acidic and over-fermented. The speed at which your leaven ripens is something you can actually control. How? If you want to buy yourself time and sleep in an extra 2–3 hours, cut down the percentage of starter in the leaven by half.

YIELD: 1 LOAF

For the whole wheat leaven
· 10g (1 tbsp plus 1 tsp) ripe sourdough starter
· 60g (½ cup) whole wheat flour
· 60g (¼ cup) cool water

For the dough
· 9g (2 tsp) large grain gray sea salt (sel de Guérande) 19%
· 385g (1 ½ cups plus 1 tbsp plus 1 tsp) lukewarm water (28–35°C / 84–95°F) 77%
· 500g (4 cups plus 2 ½ tbsp) light stone-ground wheat bread flour 100%
· 100g (½ cup plus 2 tbsp) whole wheat leaven 20%

 TIMELINE
24 h, start to finish
Day 1, Morning:
Build leaven, rest 8–9 h
Day 1, Afternoon/Evening:
Mix dough, bulk proof 4 h
Preshape, bench rest 20 min
Shape, basket rest 30 min
Refrigerate 8–15 h
Day 2, Morning:
Bake 45 min

Day 1, Morning: Make your leaven

A - Build your leaven: Hand mix the ripe starter, whole wheat flour, and cool water until smooth and homogenous to build your leaven, then let it rest, loosely covered, for 8–9 hours (or as long as the individual recipe requires).

Day 1, Afternoon/Evening (8–9 hours later): Start making your dough

B - Check your leaven for readiness: It should have doubled in size and have a domed top. It will float in water and smell creamy and ripe, not acidic.

C - Mix your dough: If your leaven is ready, in a large bowl, mix the salt with the lukewarm water until dissolved. Add the light stone-ground wheat bread flour and leaven and mix by hand until there are no dry bits of flour. Cover with a damp towel and set aside for 30 minutes.

D - Stretch and fold your dough: After 30 minutes, wet your hands and a dough scraper to prevent sticking. Use the dough scraper to release the dough from the bowl, then stretch and fold your dough over itself until it resists any more stretching. This can be done in the bowl or on a damp work surface (p. 18).

E - Bulk proof your dough: Cover and rest, repeating the stretches and folds at 30-minute intervals for the next 3 ½ hours, for a total of 4 hours (or as long as the individual recipe requires). After each subsequent rest, you'll notice your dough needs fewer and fewer stretches and folds to resist and form a nice smooth ball. As the dough gets tighter, it's nice to lift it 2-handed from the middle to let gravity stretch it downward, then turn and repeat until it forms a smooth ball. At the end of the final rest, don't fold the dough. By now, the dough should be light and puffy — very different from how it started. If you're unsure whether it's ready, pull off a small piece and see if it floats in water — just like you do to check the starter. *Note: If your dough isn't floating, this could result from a cold room or an underactive starter — give it another 30 minutes to bulk proof (rest). Remember that the opposite is also possible, and your dough may need to be shaped earlier, at the 3 ½ hour mark prior to folding.*

F - Preshape your dough: After the final rest, turn the dough out onto a floured work surface. Stretch opposing sides outward in opposite directions then fold these into the middle, overlapping each side like an envelope. Continue stretching and overlapping the sides all the way down the length of the dough. Fold all this over itself, and leave to relax, smooth-side up, for 20 minutes before the final shape. This rest is called the bench rest.

G - Shape your dough: After 20 minutes, use your bench knife to flip the preshaped dough so that it is smooth side down. Stretch opposing sides outward in opposite directions, then fold these into the middle, overlapping each side like an envelope. Fold all along this seam so it looks "stitched." Fold the top over about two-thirds of the way and press, then fold what is now the top all the way down to meet the bottom. Press to seal. Quickly scoop up the shaped loaf and put it, smooth-side down, in a floured proofing basket.

H - Basket rest your dough: Let rest at room temperature for 30 minutes, then refrigerate overnight or for up to 15 hours for the final rest. Be sure your refrigerator temperature is between 4-6°C (40-43°F) to prevent over-fermentation.

Day 2, Morning: Bake your bread

I - Preheat your oven: Preheat the oven to 250°C (500°F), along with your cast-iron pot or pizza stone or steel (pp. 22–23). Remember: A pizza stone or steel will need at least an extra 30 minutes to heat once the oven reaches temperature and you'll need to use a muffin tin or rimmed baking pan and ice to create steam.

J - Score your loaf: Once the oven is preheated, invert your loaf straight from its basket into the middle of the heated pot or stone. The smooth side of the loaf is now up. Use a sharp serrated knife or a baker's lame to score the dough (p. 22), then immediately cover the pot, if using cast iron, or toss in ice cubes if using a pizza stone or steel.

K - Bake your bread: Bake for 20 minutes, then remove the cover, lower the oven temperature to 235°C (450°F), and continue baking for another 25 minutes, or until you hear a hollow sound when you knock on the bottom of the loaf.

Malted Oat Loaf

This is a cozy bread. Both barley malt and soaked oats add a touch of warmth and beery sweetness. Malts are natural flavor boosters made from sprouted grains that have been dried and turned into powder. They're nutty and sweet and result in deeply caramelized crusts. Serve with butter and jam or as a hearty sandwich base.

Note: There are two kinds of malt, diastatic and non-diastatic. Diastatic malt is an active malt, which means it accelerates yeast activity; it's used as a dough additive. That's not the malt we want to use here. Non-diastatic malt — the kind used here — is a natural grain-based flavoring agent. You can find it at brewing supply stores or organic groceries.

YIELD: 1 LOAF

For the whole wheat leaven
- 10g (2 tsp) ripe sourdough starter
- 60g (½ cup) whole wheat flour
- 60g (¼ cup) cool water

For the porridge
- 50g (heaping ½ cup) old-fashioned oats 10%
- 100g (⅓ cup plus 1 tbsp plus 2 tsp) warm water 20%

For the dough
- 9g (2 tsp) large grain gray sea salt (sel de Guérande) 1.9%
- 350g (1½ cups plus 2 tsp) lukewarm water (28-35°C (84-95°F)) 70%
- 500g (4 cups plus 2½ tbsp) light stone-ground wheat flour 100%
- 10g (1 heaping tbsp) non-diastatic barley malt powder 2%
- 100g (½ cup plus 2 tbsp) whole wheat leaven 20%

For the crust
- 100g (heaping 1 cup) whole oats

 TIMELINE
24 hours, start to finish
Day 1, Morning:
Build leaven, rest 8-9 h
Day 1, Afternoon/Evening:
Mix dough, bulk proof 3½ h
Preshape, bench rest 20-30 min
Shape, basket rest 20 min
Refrigerate 8-15 h
Day 2, Morning:
Bake 45 min

Follow the pattern of the Daily Bread recipe (pp. 26-27).

Day 1, Morning: Make your leaven
Build your leaven and let it rest, loosely covered, for 8-9 hours (p. 26, A).

Meanwhile, prepare the porridge: Mix the 50g (heaping ½ cup) of oats and the warm water in a small bowl, cover, and let soak for 8-9 hours.

Day 1, Afternoon/Evening (8-9 hours later): Start making your dough
If your leaven is ready (p. 26, B), in a large bowl, mix the salt with the lukewarm water until dissolved. Add the light stone-ground wheat bread flour, malt, and leaven and mix by hand until there are no dry bits of flour. Cover with a damp towel and set aside for 30 minutes.

After 30 minutes, add the porridge to the dough and mix in by hand. Give the dough a set of stretches and folds until it resists any more stretching (p. 26, D). Cover and repeat the stretches and folds at 30-minute intervals for the next 3 hours, until the dough is light and airy and requires fewer and fewer folds to hold the tension (p. 26, E).

After the final rest, turn the proofed dough out onto a floured work surface and give it a preshape (p. 27, F). Let rest for 20-30 minutes.

Meanwhile, spread the 100g (heaping 1 cup) of oats on a large plate. Have a proofing basket waiting.

After 20-30 minutes, shape your dough: With wet hands, lightly dampen the surface of the dough, then use a bench knife to flip the dough onto the plate of oats. Fold and shape the dough (p. 27, G) on the plate — the oats will stick to the surface of the dough. Set the shaped loaf, smooth-side down, in the proofing basket and let rest at room temperature for 20 minutes, then refrigerate overnight or for up to 15 hours for the final rest (p. 27, H).

Day 2, Morning: Bake your bread
Place a covered cast-iron pot in the oven and preheat the oven to 250°C (500°F).

Once the oven is preheated, invert your loaf from its basket into the heated pot, smooth-side up. Score the dough (p. 27, J), then cover and bake for 20 minutes. Uncover the bread, lower the oven temperature to 235°C (450°F), and continue baking for 25 minutes, or until you hear a hollow sound when you knock on the bottom of the loaf. Because of the added moisture of the oat porridge, be sure to let this loaf properly cool before cutting.

Kasha Loaf

This one's for Frank Costanza. Buckwheat, or kasha, has a strong and earthy flavor — if you know, you know — and has been an important part of European diets since it showed up from Central Asia more than 4,000 years ago. In Northwestern France, it's ground into a gray flour and used to make savory crêpes called galettes, while in Eastern Europe, it's boiled with salt and stuffed in cabbage and dumplings. In Jewish homes, it's cooked with fried onions and bowtie pasta for kasha varnishkes. You can try, but you won't escape kasha. This bread can't either. It doubles down on buckwheat — flakes and flour — but if that isn't enough for you, add fried onions and cooked kasha on the final turn.

YIELD: 1 LOAF

For the whole wheat leaven
· 10g (2 tsp) ripe sourdough starter
· 60g (½ cup) whole wheat flour
· 60g (¼ cup) cool water

For the dough
· 9g (2 tsp) large grain gray sea salt (sel de Guérande) 1.9%
· 350g (1 ⅓ cups plus 2 tbsp) lukewarm water (28-35°C (84-95°F)) 70%
· 475g (4 cups) light stone-ground wheat bread flour 95%
· 25g (3 tbsp plus 1 tsp) dark buckwheat flour 5%
· 100g (½ cup plus 2 tbsp) whole wheat leaven 20%
· 30g (¼ cup) cooked buckwheat (optional)
· 1 yellow onion, finely diced and sautéed until golden brown (optional)

For the crust
· 100g (1 cup) buckwheat flakes (milled buckwheat groats)

TIMELINE
24 h, start to finish
Day 1, Morning:
Build leaven, rest 8-9 h
Day 1, Afternoon/Evening:
Mix dough, bulk proof 4
Preshape, bench rest 20 min
Shape, basket rest 20-30 min
Refrigerate 8-15 h
Day 2, Morning:
Bake 45 min

Follow the pattern of the Daily Bread recipe (pp. 26-27).

Day 1, Morning: Make your leaven
Build your leaven and let it rest, loosely covered, for 8-9 hours (p. 26, A).

Day 1, Afternoon/Evening (8-9 hours later): Start making your dough
If your leaven is ready (p. 26, B), in a large bowl, mix the salt with the lukewarm water until dissolved. Add the light stone-ground wheat bread flour, dark buckwheat flour, and leaven and mix by hand until there are no dry bits of flour. Cover with a damp towel and set aside for 30 minutes.

After 30 minutes, give the dough a set of stretches and folds until it resists any more stretching (p. 26, D). Cover and repeat the stretches and folds at 30-minute intervals for the next 3 ½ hours until the dough is light and airy and requires fewer folds to hold the tension (p. 26, E). *Note: At the 3-hour mark, you have the option to add kasha and onions with the final set of stretches and folds. If not adding extras, stretch and fold as usual.*

After the final rest, turn the proofed dough out onto a floured work surface and give it a preshape (p. 27, F). Let rest for 20 minutes.

Meanwhile, spread the buckwheat flakes on a large plate. Have a proofing basket waiting.

After 20 minutes, lightly dampen the top of your dough with a wet hand (to help the flakes stick) then use a wet bench knife to flip the dough onto the plate of buckwheat flakes. Fold and shape the dough (p. 27, G) on the plate — the buckwheat flakes will stick to the surface of the dough. Set the shaped loaf, smooth-side down, in the proofing basket and let rest at room temperature for 20-30 minutes, then refrigerate overnight or up to 15 hours for the final rest.

Day 2, Morning: Bake your bread
Place a covered cast-iron pot in the oven and preheat the oven to 250°C (500°F).

Once the oven is preheated, invert your loaf from its basket into the heated pot, smooth-side up. Score the dough (p. 27, J) then cover and bake for 20 minutes. Uncover the bread, lower the oven temperature to 235°C (450°F), and continue baking for 25 minutes, or until you hear a hollow sound when you knock on the bottom of the loaf. Enjoy with fresh white cheese and sharp radishes.

Seeded Plum Buns

There's a new classic baker's breakfast that leaked out of Denmark and into bakeries all over Europe — a salted butter-and-Comté sourdough bun. It's simple perfection. These nutty little buns, which get just a dash of sour sweetness from soft chopped prunes, go perfectly with the salty Comté and butter. They're some of the only breads you shouldn't bother to cool before eating. Serve them fresh from the oven for your own baker's breakfast.

YIELD: 8-12 BUNS

For the whole wheat leaven
· 10g (2 tsp) ripe sourdough starter
· 60g (½ cup) whole wheat flour
· 60g (¼ cup) cool water

For the seed mix
· 20g (3 tbsp) poppy seeds
· 20g (3 tbsp) flax seeds
· 20g (3 tbsp) pumpkin seeds
· 20g (3 tbsp) sunflower seeds (optional)
· 20g (3 tbsp) sesame seeds (optional)
· 60g (¼ cup) boiling water

For the dough
· 9g (2 tsp) large grain gray sea salt (sel de Guérande) 1.9%
· 370g (1 ½ cups plus 2 tsp) lukewarm water at 28-35°C (84-95°F) 74%
· 500g (4 cups plus 2 ½ tbsp) light stone-ground wheat bread flour or light spelt flour 100%
· 100g (½ cup plus 2 tbsp) whole wheat leaven 20%
· 50g (⅓ cup) chopped prunes 10%

For the coating
· 100g (⅔ cup) poppy seeds
· 100g (⅔ cup) flax seeds
· 100g (⅔ cup) pumpkin seeds

TIMELINE
24 h, start to finish
Day 1, Morning:
Build leaven, rest 8-9 h
Day 1, Afternoon/Evening:
Mix dough, bulk proof 4 h
Preshape, bench rest 20 min
Shape, basket rest 20-30 min
Refrigerate 8-15 h
Day 2, Morning:
Bake 30 minutes

Follow the pattern of the Daily Bread recipe (pp. 26-27).

Day 1, Morning: Make your leaven
Build your leaven and let it rest, loosely covered, for 8-9 hours (p. 26, A).

Meanwhile, prepare the seed mix: Mix the poppy, flax, and pumpkin seeds with the boiling water in a small bowl, cover, and let soak for 8-9 hours. Drain before using.

Day 1, Afternoon/Evening (8-9 hours later): Start making your dough
If your leaven is ready (p. 26, B), in a large bowl, mix the salt with the lukewarm water until dissolved. Add the light stone-ground wheat bread flour and leaven and mix by hand until there are no dry bits of flour. Cover with a damp towel and set aside for 30 minutes.

After 30 minutes, add the drained seeds and chopped prunes and give the dough a set of stretches and folds (p. 26, D) to incorporate. Cover and repeat the stretches and folds at 30-minute intervals for the next 3 ½ hours, until the dough is light and airy and requires fewer and fewer folds to hold the tension (p. 26, E).

After the final rest, turn the dough out onto a wet work surface and divide it into two even portions. Using wet hands, preshape both portions (p. 27, F) then let rest for 20 minutes.

Meanwhile, spread the poppy, flax, and pumpkin seeds for coating on a large plate. Have 2 proofing baskets waiting.

After 20 minutes, shape your dough: Use a wet bench knife to flip one portion of dough onto the plate of seeds. With wet hands, fold and shape the dough (p. 27, G) on the plate — the seeds will stick to the surface of the dough. Repeat with the second portion of dough. Place the shaped loaves, seam-side up, into the proofing baskets and let rest at room temperature for 20-30 minutes, then refrigerate overnight or for up to 15 hours for the final rest.

Day 2, Morning: Bake your bread
Place a covered cast-iron pot in the oven and preheat the oven to 250°C (500°F).

Once the oven is preheated, remove 1 shaped loaf from the refrigerator and invert it into the pot. Using your bench knife, press straight into the loaf to divide it into 4-6 even triangular portions and gently separate them. If this is too much maneuvering, cut the buns on a cutting board and place them in the pot afterward. Cover the pot and bake for 15 minutes, then uncover the pot, lower the oven temperature to 235°C (450°F) and continue baking for about 12 minutes, or until brown and crusty. Repeat for the second loaf.

Soft Whole Wheat Bread

Whole wheat bread has a reputation as a health food and not as a flavor bomb, but that is a disservice to the genre. Pain Complet, whole wheat bread, is in every French baker's repertoire and is a rich alternative to the ubiquitous baguette. Here, the addition of a small amount of butter softens the crumb of this classic loaf and smells smotheringly delicious as it bakes. While fats are usually left out of bread and reserved for soft, enriched doughs like brioche, their tenderizing effect can work wonders on rougher whole-grain loaves. If you want to keep this dairy free, substitute olive oil for the butter.

YIELD: 1 LOAF

For the whole wheat leaven
· 10g (2 tsp) ripe sourdough starter
· 60g (½ cup) whole wheat flour
· 60g (¼ cup) cool water

For the dough
· 9g (2 tsp) large grain gray sea salt (sel de Guérande) 1.9%
· 400g (1¾ cups) lukewarm water at 28-35°C (84-95°F) 80%
· 400g (3⅓ cups) whole wheat flour 80%
· 100g (¾ cup plus 1 tbsp) light stone-ground wheat bread flour, light spelt flour, or bread flour 20%
· 100g (½ cup plus 2 tbsp) leaven 20%
· 50g (3½ tbsp) unsalted butter, room temperature 10%
Optional: Substitute 35g (3 tbsp) olive oil for the butter 7%

(L) **TIMELINE**
24 h, start to finish
Day 1, Morning:
Build leaven, rest 8-9 h
Day 1, Afternoon/Evening:
Mix dough, bulk proof 4 h
Preshape, bench rest 20 min
Shape, basket rest 30 min
Refrigerate 8-15 h
Day 2, Morning:
Bake 45 min

Follow the pattern of the Daily Bread recipe (pp. 26-27).

Day 1, Morning: Make your leaven
Build your leaven and let it rest, loosely covered, for 8-9 hours (p. 26, A).

Day 1, Afternoon/Evening (8-9 hours later): Start making your dough
If your leaven is ready (p. 26, B), in a large bowl, mix the salt with the lukewarm water until dissolved. Add the whole wheat flour, light stone-ground wheat bread flour, and leaven and mix by hand until there are no dry bits of flour. If the dough feels pretty wet, don't worry — the whole wheat flour will absorb the water during the rest. Cover with a damp towel and set aside for 30 minutes.

After 30 minutes, give your dough a few stretches and folds until it resists any more stretching (p. 26, D). Gently schmear the butter into the dough, then continue to stretch and fold to incorporate the butter. If the dough tears, don't worry — it will come back together during the rest. Once the butter is fully incorporated, pick up the dough from the middle and let gravity fold it back on itself. Cover with a damp towel and let rest for 30 minutes. Cover and repeat the stretches and folds at 30-minute intervals for the next 3½ hours, until the dough is light and airy and requires fewer and fewer folds to hold the tension (p. 26, E).

After the final rest, turn the proofed dough out onto a floured surface and give it a preshape (p. 27, F). Let rest for 20 minutes. During the bench rest, lightly flour a proofing basket with whole wheat flour.

After 20 minutes, shape your dough: Use your bench knife to flip the dough, so it is smooth-side down on the work surface. Shape the dough (p. 27, G) and set it, smooth-side down, in the floured proofing basket. Let rest at room temperature for 30 minutes, then refrigerate overnight or for up to 15 hours for the final rest.

Day 2, Morning: Bake your bread
Place a covered cast-iron pot in the oven and preheat the oven to 250°C (500°F).

Once the oven is preheated, invert your loaf from its basket into the heated pot, smooth-side up. Score the dough (p. 27, J), then cover and bake for 20 minutes. Uncover the bread, lower the oven temperature to 235°C (450°F) and continue baking for 25 minutes, or until you hear a hollow sound when you knock on the bottom of the loaf.

Black Seed Potato Bread

The only European potato bread I've managed to find in the wild was in a bakery in Hungary, and I struggled so badly to make myself understood, it's a miracle I even got a hold of it. I might not have much luck finding them, but potato breads can allegedly be found all over Germany and Central Europe. Breads that incorporate potatoes have been around for centuries. In times of shortage, potatoes were an easy way to add bulk and longevity to bread, but this loaf is hardly the product of austerity — it's a show-off and demands that you treat it as such. Let it be the main event, not the sideshow. The potato gives the crumb loads of satisfying softness, while the seeds add onion-y bursts and crunch. It needs nothing more than some good olive oil and a touch of flaky salt for it to be a dinner course all its own.

YIELD: 1 LOAF

For the whole wheat leaven
· 10g (2 tsp) ripe sourdough starter
· 60g (½ cup) whole wheat flour
· 60g (¼ cup) cool water

For the dough
· 8g (½ tbsp) large grain gray sea salt (sel de Guérande) 2%
· 300g (1¼ cups) lukewarm water at 28–35°C (84–95°F) 75%
· 400g (3⅓ cups) light stone-ground wheat bread flour 100%
· 80g (⅓ cup) whole wheat leaven 20%
· 140g (1 cup) boiled, mashed, and cooled new potatoes 35%
· 5g ½ tbsp nigella seeds 1.2%
· 5g (½ tbsp) poppy seeds 1.2%
· 5g (1½ tbsp) black sesame seeds 1.2%

 TIMELINE
24 h, start to finish
Day 1, Morning:
Build leaven, rest 8–9 h
Day 1, Afternoon/Evening:
Mix dough, bulk proof 4 h
Preshape, bench rest 20 min
Shape, basket rest 20 min
Refrigerate 8–15 h
Day 2, Morning:
Bake 45 minutes

Follow the pattern of the Daily Bread recipe (pp. 26–27).

Day 1, Morning: Make your leaven
Build your leaven and let it rest, loosely covered, for 8–9 hours (p. 26, A).

Day 1, Afternoon/Evening (8–9 hours later): Start making your dough
If your leaven is ready (p. 26, B), in a large bowl, mix the salt with the lukewarm water until dissolved. Add the light stone-ground wheat bread flour and leaven and mix by hand until there are no dry bits of flour. Cover with a damp towel and set aside for 30 minutes.

After 30 minutes, give the dough a set of stretches and folds until it resists any more stretching (p. 26, D). Rest for 30 minutes, then add the mashed potatoes, along with the nigella, poppy, and black sesame seeds, and give the dough a set of stretches and folds to incorporate. Cover and repeat the stretches and folds at 30-minute intervals for the next 3 hours until the dough is light and airy and requires fewer and fewer folds to hold the tension (p. 26, E).

After the final rest, turn the proofed dough out onto a floured work surface and give it a preshape (p. 27, F). Let rest for 20 minutes. During the bench rest, lightly flour a proofing basket.

After 20 minutes, use a bench scraper to flip the dough so it's smooth-side down on the floured work surface. Shape the bread (p. 27, G) then place, smooth-side down, in the floured proofing basket. Let rest at room temperature for 20 minutes. then refrigerate overnight or for up to 15 hours for the final rest.

Day 2, Morning: Bake your bread
Place a covered cast-iron pot in the oven and preheat the oven to 250°C (500°F).

Once the oven is preheated, invert your loaf from its basket into the heated pot, smooth-side up. Score the dough (p. 27, J), then cover and bake for 20 minutes. Uncover the bread, lower the oven temperature to 235°F (450°F), and continue baking for 25 minutes, or until you hear a hollow sound when you knock on the bottom of the loaf. Allow the bread to cool before slicing.

Bialys

Spoiler alert: You won't find a bialy in Bialystock, the onion roll's namesake city — I made that drive so you don't have to. While the bialy was always more localized than its cousin, the bagel, it was almost entirely wiped out in Europe, along with the Jewish bakers who made them, and survives only in exile in pockets of East Coast America. While the flatter pletzel and more brioche-like cebularz are alive and well in Poland and the Marais in Paris, only now are bialys reappearing in Europe — though there's still no sign of them in Bialystock — thanks to a new generation of primarily Jewish-American bakers. Even if the bialy's European return is a slow one — as niche as its origins — let's call it a trend. After all, they are stand-alone breads that occupy the same snack realm as focaccia, the same brunch realm as bagels, and the same place in one's heart as grandparents and chicken soup.

YIELD: 9 BIALYS

For the dough
· Ingredients for Daily Bread leaven and dough (p. 26)

For the filling
· 2 medium red onions
· 2 tbsp olive oil
· 1 tbsp poppy seeds
· ¾ tsp table salt
· 1 tsp coarse black pepper

TIMELINE
24 h, start to finish
Day 1, Morning:
Build leaven, rest 8-9 h
Day 1, Afternoon/Evening:
Mix dough, bulk proof 4 h
Preshape, bench rest 20 min
Shape, refrigerate overnight, at least 9 h
Day 2, Morning:
Final proof 2-3 h
Shape, bake 15-20 min

Day 1, Morning: Make your leaven
Build your leaven and let it rest, loosely covered, for 8-9 hours (p. 26, A).

Day 1, Afternoon/Evening (8-9 hours later): Start making your dough
Follow the recipe for the Daily Bread, including bulk proofing (p. 26, B-E), so the dough is ready to be preshaped.

After the final rest of the bulk proof, give your dough a preshape: Turn the proofed dough out onto a floured work surface and divide it into 9 equal portions, about 84g (3 ounces) each. Gently flatten then fold up the sides of each piece of dough into the middle to give it tension. Flip these smooth-side up. Using a cupped hand, gently roll each portion of dough into a ball. Let rest, smooth-side up, for 20 minutes. During the bench rest, line a baking tray with parchment paper.

After 20 minutes, flip the preshaped balls, so they are smooth-side down. Gently flatten each ball with your palm, then repeat the process, folding the dough and shaping it into balls. Arrange the balls, 5cm (2 inches) apart, on the parchment paper-lined baking tray, lightly dust the tops with flour, and cover loosely. Refrigerate overnight, at least 9 hours.

Day 2, Morning: Bake your bread
Remove the bialys from the refrigerator and allow to rise and come to room temperature for 2-3 hours.

Meanwhile, prepare your filling: Cut the onions into very thin rounds, put in a large bowl, and toss with the olive oil, poppy seeds, salt, and pepper.

Preheat the oven to 250°C (500°F).

Once your bialys have warmed up, without lifting them off the tray, press the middle of each ball to create a depression that's about 5cm (2 inches) across. Each ball should have a roughly 2cm (¾ inch) puffed edge, so that the bialys look like small pizzas with a fat crust. In the center of each bialy, spread a generous spoonful of the onion mixture. Bake for 15-20 minutes, or until toasty brown. Eat as is, or serve with butter, cream cheese, or smoked fish.

Roasted Garlic and Lemony Labne Bialys

Every single morning of the week, Ali Jalali, my best friend's father, loads an onion bagel with clouds of labne. It's an inspired Persia–meets–Shtetl breakfast and if the combo works for Mr. Jalali and his bagels, why not these bialys? Fresh labne, soft roasted garlic, and a lemony herb sauce make these bialys even dreamier than the original. You can use store-bought labne, but making your own is so easy and the bit of extra effort required is worth it. Time your bake to pull these bialys from the oven to serve hot for brunch or as an aperitif-hour nosh.

Note: I like to make the roasted garlic and the labne on day 1, but you can wait and roast the garlic on the day you bake your bialys. When making labne, don't worry about the lack of refrigeration — this is a European cookbook, after all. But in all seriousness, yogurt is a fermented product to begin with, and the salt and lemon will keep it safe until the next day.

YIELD: 9 BIALYS

For the dough
· Ingredients for Daily Bread leaven and dough (p. 26)

For the roasted garlic
· 3 garlic heads
· 65g (¼ cup plus 1 tbsp) olive oil, plus more for brushing

For the labne
· 500g (2 cups) Greek or other thick yogurt (3-5% fat)
· 1 garlic clove, crushed with a garlic press
· ½ lemon, juiced
· 1 tbsp fleur de sel

For the lemony herb sauce
· 10g (¼ cup) fresh dill
· 42g (1 cup) fresh flat-leaf parsley leaves
· 20g (½ cup) fresh mint leaves
· 10g (¼ cup) fresh chives
· 5 sprigs fresh tarragon, leaves picked
· 1 tbsp fleur de sel or any flaky sea salt
· 65g (¼ cup plus 1 tbsp) olive oil
· 1 lemon, juiced

TIMELINE
24 h, start to finish
Day 1, Morning:
Build leaven, rest 8-9 h
Day 1, Afternoon/Evening:
Mix dough, bulk proof 4 h
Preshape, bench rest 20 min
Shape, refrigerate overnight, at least 9 h
Roast garlic / Make labne
Day 2, Morning:
Final proof, shape, bake 15-20 min
Make lemony herb sauce

Day 1, Morning: Make your leaven
Build your leaven and let it rest, loosely covered, for 8-9 hours (p. 26, A).

Day 1, Afternoon/Evening (8-9 hours later): Start making your dough
Follow the recipe for the Daily Bread, including bulk proofing (p. 26, B-E), so the dough is ready to be preshaped.

After the final rest of the bulk proof, give your dough a preshape: Turn the proofed dough out onto a floured work surface and divide it into 9 equal portions, about 84g (3 ounces) each. Gently flatten then fold up the sides of each piece of dough into the middle to give it tension. Flip these smooth-side up. Using a cupped hand, gently roll each portion of dough into a ball. Let rest, smooth-side up, for 20 minutes. During the bench rest, line a baking tray with parchment paper.

After 20 minutes, flip the preshaped balls, so they are smooth-side down. Gently flatten each ball with your palm, then repeat the process, folding the dough and shaping it into balls. Arrange the balls, 5cm (2 inches) apart, on the parchment paper-lined baking tray and lightly dust the tops with flour. Cover loosely and refrigerate overnight, at least 9 hours.

While the dough is chilling, roast the garlic. Preheat the oven to 135°C (275°F). Cut a thin slice off the top of each head of garlic, so the cloves are just barely exposed. Place each head, cut-side up, on a square of aluminum foil that's large enough to enclose the entire head. Generously drizzle the top of each head with olive oil, then wrap the foil around the garlic. Bake for about 1 hour, or until the garlic is soft and can be easily squeezed out. Use right away or store in the refrigerator for up to 4 days.

Make the labne. In a small bowl, mix the yogurt, garlic, lemon juice, and salt until smooth. Spoon into the center of a large piece of cheesecloth, then pull the sides up to make a pouch and twist tightly to close. Hang the cheesecloth pouch over your kitchen faucet or shower rod and let drip and drain overnight. Unwrap the labne and use right away or transfer to an airtight container and refrigerate for up to 1 week.

Day 2, Morning: Bake your bread
Remove the bialys from the refrigerator and allow to rise and come to room temperature for 2-3 hours.

Preheat the oven to 250°C (500°F). Once your bialys have warmed up, without lifting them off the tray, press the middle of each ball to create a depression that's about 5cm (2 inches) across. Each ball should have a roughly 2cm (¾ inch) puffed edge, so that the bialys look like small pizzas with a fat crust. Brush the center of each bialy with olive oil, then squeeze roasted garlic cloves into the center of each bialy. Bake for 15-20 minutes, or until toasty brown.

While the bialys are baking, make the lemony herb sauce. Blend the dill, parsley, mint, chives, and tarragon in a food processor until roughly chopped. Add the salt. With the processor on, gradually drizzle in the olive oil and lemon juice, blending until it has a rustic slurry texture.

Serve the bialys hot, with a large spoonful of labne and a generous drizzle of the lemony herb sauce.

Roberta Pezzella

Roberta Pezzella's story is written on her body. Starting low on her ankles and winding up her calves, it cuts across her back then around and down her sleeves. When she lifts focaccia dough, you catch flashes of a life — a moment, a place, a mentor, a favorite grain. After more than twenty years fighting for her place in the Italian bread world, it's tattooed on her soul.

Roberta's bakery, PezZ de Pane — "piece of bread" in the local dialect — sits on the sunny end of a small square in Frosinone Alto, a hilly provincial capital an hour's drive from Rome. It's a straightforward shop, where she shapes bread in full view of clients. The facade is marked simply, il forno ("the bakery"), on a green and yellow sign that looks like a relic from the Sixties but is, in fact, another of Roberta's deliberately chosen details, the work of an artisan sign maker in Rome. A former art student, Roberta's interest in typography and graphic art shows up everywhere in the bakery. Framed graffiti hangs on the walls, and handwritten labels, done in thick marker like street tags — Roberta's own writing — give her whole-grain crostate and feather-light country loaves an attitude and aesthetic all their own.

Hanging on the door is one last sign in Roberta's signature print. It's a warning to customers: They won't find rosette or filoni inside. These locally popular but cheap white breads are a far cry from Roberta's exacting ferments and shapes. Still, it's as bold as refusing to sell a baguette in France.

Nevertheless, this deters no one. A steady stream of neighbors drop by to chat while Roberta, between maneuvers at the oven, personally stuffs their morning brioches with pastry cream and jam. For Roman families passing through on their way home from seaside holidays, she slices her unsweetened chocolate loaf, toasts it in the residual heat of the oven, and then plasters it thick with butter and honey. Coos of pleasure, then silence. When was the last time they tasted bread and pastry like this? Had they ever?

Roberta is generous with her bread, which not all bakers are. "Have you ever smelled bread like this?" she asks, slicing in half a pane di Ponza, her "bread of Ponza." The Ponza, named after an island southwest of Frosinone, is one of Roberta's most important loaves. Every weekend, so long as the season allows, she closes the bakery and goes to the island to gather wild fennel. After soaking it overnight, she uses the infused water to make bread. The result is mellow anise wafting over toasted grains.

Though the bakery is brand new — it opened in the winter of 2021 — Roberta herself is an institution. Her path in food began modestly. As a teenager, just graduated from the liceo artistico — art school — and without plans for the future, she took a job selling candy at a market stand in Rome. From there, she began selling fish from another stall, and by the time she was twenty-two, she was selling fish at the local Conad, a franchised grocery store. While there, Roberta started developing an interest in food. The grocery store

had huge buying power and she was responsible for choosing all the fish. She threw herself into the trade and gained a reputation for obtaining only the best and only the freshest fish. Unsurprisingly, her counter was celebrated for its quality.

After three years, despite her success, Roberta became frustrated. There were other foods she was

in the pastry department, but during her free mornings, she strayed from the restaurant to learn bread making from Gabriele Bonci, the renowned panettiere. She knew Beck wanted to transform the restaurant's bread offerings and Bonci gave her an idea: Since Beck is German, why not make him a rye bread? Roberta ultimately created a suite of breads that are still

revamping the pastry section, making it profitable and expanding the plant-based offerings. And just as she'd done with the fish counter and the bread basket, she transformed the pastry shop. From there, she was put on bread.

At La Pergola, Roberta used ten kilos (twenty-two pounds) of flour a day. Suddenly, at Bonci's, she was using fifty to sixty times that amount. And, she was the manager, in charge of a whole team of bakers. In the jealous masculine environment, no one would help her except Franco Palermo.

> " *Within months of opening, PezZ de Pane feels so settled, as though it's always been here.*

curious about beyond fish. She could see them around the grocery store — bread, vegetables, fruits. At the checkout, she began buying the culinary magazine Gambero Rossoto to read about the restaurant world and scan for recommendations. She also started taking herself out to dinner and suddenly, she was having so many new food experiences that she decided that something needed to change. At twenty-five, Roberta dumped her boyfriend, left Frosinone, and went to Rome to attend culinary school.

In a class of thirty students, Roberta finished first, and knew exactly where she wanted to go next — La Pergola, a Roman restaurant with three Michelin stars headed by chef Heinz Beck. She started working

being served at La Pergola today. But fine dining is a demanding environment and seven years was long enough. By the time she left her post as La Pergola's head baker in 2013, Roberta was burned-out. It was around the same time that Gabriele Bonci, her old friend and mentor, called her up. Would she come run the show at his bakery, Panificio Bonci? Roberta said yes.

Panificio Bonci, though, was not La Pergola. Roberta remembers a chaotic, anarchic, all-male environment. In short, she says, it was complicated. From the day Roberta showed up, in her clean chef's jacket straight from fine dining, she was out of place and resented. Bonci put her to work

Franco was an unusual employee. A master baker who had taught Bonci to make bread, Franco came and went as he pleased. Roberta was technically his boss, but he was her guru, and took her deeper into bread making. This was her proper formation as a baker. For three years, Roberta stayed at Panificio Bonci, suffering the aggression of her colleagues but perfecting her craft. Until it became too much. She fell into a depression and left.

Contemplating her future, Roberta was lost as to where to go next. It was then that she remembered her old bosses at the Conad grocery store in Frosinone. They owned twelve stores in total, and produced

all of their own bread in a bakery in the mountains nearby. Roberta remembered that they'd always spoken about changing the grocery store's bakery offerings and she saw an opportunity: Maybe she could bring better bread to the people? Something good, healthy, not super elaborate? She convinced the owners to hire her back — not as a fishmonger this time, but as a baker.

From day one, Conad's central bakery provided its own challenges. It had been so industrialized that the workers couldn't tell one kind of flour from another. Bread was exclusively machine-shaped. Simply put, there was no craftsmanship. When Roberta took charge, she got rid of all the machinery, apart from two basic mixers, and set to work teaching the staff how to bake. She quickly discovered a familiar problem that was going to be harder to fix — the fact that she's a woman.
Slowly though, Roberta changed Conad's bread production. She taught the team to hand shape, introduced natural fermentation, and improved the flours they used. Chefs started to come from all over to intern and learn from Roberta. And most importantly, the customers at the grocery stores responded. They liked what she'd done and her breads were now in demand. Roberta had done it again.

But it couldn't last. Despite all the improvements, Conad's owners didn't want to raise their bread prices. They complained that the materials and labor were too expensive and insisted they had to cut corners. And then one day, Roberta arrived at work to find all the machinery back on the floor. The product range she'd spent years developing was destroyed. She quit, devastated and — again — unsure of where to go next.

And so she ran away to Ponza and got a job frying fish at what she describes as the worst restaurant on the island. For months, no one knew where Roberta was, but when she finally emerged, she was ready to start fresh. For the next two years, she taught, consulted, learned,

and traveled, visiting bakeries in San Francisco, Copenhagen, and Germany, despite only speaking Italian. "I always find ways to communicate," she says, smiling.

And then the pandemic hit and all of Italy went into lockdown. Overnight, Roberta's consulting work dried up. She knew she never wanted to work for anyone else again. One day, in Frosinone, she came across a closed pizzeria with a "for rent" sign in the window and that was it. She decided to open her own shop, something she'd never considered before.

Within months of opening, PezZ de Pane feels so settled, an easy part of the scenery of Frosinone. It's as though it's always been here. On an average summer morning, as

the sun starts to burn, Roberta runs out to the covered market to buy the green and pink figs she'll smash onto pizza bianca with prosciutto, as well as the plum tomatoes she'll crush on her focaccia barese. A little later, her parents drop by, handing over a lunch of fava beans for her to share with her cashier and intern during the inevitable midday siesta. Down the street is the Conad where she once sold fish.

There's a light atmosphere amongst Roberta and the two women who work with her. Tomorrow they'll all take a day off. Beach plans are discussed. A trip to Abruzzo. Roberta, as usual, will go to the island of Ponza. And when she comes back, she'll bring the last of the season's fennel.

Roberta Pezzella's Pan di Ponza ·
Wild Fennel Bread

Pan di Ponza is Roberta Pezzella's signature fennel bread. Italy famously has diverse wild greens, and wild finocchio — fennel — is abundant, especially on the island of Ponza, where Roberta forages hers. To pull all the flavor from the fennel, she soaks the greens in water then freezes both overnight to create an infusion she uses to make the bread. If you can't find wild fennel, the top green leaves of cultivated fennel will work perfectly.

YIELD: 1 LOAF

For the fennel infusion
· 70g (1 ½ cups) fennel leaves
· 375g (1 ½ cups plus 1 tbsp) water

For the whole wheat leaven
· 10g (2 tsp) ripe sourdough starter
· 60g (½ cup) whole wheat flour
· 60g (¼ cup) cool water

For the dough
· Fennel infusion (room temperature) 76%
· 9g (2 tsp) large grain gray sea salt (sel de Guérande) 1.9%
· 500g (4 cups plus 2 ½ tbsp) light stone-ground wheat bread flour 100%
· 100g (½ cup plus 2 tbsp) whole wheat leaven 20%

 TIMELINE
36 h, start to finish
Day 1, Evening:
Make fennel infusion
Day 2, Morning:
Defrost fennel infusion, build leaven, rest 8-9 h
Day 2, Afternoon/Evening:
Mix dough, bulk proof 4 h
Preshape, bench rest 20 min
Shape, basket rest 30 min
Refrigerate 8-15 h
Day 3, Morning:
Bake 45 min

Follow the pattern of the Daily Bread recipe (pp. 26-27).

Day 1, Evening: Make your fennel infusion
In an airtight container, combine the fennel and water, cover, and freeze overnight.

Day 2, Morning: Make your leaven
Build your leaven and let it rest, loosely covered, for 8-9 hours (p. 26, A).

Meanwhile, remove the infusion from the freezer and allow it to defrost at room temperature.

Day 2, Afternoon/Evening (8-9 hours later): Start making your dough
If your leaven is ready (p. 26, B), drain the fennel infusion, reserving both the fennel and the infused water. Chop the fennel and set aside. In a large bowl, mix the salt with the fennel-infused water until dissolved. Add the light stone-ground wheat bread flour and leaven and mix by hand until there are no dry bits of flour. Cover with a damp towel and set aside for 30 minutes.

After 30 minutes, give the dough a set of stretches and folds until it resists any more stretching (p. 26, D). Rest the dough for 30 minutes. Add the chopped fennel to the dough and give it a second set of stretches and folds to incorporate. Cover and repeat the stretches and folds at 30-minute intervals for the next 3 hours, until the dough is light and airy and requires fewer and fewer folds to hold the tension (p. 26, E).

After the final rest, turn the proofed dough out onto a floured surface and give it a preshape (p. 27, F). Let rest for 20 minutes. During the bench rest, lightly flour a proofing basket with whole wheat flour.

After 20 minutes, shape your dough: Use your bench knife to flip the dough, so it is smooth-side down on the work surface. Shape the dough (p. 27, G) and set it, smooth-side down, in the floured proofing basket. Let rest at room temperature for 30 minutes, then refrigerate overnight or for up to 15 hours for the final rest.

Day 3, Morning: Bake your bread
Place a covered cast-iron pot in the oven and preheat the oven to 250°C (500°F).

Once the oven is preheated, remove the shaped loaf from the refrigerator and invert it into the pot. Score the dough (p. 27, J), then cover and bake for 20 minutes. Uncover the bread, lower the oven temperature to 235°C (450°F), and continue baking for 25 minutes, or until you hear a hollow sound when you knock on the bottom of the loaf.

Tourte de Seigle Auvergnate · Rye Torte

Tourte de seigle Auvergnate is the Frenchiest of rye breads — super crusty and flavorful and very similar to the whole rye tortes of Germany, Switzerland, and Austria. Something of a gold standard among bakers, this loaf has a spiral crust that makes it almost too pretty to eat. Instead, I suggest you carry it over the Alps to a handsome shepherd — tourte de seigle makes a wonderful token of affection for that special someone. If you can't manage that, slice it thin and serve it with a cheese board.

Notes: Rye is a superfood for natural yeast, so this dough ferments quickly. However, the key to making this bread is in the delicate handling. You'll also notice this dough is made with hot water — it brings out the natural sweetness of the rye and improves the bread's final texture. This bread has a very different process than the loaves up until this point — the leaven makes up half the total dough and the final bulk proof is less than an hour with no stretches or folds.

For a variation on this loaf, I like to add a combination of any of the following ingredients during the mix: pan-toasted fennel seeds, soaked golden raisins, celery seeds, or chopped roasted garlic.

YIELD: 1 LOAF

For the rye leaven
· 70g (½ cup plus 1 tbsp) light or medium stone-ground wheat bread flour
· 70g (½ cup plus 1 tsp) medium or dark rye flour
· 20g (1 tbsp plus 1 tsp) ripe sourdough starter
· 90g (⅓ cup plus 2 tsp) cool water

For the dough
· 7g (1 ⅓ tsp) large grain gray sea salt (sel de Guérande) 2.8%
· 220g (¾ cup plus 2 tbsp plus 2 tsp) hot water at 60°C (140°F) 88%
· 250g (2 cups) dark rye flour 100%
· 250g (1 ¼ cups) rye leaven 100%

Ⓛ TIMELINE
10-11 h, start to finish
Day 1, Evening:
Build leaven, rest 8-9 h
Day 2, Morning:
Mix dough, bulk proof 40-50 min
Shape, basket rest 20 min
Bake 60 min

Day 1, Evening: Make your leaven
Build your leaven and let it rest, loosely covered, for 8-9 hours (p. 26, A). Note that this is a stiff leaven and will have a thick, pasty texture.

Day 2, Morning (8-9 hours later): Start making your dough
If your leaven is ready (p. 26, B), in a large bowl, mix the salt with the hot water until dissolved. Add the dark rye flour and leaven and mix by hand until there are no dry bits of flour. Cover with a damp towel and leave the dough for its bulk proof, 40-50 minutes.

Meanwhile, place a covered cast-iron pot in the oven and preheat the oven to 250°C (500°F). Generously flour a proofing basket.

After the bulk proof, use a wet dough scraper to gently turn the proofed dough out onto a very well floured work surface — the dough will be very delicate and have a spongy, mousse-like texture. To shape, use well-floured hands, cupped and held at a 45 degree angle, to gently spin the dough and shape it, without pressing, into a round. Do this quickly and with as few movements as possible, so you push out as little air as possible. Gently lift the round loaf — do not flip it over — and it lay in the floured proofing basket. Let rest for about 20 minutes — the surface of the dough will start to crack, which means it's ready to bake.

Once the oven is preheated, invert the loaf into the heated cast-iron pot. (This loaf needs no scoring.) Cover and bake for 20 minutes. Uncover the bread and continue baking for 20 minutes, or until a thermometer inserted in the loaf reads 98°C (210°F) — rye breads are tricky, so it's imperative to check the internal temperature on this loaf rather than just going by visual signals. Lower the oven temperature to 120°C (250°F). Remove the loaf from the pot, place it directly on the oven rack, and let it dry out for another 20 minutes. Remove the bread from the oven and let it cool completely before cutting.

GLEBA · LISBON, PORTUGAL

Diogo Amorim

Gleba — or chleba — means bread in most Slavic languages, but Diogo Amorim didn't know this when he opened his Lisbon bakery six years ago. It's not a coincidence, though, he insists. The word falls in the dictionary of many European languages and always in relation to bread. In his native Portuguese, it's an old, rarely used word for land — specifically, land used to cultivate grain for bread making. That the word has a kind of universality but is tied to grain and soil is in keeping with Diogo's bread philosophy, which he'll tell you about with the detail of an historian and the enthusiasm of a manifesto. This is what informs his bakery: the soil, the grain, and the past.

Diogo is young — only twenty-six — and he was just twenty-one when he opened Gleba, but he gives the impression of being an elder in his field. He came to baking early, after studying culinary arts in Switzerland and working at London's Michelin-starred Fat Duck. Historically, the bread at fine dining restaurants had little to do with the care and perfectionism of the cooking. Most restaurants have moved away from this, with some updating their bread offerings — turning the bread into a course of its own — and others doing away with the bread basket altogether. Diogo was lucky to encounter the former early on, getting an education in grains and natural fermentation through his work at Fat Duck.

After London, Diogo moved back to Algarve to work at Vila Joya, another fine dining establishment. While he was there, he started to think that there was something to be done in terms of bread in Portugal. Something that he could do.

"We have a great bread tradition here. Portuguese people think we have the best bread in the world here. When they travel abroad, the thing they miss the most is their bread," Diogo says. "But it's been lost. The recipes, the quality — the last fifty, one hundred years, the quality has gone down. Especially in the cities. The cheaper the better, the fastest possible."

Diogo shakes his head when he tells you this. "Yes, there is worse. But that doesn't mean the current bread has anything to do with our bread traditions. Even if we are proud of our bread, ninety-nine percent of the flour in Portugal is imported." Portugal's mediterranean climate isn't ideal for grain productivity. The hot springtime means the grains form too quickly and the resulting yield isn't very high.

"We're better at growing almonds, olives, and wine. Those are much more lucrative crops compared to grain. So the Portuguese import pretty much all our grains from France, Germany, and other countries around the world."

If it sounds like an empty lament of savoir-faire lost, it isn't. When Diogo came back to Portugal, he acted, traveling from north to south, east to west. He met with old artisans

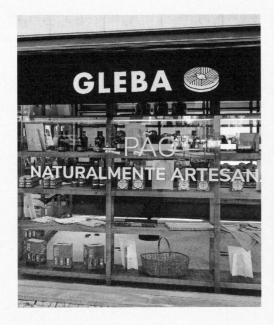

and food historians and got to know millers and bakers who maintained traditional methods and recipes. All the while, he read and researched. In this way, carefully and deliberately, Diogo learned the regional breads of Portugal, and the local grains that make them. It's this journey that centered his early baking. He wanted to do something that connected with his country's past in terms of bread.

"You cannot make an omelet without eggs, and you cannot make bread without grain. And back in the day, the only way you had to make bread was to use local grains. And these local grains and their specific characteristics were a big part of the tradition that we have right now. The recipes that were developed were developed according to the grain that was available. That's why corn was

really what created the staples that we have right now."

But those staples have been corrupted, Diogo says. "Take, for example, Alentejo bread. Alentejo is a region in the south of Portugal. When it starts being made with French wheat or Polish wheat, is it still Alentejo bread? When it is made with a completely different, very standardized wheat?"

"To put it differently," Diogo says, "if you buy a wine from Burgundy, it must be made with grapes from Burgundy, so why can you make Alentejo bread and use a completely different grain? You can't. It messes with the authenticity of the bread."

Even though Diogo knew what he wanted his bakery to be, it would only have been idealism without the

say that I was small, because I wasn't small, I was zero. I didn't even have the bakery. 'How much grain do you use per day?' the farmers would ask. 'Zero,' I'd have to say. 'And maybe when I open my bakery, I'll use sixty (about 132 pounds), a hundred kilos (about 220 pounds) a day.' Which is very very little to get someone interested."

Still, some farmers agreed. Diogo opened his bakery and bought small quantities of their grains. Because he was using only Portuguese grains from small producers, he had to mill them himself with a stone mill. At the same time, as he was building his own business, he tried to push the visibility of the farmers alongside his bread.

"We wanted to make people connect with the origins of their bread. Most people, they think of bread, they think of wheat, but they don't even know what the wheat grain is. We had to make that connection. We made those farmers visible."

> **"Diogo learned the regional breads of Portugal, and the local grains that make them.**

used in the north, where there's more rainfall and wheat is more difficult to grow. And why there are wheat loaves in the south, where wheat is more easily grown. We have soft wheats, hard wheats, wheats that are very much like rye, with very little gluten. So the characteristics of those grains are

raw materials. But he was committed to the difficult path, and convinced farmers to grow grain for him — local grain varieties for his traditional recipes. Only twenty years old and with no bakery yet to speak of, it wasn't an easy sell.

"It was very difficult at the beginning, because I couldn't even

Despite producing and selling all the bread, Diogo stuck with his plan to work only with small producers, despite the challenges that creates. Six years in, Diogo has a team of bakers and a bakery that combines the most modern technology of temperature and humidity control with the ancient methods of natural fermentation. He keeps an independent milling facility where he stores and mills his grain. He works with ten different growers, each of whom he trusts implicitly. And likewise, he appreciates the trust they put in him.

"It was hard to find and make these relationships," he says. He works with a lot of farmers from the Alentejo region. The extremely hot, dry summers mean the grain dries naturally in the fields, not in the unnaturally high temperatures of industrial drying plants. Sun drying keeps all the flavor and nutrition in the grain. "While we might not be very competitive in terms of yield, we are in terms of quality," says Diogo. Gleba uses only these local wheats, ryes, spelts, and corn, and Diogo encourages farmers to recover heritage varieties.

"We had a very small sample of a Portuguese wheat called barbela, a very ancient variety that used to be farmed here many centuries ago. We started with a one kilo (two and quarter pound) bag and now we're producing enough to produce bread."

One of the signature loaves at Gleba is the broa de milho, a dense corn bread, a staple of Portugal. There are several variations around the country, but Diogo's is very specific to the north-central region. The bread is made with white corn and rye and even up to fifty or sixty years ago, it was pretty much the only bread available in Diogo's region.

At Gleba, they use Diogo's grandmother's recipe. It's simple and straightforward and they use regional varieties of corn that were selected for bread making. Corn isn't native to Portugal. It was brought over from the Americas in the fifteenth century, but it wasn't until the eighteenth and nineteenth century that it started to be widely used and cultivated in Portugal. While some broas use yellow corn, Diogo's uses white.

"The rich used to eat white wheat bread, and the poor also wanted a white bread. So they selected white corn over more productive yellow corn — they chose white over yellow as a matter of status."

Diogo's approach to traditional breads is working. These days his business is booming and in Lisbon — a city of bakeries — his three Glebas stand out as the only places to taste Portuguese bread from a preindustrial perspective in an industrial world.

"I — we — want to make this accessible. Because we see all over the world, this healthy sourdough bread, it's only for hipsters or people who earn a lot of money. But I don't think that the bread that was consumed by our ancestors should be only for rich people. It should be for everyone. I dream of a world where most people will be able to choose to buy sourdough bread made from local grains that are sustainably grown and naturally fermented." He admits that people have to pay a little more for this, but he hopes he can help convince people that it is a choice to invest in their health and their local environment.

"I dream of a world that shifts in terms of the mentality. It's a matter of priority and caring more about what we put into our bodies, rather than, say, the kind of shoes we put on our bodies." In the meantime, Diogo and Gleba model a bakery future that looks both to the past and to the fields to change the way Portugal eats its bread.

Diogo Amorim's Broa de Milho · Portuguese Corn Torte

Broa de milho, a dense corn loaf, is a Portuguese staple. If you've never had it, get ready for a textural experience unlike any other bread. Corn was brought to Portugal from the Americas in the fifteenth century, but it took a few more centuries to popularize this bread. Baker Diogo Amorim's version of broa — his grandmother's version of broa, to be exact — is particular to the country's North Central region, where it's made with white cornmeal and rye flour. Because corn has no gluten, it gets scalded with boiling water, gelatinizing the starch in the corn. This makes the dough more cohesive (easier shaping!) and gives the bread a smooth rather than grainy texture. This recipe makes a very large loaf of bread, but the size makes for the best crust-to-crumb ratio and it can be wrapped in a cloth and stored for a week to be dipped into hearty soups and stews.

Note: *If you can't find white cornmeal, use all yellow cornmeal.*

YIELD: 1 LOAF

For the rye leaven
· 82g (⅔ cup) medium or dark rye flour
· 82g (⅓ cup plus 1 tsp) cool water
· 16g (1 tbsp) ripe sourdough starter

For the corn
· 300g (2 cups) fine white cornmeal 33.3%
· 300g (2 cups) fine yellow cornmeal 33.3%
· 600g (2½ cups) water at 100°C (212°F) 66.6%
· 18g (4 tsp) large grain gray sea salt (sel de Guérande) 2%
· 300g (2½ cups) medium or dark rye flour 33.3%
· 255g (1 cup plus 1 tbsp) hot water at 60°C (140°F) 28%
· 180g (¾ cup) rye leaven 20%

Ⓛ TIMELINE
15½–17½ h, start to finish
Day 1, Evening:
Build leaven, rest 12 h
Day 2, Morning:
Mix dough, rest 2–4 h
Shape, bake 1½ h

Day 1, Evening: Make your leaven
Build your leaven and let it rest, loosely covered, until very active, about 12 hours (p. 26, A) — a bit of sour flavor is delicious in this loaf.

Day 2, Morning (12 hours later): Start making your dough
If your leaven is ready (p. 26, B), in a large bowl, mix the white and yellow cornmeal with the boiling water until all the cornmeal is hydrated. Add the salt, rye flour, and the hot water and mix until smooth. Let the dough cool to 40°C (104°F), then add the leaven — if the leaven is mixed before the dough cools, there's a risk of deactivating it. Mix until the dough is uniform. Still in the bowl, form the dough into a ball and smooth with wet hands. Let rest for about 3 hours until the dough is puffed, and the surface cracked. Watch for these signs — it could take up to an hour less or more to be ready! When the surface is well-cracked, it's ready to shape.

Place a covered cast-iron pot in the oven and preheat the oven to 250°C (500°F).

When the dough is well-cracked, shape it using the padear process, which is used to shape doughs with no elasticity like broa. Put a generous amount of cornmeal or rye flour in a bowl and place the dough in the bowl. Rapidly rotate the bowl 90 degrees so the loaf jumps. Repeat several times to create a round loaf.

Once the oven is preheated, place the dough in the preheated pot. (This loaf needs no scoring.) Cover and bake for 1 hour and 10 minutes. Uncover the pot and continue baking for 20 minutes, or until the surface takes on a tan color. The internal temperature should read 98°C (210°F). Allow the broa to cool for at least 2 hours, or until the next day before cutting.

Neapolitan-Style Pizza

If you like your pizza to double as a pillow, read on. Neapolitan-style pizza is light and billowy and a relatively simple make-in-advance dinner. In Naples, pizza is traditionally made with a tiny amount of yeast rather than sourdough, but let's keep it natural here. The sourdough lends the dough a slight tang that is very delicious, even if it breaks from local custom.

Notes: I recommend using a stand mixer and dough hook attachment for this dough to build the proper structure, but it can be kneaded by hand. To hand knead, mix the dough with all the water until there are no dry bits of flour, then turn it out onto a lightly floured work surface and give it 10 minutes of slaps and folds until smooth (p. 84, Hand Mixing and Kneading).

Use the broiler settings on your oven to get slightly charred bubbles on the crust. If you have a home pizza oven, even better. The key to a light but moist pizza crust is a hot and fast bake.

YIELD: 3 PIZZAS

For the whole wheat leaven
- 5g (1 tsp) ripe sourdough starter
- 25g (1 tbsp plus 2 tsp) cool water
- 25g (3 tbsp cup) whole wheat flour

For the dough
- 425g (3 ⅔ cups) pizza flour (type 00) 100%
- 270g (1 cup plus 2 tbsp) water at 18–23°C (64–73°F) 63.5%
- 7g (1 ⅓ tsp) large grain gray sea salt (sel de Guérande) 1.6%
- 50g (¼ cup plus 1 tbsp) whole wheat leaven 12%
- 25g (1 tbsp plus 2 tsp) water bassinage 6%

For the toppings
- Tomato sauce (I use high-quality chopped canned tomatoes with a bit of Maldon salt)
- Mozzarella
- Veggies, ricotta, sausage — anything you like!

TIMELINE
36 h, start to finish
Day 1, Morning:
Build leaven, rest 8–9 h
Day 1, Afternoon/Evening:
Mix dough, bulk proof 3 h
Shape, refrigerate 8–15 h
Day 2, Morning:
Divide and preshape dough, rest 7–8 h
Day 2, Afternoon/Evening:
Shape dough, bake pizzas, about 5 min each

Day 1, Morning: Make your leaven
Build your leaven and let it rest, loosely covered, for 8-9 hours (p. 26, A).

Day 1, Afternoon/Evening (8-9 hours later): Start making your dough
If your leaven is ready (p. 26, B), in the bowl of a stand mixer, mix the salt with the water until dissolved. Add the flour and leaven and mix by hand until there are no dry bits of flour. Using the dough hook attachment and with the mixer on medium, knead the dough for 7 minutes. Reduce the speed to low and drizzle in the bassinage liquid. Once the bassinage liquid is absorbed, increase the speed to high and knead for 2 more minutes until the dough is soft and loose but smooth. Transfer to a lightly oiled bowl, cover with a towel, and rest for 30 minutes.

For the next 2 ½ hours, give the dough a set of stretches and folds at 30-minute intervals until it's wonderfully supple and stretchy (p. 26, E).

After the final rest, form the dough into a tight ball and set it in a lightly oiled bowl with room for expansion. Wrap airtight and refrigerate overnight or for up to 15 hours.

Day 2, Morning: Divide and preshape your dough
Divide the dough into 3 equal portions, each about 250g (9 ounces). Form these into tight balls, degassing them from the night's rest. Arrange on a lightly oiled or floured baking tray, at least 7.5 cm (3 inches) apart, then cover loosely and let rest for 7-8 hours.

Evening, Day 2: Bake your pizzas
Put a pizza stone or steel on the middle rack of the oven and preheat the oven to 250°C (500°F) for 1 hour.

Once the stone and oven are preheated, set the oven's broiler as high as it will go without smoking — my home oven goes to 300°C (575°F).

Using whole wheat flour or cornmeal for dusting, gently stretch out 1 ball of dough on a baking tray or pizza peel. The dough will be light as a feather but still strong enough to be stretched. Leave a nice puffy crust on your pizza — you didn't do all this fermenting for nothing.

Spread a thin layer of tomato sauce on top of the pizza, leaving a 2.5–5cm (1–2 inch) border around the edge. Add your mozzarella and toppings then slide your pizza onto the pizza stone or steel and bake for 5 minutes, or until the cheese bubbles and the crust gets some attractive black spots on it. (If using a real pizza oven, reduce the bake to 1-2 minutes.) Repeat to make 2 more pizzas.

Focaccia

Focaccia is an Italian classic that's even easier to make than pizza — not to mention better suited to enjoy over several days (no shade to cold pizza but...). It's salty and olive oil-rich and born from a mild, slow-rising dough that requires no complicated shaping. Focaccia's wide-open bubbly crumb is especially rewarding and a blank slate for all the topping combinations in the world. For a real treat, slice a square through the middle, when it's hot from the oven, and stuff with cheese and cured meats for crusty melty sandwich heaven.

Note: I recommend using a stand mixer and dough hook attachment for this dough to build the proper structure, but it can be kneaded by hand. To hand knead, mix the dough with all the water until there are no dry bits of flour, then turn it out onto a lightly-floured work surface and give it 10 minutes of slaps and folds until smooth (p. 84, Hand Mixing and Kneading).

YIELD: 1 FOCACCIA

For the whole wheat leaven
· 10g (2 tsp) ripe sourdough starter
· 40g (2 tbsp plus 2 tsp) cool water
· 40g (⅓ cup) whole wheat flour

For the dough
· 15g (1 tbsp) large grain gray sea salt (sel de Guérande) 3%
· 320g (1¼ cups plus 1 tbsp plus 1 tsp) water at 18-23°C (64-73°F) 66.6%
· 480g (4 cups plus 2 tbsp) pizza flour (type 00) or bread flour 100%
· 70g (⅓ cup) whole wheat leaven 14.5%
· 10g (½ tbsp) honey 2%
· 20g (1½ tbsp) olive oil bassinage 4%

For the topping
· 100g (½ cup) olive oil
· Flaky sea salt
· 1 handful pitted olives

TIMELINE
36 h, start to finish
Day 1, Morning:
Build leaven, rest 8-9 h
Day 1, Afternoon/Evening:
Mix dough, bulk proof 3 h refrigerate overnight 8 h or for up to 2 days
Day 2, Morning:
Stretch dough, rest 8 h
Day 2, Afternoon/Evening:
Bake 25 m

Day 1, Morning: Make your leaven
Build your leaven and let it rest, loosely covered, for 8-9 hours (p. 26, A).

Day 1, Afternoon/Evening (8-9 hours later): Start making your dough
If your leaven is ready (p. 26, B), in the bowl of a stand mixer, mix the salt with the water until dissolved. Add the pizza flour, leaven, and honey. Using the dough hook attachment, mix the dough on medium for 5 minutes. Reduce the speed to low and drizzle in the olive oil bassinage. The bassinage will make the dough come apart, but once it comes back together, increase the speed to high and knead for 2 more minutes, or until the dough is soft and loose but smooth. Transfer to a lightly oiled bowl, cover with a towel, and let rest for 30 minutes.

For the next 2½ hours, give the dough a set of stretches and folds at 30-minute intervals (p. 26, D-E). At the end of the 2½ hours, give the dough a final set of stretches and folds, then place in an airtight container and refrigerate overnight or for up to 2 days. (The longer the dough rests in the cold, the more profound the sour taste will be; for a milder bread, stick to an overnight rest.)

Day 2, Morning: Stretch your dough
Generously oil a 30 x 25cm (12 x 10 inch) baking pan. Turn the dough out onto the pan and gently stretch it. The dough doesn't have to fill the pan entirely — as it rises, it will expand. Cover loosely with plastic wrap or a damp towel and let it rest at room temperature for about 8 hours.

Day 2, Afternoon/Evening (8 hours later): Bake your focaccia
Preheat the oven to 235°C (450°F).

At this point, the dough will be pillowy and light. Drizzle olive oil all over the surface of the dough. Press your fingertips all over the dough, all the way down to the bottom of the pan. Sprinkle with flaky sea salt, garnish with olives or whatever topping you like, and bake for 25 minutes, or until golden brown.

Alternative topping ideas:
· Olives and fresh tomatoes
· Fresh shiso leaves and garlic confit
· Broccolini, lemon zest, and Parmesan
· Roasted eggplant, arugula, and Burrata
· Rosemary, sliced new potatoes, and flaky sea salt
· Marinated zucchini, chopped walnuts, and fresh mint

Fougasse

Fougasse is rich and airy all at once, and just about the prettiest bread there is. A signature olive bread of the South of France, you're as likely to find this leaf-shaped loaf at a roadside food truck as you are at a bakery. Its origins are in Italian focaccia, but this is a very Provençal focaccia. You typically find fougasse stuffed with regional ingredients like olives and herbs de Provence. I like to add a bit of preserved lemon and fat capers — a combo that makes the fougasse positively cry out for a cold, dry white and a tin of sardines.

Note: Like focaccia and pizza, this dough does best in a stand mixer with the dough hook attachment, but you can make it by hand. If hand mixing, mix the salt and water with the olive oil bassinage, flour, and leaven until there are no dry bits of flour. Turn the dough out onto an oiled work surface and give it 10–12 minutes of slaps and folds until smooth (p. 84, Hand Mixing and Kneading).

YIELD: 1 FOUGASSE

For the whole wheat leaven
· 10g (2 tsp) ripe sourdough starter
· 125g (3 tbsp) whole wheat flour
· 125g (1 tbsp plus 2 tsp) cool water

For the dough
· 7g (1⅓ tsp) large grain gray sea salt (sel de Guérande) 1.6%
· 240g (1 cup plus 1 tbsp) water at 18–23°C (64–73°F) 56%
· 425g (3⅔ cups) pizza flour (type 00) flour 100%
· 50g (¼ cup plus 1 tbsp) whole wheat leaven 12%
· 50g (¼ cup) olive oil bassinage 12%
· 150g (1 cup) pitted olives 35%
· 70g (¾ cup) drained and stemmed large preserved capers 16%
· ½ preserved lemon, finely chopped
· 1 tsp fresh rosemary needles
· 1 tsp fresh thyme leaves

To finish
· Olive oil for brushing or flour of your choice for dusting

TIMELINE
36 h, start to finish
Day 1, Morning:
Build leaven, rest 8–9 h
Day 1, Afternoon/Evening:
Mix dough, bulk proof 3 h
Refrigerate 8–15 h
Day 2, Morning:
Divide and preshape dough, rest 7–9 h
Day 2, Afternoon/Evening:
Shape dough, bake 15–20 min

Day 1, Morning: Make your leaven
Build your leaven and let it rest, loosely covered, for 8–9 hours (p. 26, A).

Day 1, Afternoon/Evening (8–9 hours later): Start making your dough
If your leaven is ready (p. 26, B), in the bowl of a stand mixer, mix the salt with the water until dissolved. Add the pizza flour and leaven. Using the dough hook attachment, mix the dough on medium for 5 minutes. Reduce the speed to low and drizzle in the olive oil bassinage. The bassinage will make the dough come apart, but once it comes back together, increase the speed to high and knead for 2 minutes, or until the dough is soft and loose but smooth. With lightly oiled hands to prevent sticking, transfer to a lightly oiled bowl, cover with a towel, and rest for 30 minutes.

After the first rest, give the dough a set of stretches and folds (p. 26, D), then cover and rest for another 30 minutes. Add the olives, capers, preserved lemon, rosemary, and thyme and give the dough a second set of stretches and folds to incorporate. Cover and repeat the stretches and folds at 30-minute intervals for the next 2 hours, until the dough is light and airy and requires fewer and fewer folds to hold the tension (p. 26, E).

After the final rest, form the dough into a tight ball and set it in an oiled bowl with room for expansion. Wrap airtight and refrigerate overnight or for up to 15 hours.

Day 2, Morning: Divide and preshape your dough
Divide the dough into 3 equal portions, each about 250g (9 ounces). Form each into a ball, then arrange, 7.5cm (3 inches) apart, on a lightly oiled baking tray. Cover loosely and let rest for 7–9 hours.

Day 2, Evening: Bake your bread
Preheat the oven to 250°C (500°F). Dust 2 baking trays with whole wheat flour and gently transfer each ball of dough onto them. I bake 1 tray with 2 fougasses, then a final tray with only 1 fougasse — this leaves plenty of space for the loaves to expand. To shape, stretch each ball of dough into a long oval, being careful not to crush and degas the dough — you want all those lovely air bubbles to remain intact. Next, use a dough scraper or bench knife to make decorative cuts into each oval, going all the way through the dough. Pull apart the dough at each cut, stretching the dough and creating a leaf shape. Brush each fougasse with olive oil or dust with flour, then bake for 15–20 minutes, or until golden brown and fragrant.

Xavier Netry

Five days a week, Xavier Netry wakes up before 2am and quietly dresses while his wife and five-year-old son sleep. If it's a weekday, he'll slip out the door to cross a Paris dark and empty enough to echo his own footsteps. On weekends, he passes crowds stumbling out of late night bars towards warm beds. For centuries, Parisian bakers have been rising in the middle of the night to tend to their bread. At only thirty-four years old, Xavier, a lifelong Parisian and the head baker at Boulangerie Utopie, has kept this schedule for more than twenty years.

Night work isn't an easy life, but these small morning hours are Xavier's preference — he's alone in the fournil, the part of the bakery that houses the oven. The shades of the boutique are drawn and there are no customers. The oven is already hot and groaning. Occasionally, a mouse squeaks — they're as nocturnal as bakers. But the solitude isn't what Xavier likes about the night shift. It's the work. There's always the

most to do. Enormous sourdough miches nearly two-thirds of a meter (about two feet) long have to be loaded into the oven. Spelt breads and pain de campagne that spent the night proofing go in next. Sturdy rye tourtes need to be mixed and shaped. Wilder breads, full of spices and fruits and seeds, are already pushing against their canvases while flour and salt need scaling for whole wheat loaves. And then there are the baguettes. Endless baguettes that need to be shaped, scored, and baked.

If you were a fly on that flour-dusted wall, the first thing you'd notice would be Xavier's hands. There's an economy of movement — tidy gestures that have been refined and then refined again. Nothing is wasted. Supple doughs are transported with confident fingertips and folded into smooth pillows. No matter how wet the dough, it never sticks to those fingers. No matter how soft the shaped loaf, it always makes it to the oven. There's an obvious fluency that can only be built over time.

Watching him work, it makes sense that Xavier started his life in boulangerie as a thirteen-year-old. That was when his mother fell sick and was no longer able to work. Xavier had no choice but to find a job. He was a curious thirteen-year-old though, and the men pulling bread from ovens behind the ubiquitous local bakeries piqued his interest. That he was too young to work legally didn't deter him, and when the father of a friend brought Xavier onto his team — under the table, of course — his career began.

It was a turn of fate that he credits with keeping him out of trouble and in school, but bakery life is physical work, hard on grown adults, to say nothing of a child. Nonetheless, he kept at it and simultaneously worked through the French trade

educational system, completing high school and achieving his baker's license.

By the time he was twenty-two, Xavier had worked in as many as twenty bakeries, building the toolbox he keeps in his hands. His knowledge of mixing, fermenting, and shaping expanded, and he gained confidence in his craft. Some bosses were kind, others violent and racist, but he kept working and learning the endless approaches there are to dough. All of this came to a halt when Xavier took a job at Carrefour, the French supermarket chain.

> ❝ Today, the bakery world is full of younger bakers with more attention to quality.

The Carrefour bakery was hardly a bakery — machines did everything. The work was entirely mechanical and without the artisanship Xavier had come to love. Looking back, he concedes that even that was a learning experience, especially in terms of understanding the value of craftsmanship, but at the time he felt completely disheartened. Xavier left Carrefour and quit bakery. He was only twenty-two.

Xavier spent a year out of bakeries, training as a bodyguard and working with football stars and in the Louis

Vuitton boutique, but when he was offered a job as the head baker at a large company, he went back, enticed by the responsibility. Still, it wasn't until four years later, when he was offered the chef boulanger job at the brand new Boulangerie Utopie, that he rediscovered his passion. Once there, he realized how much he'd missed the early excitement he'd had for bread making.

At Utopie, Xavier was expected to put his creativity into his work, and he started to see bread as a canvas. The owners of the bakery came from pastry backgrounds and encouraged his use of original flavor combinations. Every week for the last five years, Xavier has developed "a pain de weekend," a special weekend bread inspired by the world around him, and customers line up around the block to try his new flavors.

Xavier loves seeing the clients happy and when he has a free moment between bakes, he jumps into sales just to have a chat with the regulars. This rapport with his customers keeps him playing with flavors, always thinking about what they might like. During strawberry season, he might create a focaccia with strawberry and timut pepper. In winter, spiced apples in stone-ground sourdough. Coffee and caramel trades weeks with preserved lemons. Sometimes he takes inspiration from his family in Guadeloupe. He's made breads with the elements of creoline sauce — Antillean peppers, onion, and vinegar — or with a touch of a cocktail — rum, lime, and dried banana. Sometimes the ideas come from the weekly open air markets, other times from a meal he has in a restaurant. Xavier is always thinking, "Could I use this in a bread?"

And at Utopie, it's not just creative satisfaction he's found. He's become a mentor to his team, as well as to more than a hundred interns who have come to learn the art of bread making. The job of the boulanger has become more appealing lately — stylish, even — and he teaches an endless stream of interns at Boulangerie Utopie, shaping their experience of the craft. Whether the interns are simply passionate home bakers who come to work with him for a day or two or experienced students, Xavier calmly and gently guides these aspiring bakers in their journey, never losing his patience. He concedes that a lot of these folks don't know what they're signing up for.

"It's a job for the mentally strong rather than the physically strong," he warns. Still, there's one thing he insists upon: "If you see someone doing a good job, you need to tell them. That recognition is important. It motivates and builds passion."

In twenty years, Xavier has seen a lot of change. "The bakery world has democratized," he says, then pauses, reconsidering. "More people want good bread and more bakeries have opened in response. Today, it's full of younger bakers with more attention to quality and handwork."

"C'est un beau metier," he says. It's a beautiful profession. An inventive profession. And it keeps him crossing Paris every night while the rest of us sleep.

Xavier Netry's Pain Café Caramélisé · Caramelized Coffee Bread

There are few people from whom I've learned as much about bakery as Xavier Netry. At Paris' Boulangerie Utopie, he's king of the French classics, but his passion lies in creative bread making and a playful approach to flavor. His pain café caramélisé offers a coffee kick with a bittersweet note. The liquid in this recipe comes entirely from filter coffee and coffee-flavored caramel, while puffed rice adds a bit of crunch. It's as pleasant with sweet jams and sour chutneys as it is schmeared with pâté.

Note: Xavier uses a stand mixer with the dough hook attachment to build structure in this bread, and adds a bit of yeast to boost the primarily sourdough-based dough. However, if you wish to be a sourdough purist, skip the yeast and give the dough a 4-hour bulk proof with sets of stretches and folds every 30 minutes.

YIELD: 2 LOAVES

For the stiff leaven
· 100g (¾ cup plus 1 tbsp) light stone-ground wheat bread flour
· 50g (3 tbsp plus 1 tsp) cool water
· 20g (1 tbsp plus 1 tsp) ripe sourdough starter

For the dough
· 500g (4 cups plus 3 tbsp) white bread flour 100%
· 285g (1¼ cups) strong brewed coffee, room temperature 57%
· 150g (⅔ cup) stiff leaven 30%
· 10g (heaping ½ tbsp) table salt 2%
· 2g (¾ tsp) instant yeast or 4g (1¼ tsp) fresh yeast 0.4%
· 140g (½ cup) coffee caramel 28%
· 100g (2 cups) puffed rice 20%
· 57g (¼ cup) bassinage water 12%

For the coffee caramel
· Ingredients for Caramel (p. 264)
· 20g (¼ cup) ground coffee or 1 tbsp instant espresso powder

 TIMELINE
24 h, start to finish
Day 1, Morning:
Build leaven, rest 8–9 h
Brew coffee
Make caramel
Day 1, Afternoon/Evening:
Make autolyse, rest 1 h
Mix dough, bulk proof 1 hour
Preshape, rest 30 min
Shape, refrigerate 12–24 h
Day 2, Morning:
Bake 30 min

Day 1, Morning: Make your leaven

Build your leaven and let it rest, loosely covered, for 8–9 hours (p. 26, A).

Meanwhile, brew a pot of strong coffee and let cool while the leaven is fermenting. You will use 285g (1¼ cups) of this coffee later to make your dough.

Follow the recipe to make the Caramel (p. 264), adding the ground coffee with the cream. Set aside to cool at room temperature.

Day 1, Afternoon/Evening (7–8 hours later): Start making your dough

About 1 hour before your leaven hits peak activity, begin mixing your dough. (Note that because this is a stiff leaven, you have a larger window of peak activity, so don't stress too much!) In a stand mixer, combine only the white bread flour and coffee. Using the dough hook attachment, mix the dough on low for 5 minutes. Cover with a damp towel and let rest for 1 hour — this is your autolyse (p. 17).

After 1 hour, add the leaven, salt, and yeast and mix on low for 7 minutes. Increase the speed to medium and mix for 1 minute. Add the Coffee Caramel and puffed rice and mix on medium until incorporated, about 3 minutes. Reduce the speed to low, then drizzle in the bassinage water, and mix until completely absorbed. Cover the mixing bowl loosely with a tea towel and let rest for 30 minutes.

After 30 minutes, give the dough a set of stretches and folds (p. 26, D), then cover loosely and let rest for 30 minutes.

After the second rest, turn out the dough onto a lightly floured work surface and divide it into 2 equal portions. Preshape the dough into loose balls (p. 27, F), then let rest for 30 minutes.

After 30 minutes, shape the dough: Flip the balls of dough, so they are smooth-side down, then flatten them into thick circles. Fold the top half of 1 circle of dough down two-thirds and press to flatten. Fold the bottom half up two-thirds and press to flatten. Press the top down to meet the bottom and pinch to seal the seam. Repeat with the second circle of dough, so you have 2 oval-shaped loaves. Place a tea towel on a baking tray and generously flour the towel. Place both loaves, smooth-side down, on the towel, lifting the towel to separate the loaves. Put a heavy can or wine bottle on each side to help the loaves keep their shape. Refrigerate for 12–24 hours.

Day 2, Morning: Bake your bread

Place a covered cast-iron pot in the oven and preheat to 250°C (500°F). Place 1 of the proofed loaves, smooth-side up, on a piece of parchment paper, score the top (p. 27, J), and place in the pot. Cover and bake for 15 minutes. Uncover the bread, lower the oven temperature to 235°C (450°F) and bake for 15 minutes, or until golden brown. Repeat to bake the second loaf, raising the oven temperature and preheating the pot as needed.

Soft Salzburg Bretzeln

If you haven't had a New Year's Day hangover in Salzburg, you're probably
living a healthier life than me. However, if you have, then you know that nestled
charmingly amongst the frigid Austrian hills are precious few options to cope
with a throbbing head and a thirst for salt. Thank god for Bretzeln, large soft
pretzels with perfectly tangy skin and just enough salt. They'll fix you right
up. Pretzels hold a special place in the bakery culture of Austria and Southern
Germany, so much so that the traditional marking of a bakery is a hanging iron
pretzel. Enjoy the region's bakery heritage, whether you're hungover or not.

Note: This is a yeast-based recipe that uses a small amount of sourdough to add flavor. It's a great use of the discard you have left over from starter refreshments. While it's best to make this dough in a stand mixer with the dough hook attachment, it can be made by hand. If hand mixing, combine all ingredients except the butter in a large bowl, and mix until there are no dry bits of flour, then turn the dough out onto a lightly oiled work surface and give it 7 minutes of slaps and folds (p. 84, Hand Mixing and Kneading). Once your arms are tired, spread the softened butter onto the dough, then use a bench knife to cut it into the dough (p. 84). Once the butter is incorporated, give the dough another 5 minutes of slaps and folds until smooth. This recipe uses white bread flour, but I encourage you to experiment with spelt or other whole grain flours, keeping in mind that you may need to adjust the hydration.

YIELD: 8-9 LARGE PRETZELS

For the dough
- 480g (4 cups) white bread flour 96%
- 20g (2 tbsp plus 2 tsp cup) whole wheat flour 4%
- 6g (2 tsp) instant yeast 1.2%
- 30g (2 tbsp) ripe sourdough starter 6%
- 20g (2 tbsp plus ½ tsp) non-diastatic barley malt powder 4%
- 10g (heaping ½ tbsp) table salt 2%
- 275g (1 cup plus 2 tbsp plus 1 tsp) water at 18-23°C (64-73°F) 55%
- 35g (2 tbsp plus 1 tsp) unsalted butter, room temperature 7%

For the poaching bath
- 1,500 ml (6 ⅓ cups) water
- 30g (1 tbsp plus 2 tsp) baking soda

For the topping
- Pretzel salt, rock salt, sea salt, or other large grain salt for finishing

 TIMELINE
12 h, start to finish
Day 1, Evening:
Mix dough, rest 45 min
Divide and preshape dough, rest 15-20 min
Preshape dough logs, rest 5-10 min
Shape pretzels, rest 30 min
Refrigerate overnight
Day 2: Morning:
Soak 1-2 min
Bake 8 min

Day 1, Evening: Make and shape your dough

In the bowl of a stand mixer, combine the bread flour, whole wheat flour, yeast, ripe sourdough starter, barley malt powder, salt, and water. Using the dough hook attachment, mix the dough on low for 5 minutes, or until the dough comes together. With the mixer on low, gradually add the softened butter. Continue mixing until the butter is no longer visible. Increase the speed to medium and mix for 5 more minutes, or until the dough comes together in a smooth ball. Transfer to a lightly oiled bowl, cover with a damp towel, and let rise for 45 minutes.

After 45 minutes, divide the dough into 8-9 equal portions, each about 84g (3 ounces). Form each portion into a tight ball (p. 87). Let rest for 15-20 minutes.

After 15-20 minutes, flip each ball of dough, so it's smooth-side down. Using a rolling pin, roll out a ball of dough into a thin oval. Starting from the top of a long side, roll up the oval until you have a tight log shape. Repeat with the remaining dough and let rest for 5-10 minutes.

After 5-10 minutes, roll each log with your hands as though you're making a clay snake. Lengthen each log to be 35-40cm (14-16 inches) long with a fat middle and tapered ends. To keep the middles fat and the ends long and fine, start rolling in the middle and press down progressively harder as you move your hands towards the ends (p. 88). If the dough resists or tears, let it rest for a few minutes until it's more relaxed.

To shape the pretzels, hold both ends of a log and join them together in a twist. Fold this twist over onto the fat part of the pretzel. Next, invert the shaped pretzel onto 1 or 2 parchment paper-lined baking trays so that the ends are on the underside. Repeat for the other pretzels. Let rest at room temperature for 30 minutes, then cover and refrigerate overnight.

Day 2, Morning: Poach and bake your pretzels
Preheat the oven to 220°C (425°F).

In a large pot, bring the water and baking soda to a boil, then remove from the heat. Soak each pretzel in the hot water for 1-2 minutes, then place, twisted-side down and 3cm (1¼ inches) apart, on 1 of the parchment paper-lined baking trays. When all the pretzels are soaked, use a knife or razor to slash the fat parts of each one. Sprinkle with the pretzel salt and bake for 8 minutes, or until rich and brown. I suggest serving these slathered with butter and chopped chives or as an accompaniment to a particularly greasy sausage with mustard.

Fine Sourdough Bagels

When I opened my bakery in Berlin, I was trying to find a favorite taste on the wrong side of the world and it was proving elusive. My reference — my aspiration — was and has always been a very traditional, basement-level bagel bakery in Newton, Massachusetts: Rosenfeld's Bagels. The bagels there are chewy and slow-risen and they're boiled right in front of you. In the years since I opened, artisan bagel bakeries have boomed globally, and with them, the ethos of long fermentations and hand shaping. I like to think that Fine Bagels played a small part in Europe's bagel boom — and the century-long circular journey from Poland to New York and back. Despite the trend, bagels are a bit of a Rodney Dangerfield in the European bread world. They get no respect. Still, show me another bread that can take me home with one bite.

Notes: I prefer to make bagel dough in a stand mixer with the dough hook attachment. It's a stiff dough and hand kneading is a one-way ticket to carpal tunnel syndrome.

For a morning bake, refrigerate the shaped bagels overnight prior to the 4-hour rise. Remove them from the refrigerator early and give them the 4-hour rise in the morning, followed by boiling and baking.

YIELD: 14 BAGELS

For the whole wheat leaven
· 100g (¾ cup plus 1 tbsp) whole wheat flour
· 100g (⅓ cup plus 1 tbsp plus 2 tsp) cool water
· 30g (2 tbsp) ripe sourdough starter

For the dough
· 1kg (8 ⅓ cups) white bread flour 100%
· 520g (2 cups plus 2 tbsp plus 2 tsp) water at 18–23°C (64–73°F) 52%
· 20g (heaping 1 tbsp) table salt 2%
· 200g (1 ¼ cups) whole wheat leaven 20%
· 40g (2 tbsp) light barley malt syrup 4%

For the boiling water
· 1,500 ml (6 ⅓ cups) water
· 60g (3 tbsp) light barley malt syrup
· 19g (1 tbsp) table salt

For the topping
· Sesame or poppy seeds (optional)

TIMELINE
24 h, start to finish
Day 1: Evening:
Build leaven, rest 8–9 h
Day 2: Morning:
Mix dough, rest 4 h
Day 2: Afternoon:
Divide and shape dough, rest 4 h
Day 2, Evening:
Boil 1–2 min; bake 8–10 min

Day 1, Evening: Make your leaven
Build your leaven and let it rest, loosely covered, for 8–9 hours (p. 26, A).

Day 2, Morning (8–9 hours later): Start making your dough
If your leaven is ready (p. 26, B), in the bowl of a stand mixer, combine the bread flour, water, salt, leaven, and barley malt syrup. Using the dough hook attachment, mix the dough on low for 9 minutes, or until it forms a solid, smooth mass. *Note: This is a stiff dough, so pay attention if your mixer is straining and add an extra 20g (1 tbsp plus 1 tsp) of water as needed to loosen it.* Form the dough into a smooth ball and place in a lightly oiled bowl. Wrap airtight — this will prevent this low-hydration dough from drying out — and let it rest at room temperature for 4 hours, or until light and airy and nearly doubled in size.

Day 2, Afternoon (4 hours later): Divide and shape your dough
After 4 hours, divide the dough into 14 equal portions, about 125g (4 ½ ounce) each. Flatten each portion of dough. Roll up each portion to form a short, fat log then roll each log with your hands to elongate to about 15cm (6 inches) long. Twist the log, then press the ends together, stretching one end over the other and pinching to make a nice seal. Repeat with the remaining dough and place each shaped bagel, seam-side down, on a parchment paper-lined baking tray. Cover loosely and let rise at room temperature for 4 hours, or until light and puffed.

Day 2, Evening (4 hours later): Boil and bake your bagels
Preheat the oven to 235°C (450°F).

In a large pot, bring the water, barley malt syrup, and salt to a rolling boil. Boil each bagel for 1–2 minutes, then place, smooth-side up, on a parchment paper-lined baking tray. While the bagels are still wet, top with sesame or poppy seeds, if using. Bake for 8–10 minutes, or until golden brown. Keep these legit and serve with cream cheese, lox, capers, and onions.

Baltic Rye

Some of the most flavorful and complex rye breads in Europe come from the Baltic countries, particularly Latvia. If you've ever taken a flight out of Riga, you'll see lines of young people that live abroad sending carry-on bags packed with black bread through the X-ray machines. These unique ryes, gently sweetened with bitter molasses and caraway, are the things of perfume dreams, and born for thick wedges of smoked fish. This recipe adapts the flavors and textures of these breads for a manageable home bake. So, breathe in deep and imagine a Northern summer where the sun never goes down.

Note: This recipe, like the Tourte de Seigle Auvergnate (p. 48) uses a stiff rye leaven. Though the stiff leaven has the same hydration as our liquid starters, whole rye flour absorbs much more water, so the texture will be a thick paste. Stiff leavens are powerful and add a lifting kick to dense bread — they also have a longer window of usage when they're at their strongest, so you have a bit of wiggle room with your timing. But, beware: A stiff leaven can get very sour, very fast.

YIELD: 1 LOAF

For the stiff rye leaven
- 50g (⅓ cup plus 1 tbsp) medium or dark rye flour
- 50g (3 tbsp plus 1 tsp) cool water
- 15g (1 tbsp) ripe sourdough starter

For the dough
- 1½ tsp caraway seeds 1%
- 1½ tsp fennel seeds 1%
- 10g (2¼ tsp) large grain gray sea salt (sel de Guérande) 2%
- 480g (2 cups plus 1 tbsp plus 1 tsp) water 95%
- 50g (2½ tbsp) blackstrap or unrefined molasses 10%
- 250g (2⅓ cups plus 2 tbsp) light rye flour 50%
- 100g (¾ cup plus 2 tsp) dark rye flour 20%
- 150g (1¼ cups) light stone-ground wheat bread flour 30%
- 100g (½ cup plus 2 tbsp) stiff rye leaven 20%

 TIMELINE
24 h, start to finish
Day 1, Evening:
Build leaven, rest 8–9 h
Day 2, Morning:
Mix dough, bulk proof 3 h
Day 2, Afternoon (3 hours later):
Shape dough, rest 3–3½ h
Day 2: Evening:
Bake 1 h

Day 1, Evening: Make your leaven
Build your leaven and let it rest, loosely covered, for 8–9 hours (p. 26, A).

Meanwhile, toast the caraway and fennel seeds in a frying pan over medium heat, agitating the pan occasionally, for 5–10 minutes, or until they take on a deeper color and aroma. Remove from the heat and let cool.

Day 2, Morning (8–9 hours later): Start making your dough
If your leaven is ready (p. 26, B), in a large bowl, mix the salt with the water and molasses until dissolved. Add both rye flours, the light stone-ground wheat bread flour, and the leaven and mix by hand until the dough is smooth and has a batter-like consistency with no chunks — it will be very loose and sticky with almost no gluten development. Loosely cover the bowl and let it rest for 1 hour. Add the toasted caraway and fennel seeds and give the dough a set of stretches and folds — don't worry if the dough feels very wet and falls apart when you pull it up to stretch. Cover and repeat the stretches and folds at 30-minute intervals for the next 2 hours. The dough will gradually gain some stretch, but it will still be sticky and loose.

Day 2, Afternoon (3 hours later): Shape your dough
After the final rest, lightly oil a loaf pan with a pastry brush. You have 2 options for shaping the loaves.

The first option is simply to pour the dough from your mixing bowl into your oiled loaf pan. Using a dough scraper or wet hand to assist, scrape the bowl to loosen the dough, then invert it into the loaf pan. Smooth the top with a wet hand then gently sift some rye flour on top.

The second option is for the more confident shaper but yields even better results. Generously flour your work surface with dark or medium rye flour. Use a dough scraper or wet hand to scrape the bowl to loosen the dough, then pour it out onto the floured surface. Fold in each side of the dough to create a rounded oval then quickly lift and flip the dough, so it is smooth-side up. Place the dough in the oiled loaf pan, keeping the long side of the oval in line with the length of the pan. Don't worry if it doesn't fill the entire pan — it will spread.

Let the dough rest for 3–3½ hours, or until it has gained about 50 percent more volume and the floured surface begins to crack.

Day 2: Evening (3–3½ hours later): Bake your bread
Place a small metal baking tin in the bottom of the oven, set a rack in the middle of the oven, and preheat the oven to 250°C (500°F).

Score the dough lengthwise across the middle (p. 27, J). Set the loaf pan on a middle rack, then toss several ice cubes into the hot metal baking tin. Close the door quickly, so the oven fills with steam, and bake for 20 minutes. Lower the oven temperature to 225°C (440°F) and continue baking for 10 minutes. Carefully remove the loaf from the pan, place it directly on the oven rack, and continue baking for 10 minutes to help the bread develop color on all sides. Lower the oven temp to 100°C (215°F) and continue baking for 20 minutes to dry the crumb. If the top crust of your loaf gets too dark, loosely cover it with aluminum foil. Rye bread can look done on the outside but be sticky and uncooked on the inside. If you're not sure, a thermometer inserted into the middle of the loaf should read at least 93°C (200°F). Let the loaf cool completely before cutting or even wait until the next day. Your patience will be rewarded! The bread will stay good for a week, and the flavor will deepen each day.

Monika Walecka

Before you see Monika Walecka's baking, you smell it. On a quiet side street in the Żoliborz district of Warsaw, the scent of bread and pastries teases the hungry visitors to Cała w Mąca piekarnia ("whole flour bakery"). It's the notes of at least fifteen different items that merge into a scent of pure goodness — hearty breads, flaky whole-grain danishes, fruit and cream brioches, savory roasted vegetable toasts. Behind a sign featuring a fierce bread-yielding mermaid (a take on Warsaw's coat of arms) and a fertility goddess sculpted in dough, there's a team of women hustling bread from the oven, plaiting challahs, and filling molds with stiff whole rye dough. The variety is extraordinary. And Monika's breads are beautiful, all bubbly interiors and deeply browned crusts. But appearance isn't the priority, here — it's flavor.

"I use flour like spices," Monika explains. "So here," she says, holding up a bagel, "Einkorn with whole rye flour. Every bread has to have a solid addition of whole-grain flour. Even if I have to sacrifice some crunch or texture, I add more and more different grains. It's our rule here, at least thirty percent whole grains, all Polish flour." And so the breads are distinctly nutty — with just a touch of tang — but perfectly light and balanced, much like her combination of technique and intuition.

But it isn't just the flavor that Monika emphasizes, it's also the aromas. She's a perfume collector, and has been since she was in high school, when her mother bought her her first bottle, Organza by Givenchy. As soon as she left school and got a job, she set a little aside every month for a new bottle. "Perfumes are like fairy tales, it's a very narrative world and a huge inspiration for what I do."

With Monika's love of perfume, every Sunday, Cała w Mąca sets aside bread and becomes Cukiernia Tonka, where she and her team can explore the pastries and flavors they don't have space to produce the rest of the week.

"I always wanted to create pastries that were inspired by the tones of perfumes. You even have a category of perfumes called "gourmand," which have notes like vanilla and citrus that are super pronounced. Tonka is a link between the perfume world and the pastry world, because it's an ingredient used in both. To me, it's the most beautiful spice, it's not a particular smell, but rather a feeling. Whether it's hot or cold, it changes; it's never the same."

Tonka is a very personal side project, where Monika can emphasize the links between scent and taste with pastries like her Cake of a Lady, inspired by the perfume Portrait of a Lady by Frédéric Malle.

"The accords are a mixture of red berries, currants, rose, and root spices," explains Monika. "The cake

we layer like an opera cake: It's génoise soaked with cinnamon and cloves then smeared with crushed black currants and a mascarpone cream with locally made rose petal jam. We cover the whole thing with an Italian meringue."

And so, just as her bread has rules, so does her pastry. All the pastry is made with an incorporation of old bread. The strudel is layered with breadcrumbs from dried challah. The cheesecake crust is a mix of browned butter and ground country loaf. Even the financiers — little tea cakes — are made with remnants of the bakery's production. Through this, the end result is given a complexity and richness that hits every part of the tongue.

Nevertheless, Cała w Mąca and Cukiernia Tonka are a long way from the start of Monika's culinary career, one that began seventeen years ago, back in the days when food magazines and blogs were just starting out in Poland, and there was a growing new interest in food creativity.

"I was a very traditionally raised girl, my mother would cook everything from scratch, traditional home cooking," says Monika. "But

then I discovered this culinary world and said, 'Woah, there's more than schnitzel and potatoes.'" At the time, she was working as a producer for MTV and going to a lot of techno parties.

"And suddenly I felt like, I'm done with that. I want to do something new. I was looking for every occasion to cook." Monika started her own food blog, developing recipes and taking photos, learning as she went. This grew into writing food columns

and working as a professional recipe developer, which she was able to continue when her husband's job transferred them to Prague.

She was in the Czech Republic capital when Chad Robertson's famous 2010 cookbook, *Tartine Bread*, was published and she got her hands on a copy.

"Yes, I'm one of those Chad Robertson kids," Monika says, laughing and rolling her eyes at herself. "But really, I had never made bread like this before, and I fell in love." Serendipity kicked in when

her husband called her one day from work. He'd gotten an offer to move to California.

"And I thought, 'Shit, that's where Tartine is.' That was literally my first thought." The couple packed up and flew halfway around the world. Their first stop? The bakery.

"I tried all of the stuff — the cookies, the pastries — it was out of this world to me. But also, I finally got to try the bread. And I thought, 'Hey, my bread is good, but this is

> ## " *The pastry has a complexity and richness that hits every part of the tongue.*

next level. Why am I making the bread from the book, but it's not as good?'" This question consumed Monika's life for the next few years in San Francisco. "Every day I baked bread. Every day I read about bread. I would only think about bread." But finding her place in the clannish world of San Francisco sourdough bakeries wasn't easy.

"And I was in a foreign country, I wasn't super confident with my English. I had my CV that in Poland looked quite impressive, but there I was no one. Just a girl out of her world in San Francisco, the coolest city in the world." She was turned away from everywhere she applied. She had no professional experience, and didn't know how to behave in a professional kitchen. "I had no idea about anything, really. But I was very persistent."

To improve her skills, Monika took a course at the San Francisco Baking Institute. To increase her visibility, she used photography and social media to make a name for herself, baking and shooting at home. At last, people from the baking industry started to notice her.

"Finally, if I knocked on a door, they would say, 'OK, at least you can learn.' And I learned. It was my time and place to learn everything I could, because I knew I wouldn't stay in San Francisco forever."

Every day she would go to work at Marla Bakery, then come home, refresh her starter, mix dough, nap, shape bread, sleep, go back to work in the bakery, and repeat. Weekends she spent staging at restaurants and bakeries. For two years, she dedicated herself to her craft. And so, when it finally came time to return to Poland, Monika was ready for her own project. A week after arriving back home, she rented space in a semi-industrial bakery and went to work. The plan was to emulate the bakers she'd come to know in California, who baked without a storefront and sold at farmers' markets once or twice a week.

"I didn't want a daily bakery, I appreciated my freedom." Monika baked her breads and pastries twice a week and sold them at the Forteca Kręgliccy, a farmers' market in an old fortress in Warsaw. Of course, baking twice a week meant working five days a week. Before market days, she would stay up baking all night long, pumping techno to keep herself awake. When she could, she pulled an old army cot out from behind the refrigerator to take a short nap. It was a brutal schedule, but Warsovians loved her bread. After a crazy marathon of two years baking on her own, however, Monika knew she needed to change her way of working.

"You are there for bread, but you can't let the bread rule you. If you want to do the bread for many years, take care of the balance. This work is physically demanding and working at night is so unhealthy. So I started thinking, 'OK, maybe it's not so bad to have a bakery.'"

And so, just before the pandemic hit in 2019, Monika opened her bakery. She brought along her right-hand baker, Karolina Bonska, a young bread maker with smooth competence and skill, and expanded the team. There are now thirteen women working in Monika's bright ground-floor bakery, each of them organized in their tasks.

"Yes, we're girls only and we have a really nice work environment. We don't argue, we cooperate. This is because we're friends and we respect each other. I'm really pushing the girls to become better bakers, as I pushed myself. It's a huge satisfaction to me to see someone who could barely roll a ball of dough and now they make these beautiful loaves. It's a bit like being a mother, watching those kids grow into amazing grown-ups," Monika says, all pride and no condescension. "I like to showcase that women can do bread as well as any man. I think we do a pretty good job of that."

And so, it would seem, Monika has found her balance — not just in bread, but in life. And one day, she hints, there might be a perfume that smells just like it.

Monika Walecka's Ratatouille Béchamel Toasts

In Monika Walecka's Warsaw bakery, she respects the life cycle of bread and incorporates unsold loaves into many of her offerings, both sweet and savory. Her ratatouille béchamel toasts are luxurious and melty — a testimony to her culinary tendencies — and a wonderful way to use up a loaf gone just a bit stale.

YIELD: 3-5 TOASTS

- 50g (3 ½ tbsp) unsalted butter
- 70g (½ cup plus 1 tbsp) whole-grain emmer flour (rye, spelt, or einkorn works here, too!)
- 400g (1 ¾ cups) whole milk
- 1 garlic clove, crushed and peeled
- Pinch table salt
- Pinch freshly ground nutmeg
- 3-5 thick slices day-old bread
- 300g (about 3 cups) cooked vegetables, such as zucchini, eggplant, squash, tomato, or mushrooms
- 113g (1 cup) shredded Gruyère, mozzarella, cheddar, or other meltable cheese

Preheat the oven to 175°C (350°F).

To make the béchamel, melt the butter in a medium saucepan over low heat. Add the emmer flour and stir to combine. Once the mixture is bubbling, slowly add the milk while whisking. Continue cooking and whisking until the sauce thickens, then add the garlic and season with salt and nutmeg. Remove from the heat.

Arrange the bread on a parchment paper–lined baking tray and slather each slice with the béchamel. Spoon a generous portion of the cooked vegetables onto the bread, top with the shredded cheese, and bake for about 10 minutes, or until crisp and golden.

Whipped Kefir Butter for Bread

For every bread, there is a butter. The peak of good butter is the small farm-produced cultured butter — fermented, molded, and salted with large crystals — that can taste more like a cheese than butter. Dairy like this is as seasonal as fruit, with its characteristics depending on the cows' diet, which is, of course, whatever the season has to offer. If you manage to get a hold of butter like this, please don't touch it! Just put it on your bread and enjoy. It's perfect as it is. So why bother with a recipe? Didn't I just tell you not to touch your butter? Well, let's face it. Most of us don't live next door to happy dairy cows. So, for any other butter, there's room to play. And whipped milk kefir butter is a stable, tangy spread for toast, sandwiches, or hot bread. If I'm whipping butter, I make it the same day I want to use it and keep it at room temperature. Once it goes back in the fridge, it'll solidify and you'll lose all that texture.

YIELD: 320G (ABOUT 1¾ CUPS)

· 250g (1 cup plus 2 tbsp) unsalted butter, softened
· 70g (¼ cup plus 2 tsp) milk kefir, room temperature
· Maldon salt or fleur de sel

In a stand mixer fitted with the whisk attachment, whip the butter on high until very soft and fluffy. Reduce the speed to low and drizzle in the kefir. Return the mixer to high and whip until pale and shiny. Season with the salt.

FLAVORING IDEAS:

Fig and Olive Oil Butter
· 2 tbsp olive oil
· 4 soft dried figs, finely chopped

In the final minute of whipping the butter, reduce the speed to low and drizzle in the olive oil. Once the butter is uniform, stir in the figs by hand.

Coffee and Date Butter
· 3 tbsp espresso or 1 tsp instant espresso powder
· 4 Medjool dates, pitted and finely chopped

Add the espresso or espresso powder to the kefir before drizzling into the butter and whipping. Once the butter is uniform, stir in the dates by hand.

Millefiori Butter
· 3 tbsp edible flower petals, such as chamomile, cornflower, borage, or nasturtium
· 1 tbsp honey

Once the butter is fully whipped, stir in the flowers and honey by hand.

Green Peppercorn and Chile Butter
· 4 fresh green chiles, finely chopped
· 1 tbsp fresh green peppercorns
· 1 tsp lemon zest
· 1 tsp sumac

Once the butter is fully whipped, stir in the chiles, peppercorns, lemon zest, and sumac by hand.

Miso Maple Butter
· 1 tbsp red miso
· 1 tbsp maple syrup or maple sugar

Whip the miso and maple syrup with the butter before adding the kefir.

Anchovy and Olive Butter
· 2 tbsp anchovy paste
· 2 tbsp finely chopped pitted olives

Whip the anchovy paste with the butter before adding the kefir. Once fully whipped, stir in the olives by hand.

Buckwheat and Fried Onion Butter
· 2 tbsp toasted buckwheat
· ½ yellow onion, sliced, fried, and cooled

Once the butter is fully whipped, stir in the buckwheat and onion by hand.

CHAPTER 2

Brioches and Enriched Doughs

That's Rich: Working with Enriched Doughs

If weekdays are for bread, weekends are for brioche. These sweet and soft breads, enriched with butter, eggs, sugar, or oil — earning them the name enriched dough — occupy a special place between bread and pastry. There's no end to the regional differences you'll find with these doughs, whether across the European continent or around the world. Crush in some cardamom, and you're in Sweden; spoon on egg custard, and it could be Portugal; throw on some streusel, and now it's Poland. These are some of the most fun doughs for getting creative, as they can take on endless shapes and fillings.

The recipes in this chapter are all built on three base doughs: brioche, challah, and milk bread, which are, respectively, the butteriest, the eggiest, and the sweetest. They're interchangeable in recipes, as long as their individual proofing times are respected. Master even one of these doughs, and you'll have a base on which to create infinite sweet and seasonal breads.

Baking with Yeast

For a powerful rise in the face of heavy fats and solids from enriching ingredients like milk, eggs, or butter, the recipes in this chapter use yeast. If you read the bread chapter, you might think I hate yeast. Far from it. For me, it's all about the how and when with yeast. While many of the new-wave bakers are purists and avoid yeast altogether — even for enriched doughs — and instead favor stiff and robust sweet sourdoughs, I suggest keeping an open mind. Yeast can be a gratifying way to create consistent results. It also offers an especially forgiving method for learning the tactile aspects of bread making, as long as you remember that dough-making isn't a game of speed. Even when using yeast, it's good to slow down the fermentation with an overnight rest in the fridge, which will improve the final product's flavor, digestibility, shaping, and shelf-life. I recommend

this step for brioche and milk dough, but not challah, which you'll see in the recipes.

Adding Sourdough

If you have a sourdough starter you're refreshing regularly, you'll have leftover starter from refreshments. I like to add up to ten percent of ripe starter to all enriched doughs for flavor, as well as softness and longevity in the final bread.

What Kind of Yeast?

All the recipes in this chapter call for instant yeast, which can be added directly to flour with no need to activate it in warm water. Instant yeast is the simplest yeast to use and widely available. Just don't confuse it with active dry yeast; they look identical but behave differently.

There are three kinds of yeast— instant, active dry, and fresh. Because active dry yeast requires warm water and sugar to feed and activate it, I take this option off the table. The warm water and extra sugar can throw off a recipe.

Fresh yeast, however, is an excellent alternative for instant yeast. Simply double the quantity of instant yeast to convert to fresh. For instance, 10 grams (1 tbsp plus ¼ tsp) of instant yeast can be substituted for 20 grams (2 tbsp) of fresh yeast. If you want to use fresh yeast, note that it must be stored in the refrigerator and kept in a dry, airtight container or wrapping. Fresh yeast should be crumbly and have a very light chalk color and a mild odor. If it gets gummy, dark, or has a strong odor, don't use it. It has expired, and its potency will be diminished.

Yeast, like salt, is a small-quantity, high-impact ingredient. While imperial measurements are provided, you'll have far more consistency and accuracy if you weigh your yeast with a precise kitchen scale.

Mixing and Kneading

Mixing and kneading your dough are two parts of the same process. For simplicity's sake, mixing is

the process of bringing your base ingredients together to form a cohesive dough, or incorporating an ingredient into an existing dough. Kneading is the continued working of that dough to achieve a desired texture and strength.

Measuring and laying out your ingredients before you begin the mix is always a good idea — especially if you're as forgetful as I am. Once you've started mixing your dough, it can be hard to figure out if you've forgotten an ingredient. When mixing enriched doughs, it's essential to respect the order of ingredients. For example, butter can impede dough development, so it's often added halfway through the mix. Because of the fat content and milk solids in enriched doughs, we have to work them differently than sourdough breads. While enriched doughs can be both mixed and kneaded by hand, I recommend using a stand mixer with a dough hook attachment both for ease and tidiness, but also because it helps you develop a strong gluten network that will allow the final dough to hold its shape without the workout. All the recipes in this chapter provide the timing for machine mixing (p. 89).

Hand Mixing and Kneading

Kneading enriched doughs by hand is hard work, requires a bit of technique, and you will have to add a few extra minutes to the work. Begin by forming a well in your dry ingredients. Add liquids to the well (1) and then mix little by little, taking flour from the sides of the well until all your dough has come together in a shaggy mass (2-3). Using your bench knife, "cut" the dough repeatedly, top to bottom — this will develop the gluten network (4-6). Once the dough has come together and developed a bit of stretch, continue to work the dough by slapping and folding. To slap and fold, hold one end of your dough and slap the dough lengthwise onto the work surface to stretch it (7). Then fold the portion you're holding over the opposite end (8). Rotate

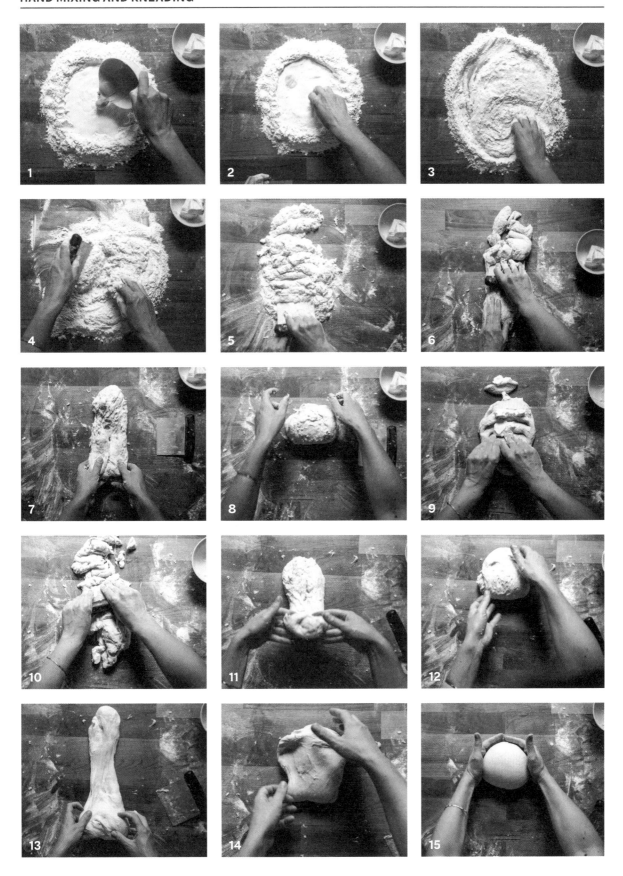

the dough by 90 degrees and repeat. As the dough becomes stronger and smoother, begin incorporating the butter, using your bench knife to "cut" the butter into the dough (9-10). Once sufficiently incorporated, slap and fold again (11-14) until the dough is smooth and shiny (15) and passes a windowpane test (see below).

Temperature

When using a stand mixer, keep in mind that the speed of the mixer impacts the temperature of the dough. Once well-mixed, a perfect temperature for an enriched dough to hit is 26°C (79°F) and checking that temperature with a digital instant-read thermometer is one of the ways you can see if your dough is ready.

Dough that is overheated — often by the process of mixing or simply the weather — can begin to break down and result in a flatter final product. On hot days, cold tap water and chilled flour can bring down the temperature of your dough and allow for a longer mix. For our most intensely mixed recipe — brioche — chilled butter helps to keep the temperature in check.

The Windowpane Test

It's not only the temperature that will tell you that your dough is done. There are also simple visual clues that signify good dough development. When an enriched dough is mixed and kneaded properly, it will have a glossy finish and will pull away cleanly from the sides of the bowl or work surface.

SHAPING A BALL

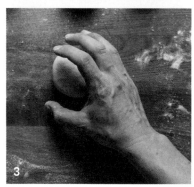

But the best test is the windowpane test. To do this, pinch off a tiny morsel of dough, hold it up to a light, and gently stretch it out so that it's thin and translucent. If the dough is extensible — stretchy — enough that it doesn't rip easily and creates a nice thin sheet, it's ready.

Bulk Proof

Like the sourdough breads in Chapter 1, enriched doughs go through a bulk proof (rise) before they are divided and shaped. However, unlike sourdough, these doughs don't need to undergo stretches and folds during the bulk proof stage. Further, the bulk proof stage can be done overnight in the refrigerator between 4-6°C (40-43°F). While the recipes provide both room temperature bulk rises and refrigerated bulk rises, I always recommend the slow refrigerator method except for challah dough.

Why You Should Do a Cold Bulk Proof

While it's perfectly fine to bulk proof your dough at room temperature, if

you have the time, it's best to bulk proof your dough overnight in the refrigerator. One main reason to do this is so you can make your dough ahead and be ready to assemble and bake it in the morning — or any time in the following 48 hours. But it's more than that. The slow cold rise will improve the flavor and digestibility of the final product and the longer time helps dissipate any unwanted yeasty flavor. Further, in their room temperature form, these doughs are very soft, which means precise shaping can be fussy and sticky. The cold temperature will stiffen the dough to create a clay-like texture that is easily moldable, making balls, braids, and any other shape easy to form. If you choose the quick-and-dirty room temperature bulk proof, the shaping will be more difficult.

Airtight Proofing Without the Waste

Many stages of making enriched doughs require the dough to have an airtight cover to prevent drying. While plastic wrap is often the easiest choice, there are more ecological options. My tried-and-true method is to slide my bowl of dough or tray of bread into a large plastic shopping bag — any ordinary one from the supermarket will do — and tie off the end, keeping the bag super loose so it doesn't actually touch the dough. You can flip the bag inside out to dry off any accumulated humidity when the proof is done, then reuse the bag over and over. Keep this tip in mind for the laminated doughs (Chapter 3) and tarte recipes (Chapter 4) as well. Reusable beeswax wraps or inverted airtight food storage boxes are another great way to reduce waste in the kitchen.

Preshaping and Shaping

Shaping enriched doughs is all about tension. As much as the dough rises during the bulk proof, in shaping, it needs to be degassed (all the air is pressed out) and then tightly reformed to give it strength for the final rise. This process is done twice — first in the preshaping stage and secondly in the shaping stage. These stages are generally done between 10 and 20 minutes apart — recipes will specify — which is just enough time for the dough to relax so you can add more tension.

When preshaping and shaping, there are two sides to each shape: the smooth side and the seam side. The smooth side is the side where no dough meets, while the seam side is where the dough comes together and is sealed.

Shaping a ball: The preshape of a ball is...a ball! To form a ball, flatten your portion of dough with the palm of your hand on an unfloured or just barely floured work surface (1) — you're going to want a bit of friction. Fold in the sides of the dough tightly, so that they meet in the middle (2) — that's your seam. Now flip the folded dough so that the seam side is down and the smooth side is up. Hold your hand like a cage around the dough and move it in circles (3), tightening the ball as you go (4). *Note: When shaping a ball from a preshaped ball, you'll flip it so that it is smooth-side down before flattening and giving the final shape.*

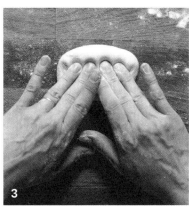
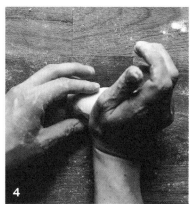

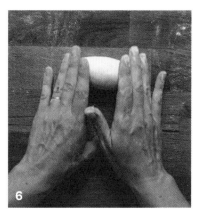

Shaping a navette (photos p. 87):
The navette is a tapered oval shape — it's a cute way to fancy-up your individual rolls and brioches. The preshape of a navette is a ball. To shape the navette from a preshaped ball, simply flip the ball so it is smooth-side down, then flatten it into a circle (1). Fold the top half of the circle to the middle (2). Do the same with the bottom half (3), then fold the top down to meet the bottom (4). Press to seal the seam where the top meets the bottom, then flip so it is seam-side down (5). Gently roll with your hands to elongate (6), starting light in the middle then pressing the ends of the dough while still rolling to create little points (7).

Shaping a tress for a braid: The foundation of every braided bread is a well-made tress. The preshape for a tress is a loose navette or elongated ball. After the preshape, flip the dough so it is smooth-side down, then press it flat into an oval (1). Fold the top to meet the middle (2), then the bottom to meet the middle (3), then fold the top down to meet the bottom (4). Press to seal the seam where the top meets the bottom, then flip so it is seam-side down (5). Gently roll with your hands to elongate the dough like you're making a clay snake (6), starting with light pressure in the middle and applying progressively more pressure as you move your hands towards the ends of the tress (7). If, at any time, the dough resists too much or rips before it reaches your desired length, let it relax for a couple minutes, then continue.

Egg Washes

Part of what gives enriched doughs their appeal is their shiny golden crusts, which are achieved by gently brushing the surface with an egg wash. Brush it on once before the final proof, then again right before the bake — not only will it enliven the appearance of the final product, it will help retain moisture in the dough as it proofs. These egg washes are interchangeable, but the recipes make recommendations — the effect will just be different.

SHAPING A TRESS FOR A BRAID

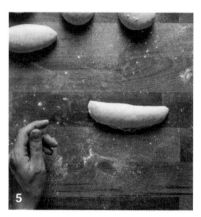
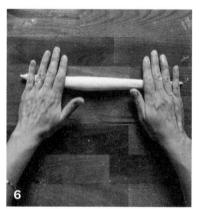
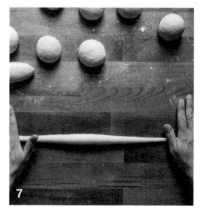

Dark egg wash: Combine 1 large egg and 1 large egg yolk and whisk well. This formula makes an exceptionally shiny, rich egg wash that's ideal for challah.

Light egg wash: Combine 1 large egg and 3 tbsp whole milk and whisk well. This formula makes a light, golden egg wash with a bit of shine; it's ideal for small buns where you want a paler appearance and a softer crust.

The Final Proof

The final proof (rise) of your dough happens when your products are already shaped and placed on their trays or molds. This should happen at room temperature. To prevent drying and cracking of the egg wash, I like to cover my dough with a large reusable plastic box. Remove the box 15 minutes before the proof is done, allowing the surface to dry just enough so it's not too sticky for the final coat of egg wash. Nicely proofed dough that's ready for the oven, will be exceptionally light and delicate and nearly doubled in size yet will hold its shape and not collapse. A tap to the surface will spring back about halfway, very slowly. In hot weather, you might find the proof time has to be slightly reduced, while in the cold, it's the opposite — that's because heat speeds up fermentation and cold slows it.

The Bake

The best bakes for properly proofed enriched dough are on the short and hot side with the convection or fan settings turned on — when it comes to baking, dragging things out can also dry things out. Everyone's oven is different, though, so if the bake times in the recipes don't work for you, adjust them to suit your oven. Further, home ovens often give incorrect temperature readings, so if the recommended temperatures don't work, either check your temperature with an external oven thermometer or just play with your settings. Because of the variation in home ovens, the first time you bake off any new recipe, I recommend keeping a close eye on what's baking rather than just following the clock.

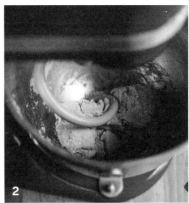

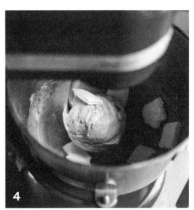
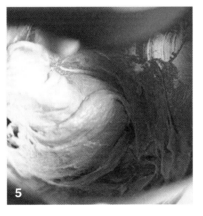

Base Recipe: Basic Brioche Dough

Brioche is the richest of our three base enriched doughs and takes almost all its moisture from eggs and butter. Like milk bread, brioche dough is best made ahead and allowed to bulk proof in the refrigerator overnight. Chilling stiffens the buttery dough and creates a malleable dough that, once baked, is incredibly light and melts on the tongue. Make a classic Brioche Nanterre (p. 94) or use it for braids, babkas, or any other recipe that calls for an enriched dough. For a subtle variation, add a splash of fleur d'oranger (orange blossom water) or anise extract alongside the vanilla.

Note: Resist any temptation to use warm butter to make brioche — the dough will heat up too much during mixing and won't form properly.

YIELD: ABOUT 735G (26 ¼ OUNCES) DOUGH OR 1 LARGE BRIOCHE LOAF

For the dough
· 350g (2 ¾ cups plus 2 tsp) all-purpose flour 100%
· 66g (⅓ cup) granulated sugar 19%
· 5g (1 ¾ tsp) instant yeast 1.4%
· 5g (¾ tsp) table salt 1.4%
· 2 large eggs 28.5%
· 90g (⅓ cup plus 1 tbsp) cold water 26%
· 10g (2 tsp) pure vanilla extract 3%
· 14g (1 tbsp) fleur d'oranger (orange blossom water; optional) 4%
· 100g (7 tbsp) unsalted butter, cubed and cold 29%

 PROOFING TIMELINE
Cold bulk proof: 30 min at room temperature, plus 8–48 h in the fridge
Room temperature bulk proof: 1 h and 15 min
Preshape: 20 min
Final proof: 2 ½ h

A - Mix and knead your dough (photos p. 89)
In the bowl of a stand mixer fitted with the dough hook attachment, combine the all-purpose flour, granulated sugar, yeast, salt, eggs, cold water, vanilla, and fleur d' oranger, if using, and mix on medium for about 5 minutes, or until the dough comes together in a solid, medium-stiff mass (1–2).

Reduce the speed to low, then gradually add the butter, a few pieces at a time (3–4). As the butter incorporates, the dough will start to come apart (5). Continue mixing for about 5 minutes, or until the dough comes back together and there is no visible butter (6). Increase the speed to medium-high and knead for 5–7 minutes, or until the dough is glossy, pulls away cleanly from the sides of the bowl (7), and passes the windowpane test (8 and p. 86).

Note: If mixing and kneading by hand, give the dough 7 minutes of slaps and folds (p. 84, Hand Mixing and Kneading) before incorporating the butter. Continue the slaps and folds until the dough is smooth and shiny, no longer sticks to the table, and passes the windowpane test, which can take up to 12 minutes.

B - Bulk proof your dough
Option 1: Cold (recommended): Form the dough into a ball and let it rest at room temperature for 30 minutes. Reform the dough into a ball, then place it in a lightly oiled bowl with room for expansion, wrap airtight, and refrigerate overnight or for up to 2 days. It will expand and stiffen during that time.

Option 2: Room temperature: Form the dough into a ball, then place it in a lightly oiled bowl with room for expansion, wrap airtight, and let rest at room temperature for 1 hour and 15 minutes. Once properly risen, the dough will have almost doubled in size and when pressed with a finger, the dough will spring back slowly. *Note: If the dough collapses under your finger with no spring back, it's been over-proofed, and your final loaf will be flatter and lose its shape easily.*

C - Divide and shape your dough (1 hour and 15 minutes later for room temperature bulk proof; 8–48 hours later for cold bulk proof)
After the bulk proof, your dough is ready to divide, shape, and use for any of the recipes in this chapter. Preshape according to your chosen recipe and wait 20 minutes between the preshape and final shape. Once the dough is shaped, brush it with the egg wash to maintain moisture during the final proof.

D - The final proof
The final proof of brioche takes 2 ½ hours. The larger the item and the warmer the room, the faster it will proof. The rules, however, are the same. The fully proofed dough will be almost doubled in size, soft to the touch, and will not lose but maintain its shape. It will spring back slowly when pressed with a finger. Always brush with egg wash a second time before baking.

Base Recipe: Basic Challah Dough

While tender and luscious like brioche and milk dough, challah contains no dairy. Instead, it gets its soft and cakey yet pull-apart crumb from egg yolks and oil. And, because challah has no solid fats, it rises much faster than the others. For this reason, challah is the only dough I prefer to proof at room temperature, with no refrigeration. Though it is totally possible to proof challah overnight in the refrigerator, it can have a tendency to over-proof if your refrigerator isn't cold enough. An over-proofed dough can mean a flatter loaf that doesn't hold its shape, so if you are refrigerating the dough overnight, keep the temperature as low as possible, ideally 4°C (40°F).

Note: This recipe uses egg yolks only. Save the extra egg whites in the fridge or freezer to use in meringues, sponge cakes, or omelets.

YIELD: ABOUT 1KG (2 ¼ POUNDS) DOUGH OR 2 CHALLAH LOAVES

For the dough
· 235g (1 cup plus 2 tsp) cold water 39%
· 6 large egg yolks 18%
· 35g (3 tbsp) neutral oil (or olive oil) 5.8%
· 10g (2 tsp) pure vanilla extract 1.7%
· 600g (5 cups) all-purpose flour 100%
· 66g (⅓ cup) granulated sugar 10%
· 10g (heaping ½ tbsp) table salt 1.7%
· 8g (2 ½ tsp) instant yeast 1.3%

 PROOFING TIMELINE
Cold bulk proof: 8–24 h
Room temperature bulk proof: 50 min
Preshape: 10 min
Final proof: 1 ½ h

A - Mix and knead your dough
In the bowl of a stand mixer fitted with the whisk attachment, combine the cold water, egg yolks, oil, and vanilla. Add the all-purpose flour, granulated sugar, salt, and yeast, then switch to the dough hook attachment, and knead on low for about 9 minutes, or until the mixture forms a smooth, medium-stiff mass that doesn't stick to the sides of the bowl. Increase the speed to medium-high and knead for about 1 minute. Remove the dough from the bowl and form it into a tight ball. When formed into a ball, the texture will be smooth and a bit stiff but not glossy like the Basic Brioche Dough or Milk Dough.

Note: If mixing and kneading by hand, give the dough 12-15 minutes of slaps and folds until smooth (p. 84, Hand Mixing and Kneading).

B - Bulk proof your dough
Option 1: Room temperature (recommended): Place the ball of dough in a lightly oiled bowl with room for expansion, cover with a damp towel, and let rest at room temperature for about 50 minutes. Once properly risen, the dough will have almost doubled in size and when pressed with a finger, the dough will spring back slowly. *Note: If the dough collapses under your finger with no spring back, it's been over-proofed, and your final loaf will be flatter and lose its shape easily.*

Option 2: Cold: If you prefer to make your dough in advance, form the dough into a tight ball, then place it in a lightly oiled bowl with room for expansion, wrap airtight, and refrigerate overnight or for up to 24 hours. It will be puffed and a bit stiffer after refrigeration. Unlike the brioche or milk dough, this dough should not be pushed any longer than 24 hours in the refrigerator.

C - Divide and shape your dough (50 minutes later for room temperature bulk proof; 8-24 hours for cold bulk proof)
After the bulk proof, your dough is ready to divide, shape, and use for any recipe in this chapter. Preshape according to your chosen recipe and wait 10 minutes between the preshape and final shape. Once the dough is shaped, brush it with the egg wash to maintain moisture for the final proof.

D - The final proof
The final proof of challah takes 1–1 ½ hours, which is shorter than for Basic Brioche Dough or Basic Milk Dough. The larger the item and the warmer the room, the faster it will proof. The rules, however, are the same. The fully proofed dough will be almost doubled in size, soft to the touch, and will not lose its shape. It will spring back slowly when pressed with a finger. Always brush with egg wash a second time before baking.

Base Recipe: Basic Milk Dough

Milk dough is essential to every baker's toolbox. If Goldilocks were testing recipes, milk dough would be the perfect medium dough. Taking its softness and sweetness from milk, it's lighter and more neutral than a brioche. It's also versatile, easily transformed by spices or fillings, and a delight to shape once it's cold. Because the recommended refrigerated bulk proof causes the butter in the dough to stiffen, you'll have a clay-like consistency that's easy to form into balls, braids, and other shapes. Use milk dough as a base for simple buns or sandwich loaves or dress it up with chocolate chips and spices. Swap it out for any of the recipes in this chapter that call for brioche or challah.

Note: Once you've mastered this recipe, experiment by substituting all or part of the all-purpose flour with spelt or stone-ground wheat flour, or substitute up to 30 percent of the all-purpose flour with whole wheat or whole spelt flour.

**YIELD: ABOUT 1KG
(2 ¼ POUNDS) DOUGH
OR 12 INDIVIDUAL BUNS**

For the dough
· 520g (4 ⅓ cups) all-purpose flour 100%
· 20g (1 ½ tbsp) granulated sugar 3.8%
· 7g (2 ¼ tsp) instant yeast 1.3%
· 9g (heaping ½ tbsp) table salt 1.7%
· 240g (1 cup plus 1 tbsp) whole milk, cold 46%
· 2 large eggs 19%
· 100g (7 tbps) unsalted butter, cubed and room temperature 19%

PROOFING TIMELINE
Cold bulk proof: 30 min at room temperature plus 8-48 h in the refrigerator
Room temperature bulk proof: 1 h
Preshape: 20 min
Final proof: 2-2 ½ h

A - Mix and knead your dough

In the bowl of a stand mixer fitted with the dough hook attachment, combine the all-purpose flour, granulated sugar, yeast, salt, cold milk, and eggs and mix on medium-low for 6 minutes, or until the mixture comes together in a solid, medium-stiff mass with no dry bits. Reduce the speed to low, then gradually add the butter, a few pieces at a time. Continue mixing until no butter is visible, then increase the speed to medium and knead for 5-7 minutes, or until the dough pulls away from the sides of the bowl, forms a smooth, shiny ball, and passes the windowpane test (p. 86).

Note: If mixing and kneading by hand, give the dough 5-7 minutes of slaps and folds (p. 84, Hand Mixing and Kneading) before incorporating the butter. Continue the slaps and folds until the dough forms a smooth, shiny ball and passes the windowpane test, which can take up to 10 minutes.

B - Bulk proof your dough

Option 1: Cold (recommended): Form the dough into a ball and let it rest at room temperature for 30 minutes. Reform the dough into a tight ball, then place it in a lightly oiled bowl with room for expansion, wrap airtight, and refrigerate overnight or for up to 2 days. It will expand somewhat and stiffen during that time.

Option 2: Room temperature: Form the dough into a ball, then place it in a lightly oiled bowl with room for expansion, wrap airtight, and let rest at room temperature for 1 hour. Once properly risen, the dough will have almost doubled in size and when pressed with a finger, the dough will spring back slowly. *Note: If the dough collapses under your finger with no spring back, it's been over-proofed, and your final loaf will be flatter and lose its shape easily.*

C - Divide and shape your dough (1 hour later for room temperature bulk proof; 8-48 hours later for cold bulk proof)

After the bulk proof, your dough is ready to divide, shape, and use for any of the recipes in this chapter. Preshape according to your chosen recipe and wait 20 minutes between the preshape and final shape. Once the dough is shaped, brush it with the egg wash to maintain moisture for the final proof.

D - The final proof

The final proof of milk dough takes 2-2 ½ hours. The larger the item and the warmer the room, the faster it will proof. The rules, however, are the same. The fully proofed dough will be almost doubled in size, soft to the touch, and will not lose but maintain its shape. It will spring back slowly when pressed with a finger. Always brush with egg wash a second time before baking.

VARIATIONS:

Citrus Milk Dough
· Ingredients for Basic Milk Dough
· Zest of ½ lemon or orange

Follow the base recipe, adding the lemon or orange zest with the butter. Citrus zest has a tendency to give dough a mousse-like texture, making it more difficult to work. Proofing overnight in the refrigerator will mitigate this unwanted side effect by stiffening the dough.

Cardamom Milk Dough
· Ingredients for Basic Milk Dough
· Seeds from 4-5 cardamom pods, crushed

Follow the base recipe, adding the crushed cardamom seeds with the flour. This version can be proofed at room temperature or overnight in the fridge.

Raisin and Candied Orange Peel Milk Dough
· Ingredients for Basic Milk Dough
· 50g (⅓ cup) raisins
· 50g (3 tbsp plus 1 tsp) water
· 2 tbsp kirsch, rum, or slivovice
· 2 tbsp candied orange peel, finely chopped

Prior to mixing your dough, combine raisins, water, and kirsch, rum, or slivovice in a small bowl and let soak for 8-12 hours, or until plump. Drain the raisins and let dry on a towel. Follow the base recipe, adding the raisins and the candied orange peel during the final 2 minutes of the mix. Bulk proof overnight in the fridge.

Brioche Nanterre

Brioche Nanterre is the classic French brioche loaf — split down the middle and soft as a feather. For the best brioche flavor, always use the highest quality butter. Serve this loaf with clotted cream and jam, cut into thick slices and layered with cheeses and crisp greens, or broiled into tuna melts — brioche takes sandwiches to a level of luxury of which even Marie Antoinette could approve.

YIELD: 1 LOAF

For the dough
· Ingredients for Basic Brioche Dough (p. 90)

For the egg wash
· 1 large egg, plus 1 large egg yolk, whisked

For baking
· 20g (1 ½ tbsp) unsalted butter, thinly sliced and cold

Follow the recipe for the Basic Brioche Dough, including cold bulk proofing (p. 90, A–B).

After the bulk proof, divide the dough into 3 equal portions, about 240g (8 ½ ounces) each. If the dough sticks to the work surface, use a bench knife to assist or just the tiniest bit of flour — too much extra flour will make preshaping difficult. Shape each portion into a tight ball, then rest, seam-side down and loosely covered at room temperature, for 20 minutes. While the dough rests, lightly grease and line a loaf pan with parchment paper.

After 20 minutes, lightly flour the work surface and flip the balls of dough, so they are smooth-side down. With a rolling pin, roll each ball into a long, flat oval. Starting from the top of each oval, roll them up tightly into fat logs. Arrange the logs in the prepared loaf pan, so the spiral sides of the logs line up with the long sides of the pans, the seams are tucked underneath, and the logs have equal distance between them — they will expand as they rise. Brush with the egg wash and let rest at room temperature for 2 ½ hours.

Preheat the oven to 170°C (340°F) (preferably convection setting).

After 2 ½ hours, the brioche rolls will have risen and joined into a single loaf. Brush with egg wash a second time. Dip the tip of a pair of kitchen scissors into water or your remaining egg wash to prevent sticking and hold the scissors straight up and down and directly above the loaf. Make confident, 4cm (1 ½ inch) deep cuts in a line down the long direction of the loaf pan, snipping the length of each roll to create a continuous score along the top of the loaf. Quickly slide the thin slices of butter into this split — while the bread bakes, the butter will melt and help the seam open and separate. Bake for 40 minutes, or until a thermometer inserted in the middle of the brioche reads 93°C (200°F).

Note: Wrapped in a dishcloth, brioche will stay fresh all week; any forgotten bits can go straight into Brioche Bread Pudding (p. 136) or Twice-Baked Almond Pain Perdu (p. 135).

Berliners

Just about every country in the world has some form of doughnut. I grew up in Massachusetts, the cradle of both Dunkin' Donuts and the Kennedy who famously called himself a doughnut — Berliner — in front of the Berlin wall, so they are hardly special occasion foods to me, but across the European continent, doughnuts mean holidays. New Year's Day, Winter Carnival, summer beach vacation — you name it. So, how about you party like you only get these once a year and make your own?

Notes: While any of the base doughs in this chapter will work, challah makes the softest, fluffiest doughnuts. It's what we use at Fine Bagels for our Hanukkah sufganiyot, because it's the dough least prone to burning. Why? It contains no butter, which has a lower smoke point than oil.

Use a thermometer to check the oil temperature as you fry each batch. If the oil is too hot, your doughnuts will be dark on the outside but raw on the inside, and if it's too cool, your doughnuts will be greasy. It's a good idea to sacrifice your first doughnut as a tester to check they're cooked all the way through.

For hot morning doughnuts, make the dough the night before and chill in the fridge overnight. These doughnuts can be glazed or dusted in granulated sugar or confectioners' sugar — or you can make some of each. They can also be filled with Pastry Cream (p. 262), Jam (p. 260), or another filling of your choice.

YIELD: 14 DOUGHNUTS

For the dough
· Ingredients for Basic Challah Dough (p. 91)

For glazing
· 56g (½ cup) confectioners' sugar
· 2 tbsp hot water
· ½ tsp pure vanilla extract

For frying
· Neutral oil, such as canola, sunflower, or safflower

For dusting
· Confectioners' sugar
· Granulated sugar

For the filling
· Pastry Cream (p. 262), Jam (p. 260), or filling of your choice

Follow the recipe for the Basic Challah Dough, including cold bulk proofing (p. 91, A-B).

After the bulk proof, divide the dough into 14 equal portions, about 84g (3 ounces) each. Preshape into tight balls (p. 87), then rest, seam-side down and loosely covered, at room temperature, for 15 minutes.

After 15 minutes, flip the balls of dough, so they are smooth-side down, then flatten and reshape into tight balls. Set each ball, smooth-side up, on an individual square of parchment paper and let rest at room temperature for 1½ hours.

While the dough is resting, make your glaze, if using: In a small bowl, combine the confectioners' sugar, hot water, and vanilla and whisk until smooth.

About 15 minutes before the final proof ends, prepare the oil for frying: Fill a large saucepan with 7.5cm (3 inches) of oil and bring to 170°C (340°F) over medium heat. Line a baking tray with paper towels or a wire rack.

Once the oil is hot, working in batches, carefully lower the doughnuts into the oil and fry, flipping once, for about 3 minutes per side, or until nicely browned all over. Transfer to the paper towels or wire rack and repeat to fry the remaining doughnuts, adjusting the heat as needed to keep the oil at 170°C (340°F).

While the doughnuts are still warm, roll them in confectioners' sugar or granulated sugar, or a mixture of the two, or drizzle them with the glaze. Let cool completely.

Once the doughnuts are cool, fill a piping bag fitted with a medium round pastry tip with Pastry Cream (p. 262), Jam (p. 260), or the filling of your choice. Push the tip through the pale line around the middle of each doughnut and fill generously. *Note: If you don't have a piping bag, simply slice the doughnuts in half like hamburger buns and spread the filling by hand.*

Zara Boréas & Mia Boland

Copenhagen bakeries have a reputation. A very good reputation. They're something of a gold standard when it comes to ecologically-minded yet impossibly hip sourdough bakeries, where the quality of bread is as high as the design. Bakers flock here from around the world to perfect their craft and slip prestigious stages onto their resumes, while tourists come to wait in line for the famed cardamom buns and innovative viennoiseries. It's thrilling, but in such bakery-density, it can be hard to sort out the hype from the heart.

There's a small peninsula off the southern bit of Copenhagen, away from the polished Scandinavian boutiques and jammed bike lanes, and away from the big food money and investment. It's an old shipyard, in fact, practically an island. In this district you can take a breath from the hyper-designed city center. Here, dirt walking paths mingle with industrial zones and boat sheds are converted into homes. It's a bit overgrown with charm — poppies and wild strawberries come up through cracks in the sidewalks — but people live and work here. And that's just what Zara Boréas and Mia Boland wanted for Lille, their bakery — a real-life community.

Built into the former wood and cement workshop of an architecture school, Lille holds something soft and industrial all at once. "It made sense to be out here," Zara says. "We really wanted to add something to an existing community. By being out here, we could. There's a harbor and houseboats all around. And we thought, well, here we can make a much bigger difference than if we opened just another bakery in the city center. Before this, everyone

from the neighborhood had to bike really far to get their bread."

Lille means "small" in Danish, but Zara and Mia's vision for the bakery isn't. When you enter the bakery, you hear laughter from bakers and chefs working together, topping focaccia with crisp sweet fava leaves or spreading butter on cake-like Danish rye bread. They're drenched in the warmth and daylight that comes in from big industrial windows and that radiates off the central oven. The obvious pleasure the staff takes in their work was one of Zara and Mia's founding hopes for Lille.

Mia and Zara met five years ago, when they both found themselves in Copenhagen working at 108, a fine dining restaurant in the Noma group. Mia came to 108 having already worked in kitchens around the world. She started as chef de partie and

rose to sous chef. Meanwhile, Zara was part of the team that launched the restaurant itself. She came from a background in rural development and sustainability, as well as in restaurants.

For Mia and Zara, their meeting was fortuitous. They'd both had some tough experiences in the restaurant world and wanted to create something that felt … different. They were driven to create something less rigid, a place where people wanted to work and where they could have fun. Mia puts it plainly: "a nice environment with nice people."

Neither Zara nor Mia are bakers by trade. They initially opened the space with Jesper, a baker they also met at 108. "In the beginning, we built the place on strong pillars," they explain. Jesper did all the baking,

Mia all the food, and Zara was in charge of running the business and front of house.

"We had very clear visions for what we wanted the bakery to be. Also what kind of bread. Since only Jesper did the baking, we had to make it very simple. We had to decide what we really wanted to offer and how to do the best we can with the limitations of space and hands. So, we had to choose what we wanted. A simple range of bread. And then we drew from our childhoods." And indeed, the shelves are stocked with nostalgic sausage rolls from Mia's Australian childhood, as well as Portuguese Berliners from Zara's.

Now the girls are a little bit more open to change. Their team is bigger and their space is larger. They also have an incredibly talented staff and know it's important to give talented people space to experiment and push themselves.

Both Zara and Mia are modest about what they do. Though they don't shout about it loudly, the raw materials the bakery and kitchen use — the vegetables, butter, and flour — are sourced from the same small and local organic farmers as the elite fine dining establishments in the city center. When they talk about the pig farmer who provides their

ham, or the producer who supplies their greens, Zara and Mia use first names only, as well as plenty of awe and affection. "We feel that quality, in terms of food, should have a more democratic approach. We want to bring it to everyone for an affordable price."

Working directly with farmers means a menu that changes daily, according to availability and the season. "Summer is definitely the high-point of the year, there's so much growing and available," Mia says, excited.

Their love of local produce and like-minded farmers led them to help launch Copenhagen's first true farmers' market, on the doorstep of the bakery. The market started as a way to celebrate the first anniversary of the bakery — they invited all their suppliers — but now happens every second Sunday of the month and features twenty different stands. It's an honest farmers' market, a place for people to

used furniture and equipment, and they had things repaired rather than simply replacing them. This was partially due to their limited budget but also a deliberate choice.

"We can tell you the story of every item in the bakery, where it came from, how far we traveled to carry it back. To construct and buy, we

are still touched to see customers coming in, showing friends the place, and telling them, "This is my bakery."

And over the years, Lille has stayed good to its promise — they have become a true community space. The farmers' market launched for their anniversary has grown into its own independent organization, run by volunteers, including Mia. And it's not just through the bread and the farmers' market that they build connections, but also through concerts organized by local performers and enormous dinners at the bakery's enormous tables. The bakery is a central meeting point in this unique neighborhood, and a beautiful outlier in a city of bakeries.

" *Zara and Mia know it's important to give talented people space to experiment.*

buy their food and engage with the people who grow it. "It tries to focus on food, not food as entertainment," says Zara. "No gimmicks."

On summer mornings, bakery customers line up enthusiastically, building to the lunchtime rush. But many are not just customers — they're investors. When Zara and Mia started the bakery, they couldn't find an investor who matched their vision of a less-constructed, local bakery, so they pooled every last penny they had to open independently. Everything in the bakery was secondhand. Instead of buying new, they found

bartered a lot, but it made it what it is," Zara says. "We really wanted to prove that it was possible. A lot of people will tell you it's impossible to open a place in Copenhagen without investment, but it is. You just have to make do with what you have."

Limited by their resources, Zara and Mia found they couldn't afford an oven — the most expensive part of any bakery — so they knocked on neighbors' doors, put up fliers, and spoke with other local businesses. And these are the people who donated. Their neighbors were their investors and by enlisting their help, they created a community for Lille before it even opened. Mia and Zara

"We were looking for space for a year. We were really obsessed with this area," Zara says. "I thought it was so beautiful and getting a spot was a very lucky break. We just wrote and they had a space available. So I called Mia and said, 'Okay, you need to take twenty minutes off work and come with me.' And I remember this perfectly. We just looked at each other and said, 'Okay, it's here. We found it.'"

Lille Bakery's Raspberry Sugar Berliners

One of the most luscious treats at Zara and Mia's Lille Bakery in Copenhagen are the doughnuts — inspired by ones Zara enjoyed during childhood summers spent at the beach in Portugal. Freshly fried then stuffed with cream each morning, Zara and Mia's doughnuts are rolled in sugar infused with freeze-dried raspberries for a very special twist. Mia says the raspberries give a nice acidity, but she also recommends mixing the sugar with different spices, dried lemon zest, or just keeping it plain and simple. Use any of the base doughs in this chapter, bulk proofed then shaped, or the Lille dough recipe here.

Notes: Part of what makes these Lille Berliners special is the distinct cream filling. At Lille, they like to mix their homemade seasonal jams with whipped cream to make a light filling that's easy to pipe. When I visited, they were using black currant and bay leaf jam. You'll notice the technique for making these doughnuts differs from the one used in the previous recipe on p. 96 — different bakers, different methods!

These doughnuts can be glazed or dusted in granulated sugar or confectioners' sugar — or you can make some of each. They can also be filled with Pastry Cream (p. 262), Jam (p. 260), or another filling of your choice.

YIELD: 17 DOUGHNUTS

For the dough
- 380g (3 ¼ cups) all-purpose flour
- 50g (¼ cup) superfine sugar
- 4g (heaping ½ tsp) table salt
- 4 large eggs
- 80g (⅓ cup plus 1 tsp) water
- 8g (2 ½ tsp) instant yeast
- 90g (6 ½ tbsp) unsalted butter, cubed and cold

For the raspberry sugar
- 200g (1 cup) granulated sugar
- 2 tsp powdered freeze-dried raspberries

For the cream filling
- 500g (2 ¼ cups) heavy whipping cream
- 2 tbsp jam

For frying
- Neutral oil, such as canola, sunflower, or safflower

In the bowl of a stand mixer fitted with the dough hook attachment, combine the all-purpose flour, superfine sugar, and salt. Add the eggs, water, and yeast and mix on low until combined. With the mixer on low, gradually add the butter, a few pieces at a time, mixing until the butter is no longer visible. Continue kneading until the dough is smooth and shiny. Transfer to a lightly oiled bowl with room for expansion, cover with a damp towel, and let rest at room temperature for 1 hour, or until doubled in size.

Once the dough has doubled in size, punch it down and divide it into 17 equal portions, about 50g (1 ¾ ounce) each. Roll the dough into smooth balls (p. 87), then place on an oiled baking tray, cover with a damp towel, and let rest at room temperature for up to 1 hour, or until light and puffed.

While the dough is resting, make the raspberry sugar: In a small, shallow bowl, whisk together the granulated sugar and powdered freeze-dried raspberries. Set aside.

Make the cream filling: Whip the heavy whipping cream to soft peaks then gently fold in the jam. Transfer to a piping bag fitted with a medium round tip and keep in the fridge until ready to use.

About 15 minutes before the final proof ends, prepare the oil for frying: Fill a large saucepan with 7.5cm (3 inches) of oil and bring to 170°C (340°F) over medium heat. Line a baking tray with paper towels or a wire rack.

Once the oil is hot, working in batches, carefully lower the doughnuts into the hot oil and fry, flipping once, for 1-2 minutes per side, or until golden all over — when the doughnuts stop bubbling, that's a sign that they're cooked in the middle. Transfer to the paper towels or wire rack and repeat to fry the remaining doughnuts, adjusting the heat as needed to keep the oil at 170°C (340°F).

While the doughnuts are still warm, roll them in the raspberry sugar.

Set on a platter or tray and either eat straight away without the filling or let cool, stuff with the cream, and enjoy.

Challah

Who in this world hasn't polished off an entire challah by themselves? When I moved to Europe, my heart stopped every time I saw a shiny braid in a bakery. "What else could it be but challah?" I thought. My mistake — and my disappointment. In fact, there are plenty of breads that look like challah but aren't challah. It turns out that just about every European country has its own braided egg bread. Czechs have vanočka, Poles have chałka, Greeks have tsoureki — the list goes on. We've all given to and borrowed from each other to the point where braided egg bread is special to everyone. But, I still can't eat a whole vanočka. Or chałka. Or tsoureki. So sometimes only challah will do.

Note: The key to a nicely shaped challah is to not braid it too tightly. The strands of the braid need space to expand, and if it's too tight, the individual tresses will flatten into each other.

YIELD: 2 LOAVES

For the dough
· Ingredients for Basic Challah Dough (p. 91)

For the egg wash
· 1 large egg, plus 1 large egg yolk, whisked

Follow the recipe for the Basic Challah Dough, including cold bulk proofing (p. 91, A–B).

After the bulk proof, turn out the dough onto a clean work surface. The dough won't be sticky and the rolling process will benefit from a bit of friction, so don't give in to the temptation to heavily flour your work surface. Divide the dough into 12 equal portions, about 90g (3 ¼ ounces) each. Preshape each portion into a ball (p. 87), cover with a towel, and let rest at room temperature for 10 minutes.

After 10 minutes, it's time to shape your tresses, the long logs that will form the braid (p. 88). Flip a ball of dough over so it's smooth-side down and use your hand to flatten it. Fold the top half of the dough over itself so the edge meets the middle. Repeat with the bottom half then fold the top over to touch the bottom and seal to create a tight sausage-like shape. This step gives your braids the strength to hold their shape in the final loaf. Roll the sausage from the center outwards to elongate it, applying progressively greater pressure as you roll outward to give the tress a tapered shape. The tress should be about 35cm (14 inches) long. Repeat with the remaining balls of dough to create 12 tresses.

Braid your challahs: To braid 2 (6-strand) challahs, divide the tresses into 2 groups of 6. Set aside 1 set of 6 tresses. Arrange the remaining 6 tresses vertically in front of you on a clean work surface. Keep the tresses separate but pinch the top ends together and press until flat — this is where you will start your braid. Label each tress position, left to right, as 1–6. The positions stay static, but the tresses move, so if you put tress 6 over tress 1, then tress 6 becomes tress 1 and tress 1 becomes tress 2. Braid according to this pattern:
Tress 2 over 6 — Tress 1 over 3 — Tress 5 over 1 — Tress 6 over 4
Repeat until the challah is fully braided, then press the ends together and tuck both ends under the loaf. Gently push the ends of the loaf towards each other to give the challah a nice shape and gently roll the challah on the work surface.

Repeat with the remaining tresses to braid a second challah. Place both shaped challahs on a parchment paper–lined baking tray and brush with the egg wash. Let rest for the final proof at room temperature for 1 to 1 ½ hours, or until the dough has almost doubled in size but isn't sinking or losing its shape and springs back slowly when pressed with a finger.

Preheat the oven to 170°C (340°F) (preferably convection setting).

After the final proof, brush the dough with egg wash a second time and bake for 25 minutes, or until the challah is golden brown and a thermometer inserted in the middle reads 93°C (200°F). Once cool, serve immediately or store for up to 3 days in an airtight container.

Toasted Sesame and Date Challah

This challah has an intense sesame flavor thanks to toasted sesame oil and toasted sesame seeds, and is inspired by the braided holiday breads in Central and Southern Europe that are stuffed with fruits and preserves. Here, there's a touch of sweetness from chopped Medjool dates and some color from fresh herbs. Use this challah to soak up garlicky dips and marinated meats at your summer Shabbos table and beyond.

Note: If your dates are particularly soft, to prevent them falling apart during the mix, chop them, then put them in the freezer for about 30 minutes. This will help them hold their shape.

YIELD: 2 LOAVES

For the dough
- 50g (⅓ cups) sesame seeds
- 240g (1 cup plus 1 tbsp) water
- 6 large egg yolks
- 35g (3 tbsp) toasted sesame oil
- 600g (5 cups) all-purpose flour
- 50g (¼ cup) granulated sugar
- 10g (heaping ½ tbsp) table salt
- 8g (2 ½ tsp) instant yeast
- 144g (1 cup) chopped pitted Medjool dates
- 1–2 tbsp chopped fresh tarragon leaves
- 1–2 tbsp chopped fresh rosemary needles

For the egg wash
- 1 large egg, plus 1 large egg yolk, whisked

For the topping
- 150g (1 cup) toasted sesame seeds
- 3 sprigs fresh tarragon
- 2 tbsp chopped fresh chives or borage flowers
- Fresh herbs and edible flowers, for garnish

In a dry pan, toast all of the sesame seeds — the 50g (⅓ cup) for the dough and the 150g (1 cup) for the topping — over medium heat, shaking occasionally to prevent burning, for about 5 minutes, or until golden and aromatic. Let cool then divide into 50g (⅓ cup) for the dough and the 150g (1 cup) for the topping.

In the bowl of a stand mixer fitted with the dough hook attachment, combine the water, egg yolks, and sesame oil. Add the all-purpose flour, granulated sugar, salt, and yeast and knead on low for 9 minutes. Add 50g (⅓ cup) of the toasted sesame seeds, along with the dates, tarragon, and rosemary and mix for 1–2 minutes, or until incorporated. Increase the speed to medium-high and knead for 1 more minute. Remove the dough from the bowl and form it into a ball. Place in a lightly oiled bowl with room for expansion, cover with a damp towel, and let rest at room temperature for about 50 minutes, or until the dough has almost doubled in size and springs back slowly when pressed with a finger. *Note: If the dough collapses under your finger with no spring back, it's been over-proofed, and your final loaf will be flatter and lose its shape easily.*

After about 50 minutes, divide the dough into 12 equal portions, about 120g (4 ¼ ounces) each. Form each portion into long tapered tresses, about 40 cm (16 inches) long (p. 88). Braid according to the instructions for Challah (p. 104), then arrange each loaf on a parchment paper–lined baking tray, brush with the egg wash, and let rest for the final proof at room temperature for 1 ½ hours, or until the dough has almost doubled in size but isn't sinking or losing shape and springs back slowly when pressed with a finger.

Preheat the oven to 170°C (340°F) (preferably convection setting).

After the final proof, brush the dough with egg wash a second time and top with the remaining 150g (1 cup) of toasted sesame seeds, followed by the tarragon and chives. Bake for 25 minutes, or until the challah is golden brown and a thermometer inserted in the middle reads 93°C (200°F). Remove from the oven, then tuck edible flowers and herbs between the braids.

Soft Stone-Ground Butter Rolls

I love dinner rolls — or rather, I love spoiling my dinner with dinner rolls, especially these. Toasting grains adds subtle, malty flavor to any bread, including those made with enriched dough like these pull-apart rolls that combine roasted cornmeal and stone-ground wheat flour. Make the dough a day ahead, then shape and proof a couple of hours before dinnertime. This is a variation on the Basic Milk Dough (p. 92) and the method is the same. For a different flavor profile, toast dark buckwheat flour or kamut flour and use in place of the cornmeal. Use the same dough for navette-shaped sandwich breads or round hamburger buns. This is one of the recipes where I especially like to add a bit of sourdough for extra softness in the rolls (p. 84).

YIELD: 12 ROLLS

- 80g (½ cup) fine cornmeal
- 475g (4 cups) light stone-ground wheat flour
- 20g (1 ½ tbsp) granulated sugar
- 9g (½ tbsp) table salt
- 7g (2 ¼ tsp) instant yeast
- 120g (½ cup plus 1 ½ tsp) whole milk
- 120g (½ cup plus ½ tbsp) water
- 2 large eggs
- 50g (¼ cup) sourdough discard (optional)
- 100g (7 tbsp) unsalted butter, room temperature

Preheat the oven to 165°C (325°F) (preferably convection setting).

Spread the cornmeal on a parchment paper-lined baking tray and bake for about 10 minutes, or until lightly browned and starting to smell toasted. Set aside to cool.

In the bowl of a stand mixer fitted with the dough hook attachment, combine 40g (¼ cup) of the cooled cornmeal with the light stone-ground wheat bread flour, granulated sugar, salt, yeast, milk, water, eggs, and sourdough discard, if using. Mix on medium-low for 6 minutes, or until the dough has come together in a medium stiff mass. With the mixer on, gradually add the butter, a few pieces at a time. Continue mixing until no butter is visible, then increase the speed to medium-high and knead for 5 minutes, or until the dough starts to pull away from the sides of the bowl. Form the dough into a ball, place in a lightly oiled bowl with room for expansion, loosely covered with a damp towel, and let rest at room temperature for 30 minutes.

After 30 minutes, flatten the dough to degas it, then reshape into a tight ball. Return the dough to the lightly oiled bowl, cover airtight, and refrigerate for 8-48 hours.

After 8-48 hours, divide the dough into 12 equal portions, about 84g (3 ounces) each. Flatten and preshape into balls (p. 87), then let rest at room temperature for 20 minutes.

After 20 minutes, flatten the dough again and reshape into balls, then arrange in a parchment paper-lined brownie tray or round springform pan, leaving just enough room for expansion — about 2cm (¾ inch) — in between. Cover loosely with a damp towel and let rest at room temperature for 2 hours, or until the dough is puffed and light and springs back slowly when pressed with a finger. At this point in the rise, the buns should be gently touching — this will create the pull-apart effect once baked.

Preheat the oven to 170°C (340°F) (preferably convection setting).

With a sieve, gently dust the buns with the remaining toasted cornmeal. Bake for 20 minutes, or until the buns are golden brown.

Alberto Miragoli

Every baker has a touch of the pyromaniac in them — and Alberto Miragoli is no exception. The name of the Madrid bakery he co-owns with his brother Guido, Ciento Treinta Grados ("One Hundred and Thirty Degrees"), was influenced by Ray Bradbury's classic 1953 novel, *Fahrenheit 451*. If 451 degrees Fahrenheit is the temperature at which paper ignites, 130 degrees Celsius is approximately the temperature when the Maillard reaction — the chemical reaction responsible for Alberto's deeply browned crusts and his brother's richly roasted coffee — occurs.

Alberto's breads are light and voluminous, full of aroma but with barely a hint of sour thanks to a carefully maintained rye starter. Yet it's his crusts that really stand out. Crispy to the point that there's a delicate shatter when you bite — a pleasing sensation to contrast the chew of the interior — it's technique that gives these loaves this special quality. Alberto protects them with generous dustings of flour, a method that allows for a longer bake and greater crust caramelization without burning.

After they're pulled from the oven, these signature loaves that Alberto has affectionately named The Dirty White and The Raf (Rough) go on racks to be sold alongside porridge loaves, sesame boules, classic baguettes, and ciabattas. In front of the bread, there's a spread of pastries — classic Spanish palmitas and gâteaux Basques next to Italian maritozzi and French chocolatines. Across from the pastry, home-ground nut butters are stacked neatly next to bags of the coffee Alberto's brother roasts. Everything smells like butter.

Looking at the line snaking out the door on a Sunday morning, you'd be right to be skeptical when Alberto, who won the award for Madrid's best bread in 2020, tells you it wasn't an overnight success. They're one of a handful of sourdough bakeries in the city, all established in the last few years. And even if the scene is starting to boom, it's still niche. The artisan bread revolution is new to Spain, a country where gas stations are one of the biggest bread sellers. Popular breads include pistoles, white baguette-like breads, and candeal, tight-crumbed low-hydration loaves pressed compact through a shaping machine. Alberto makes neither.

Early on in the business, people asked Alberto if he sold "normal" bread, something more pale. They weren't looking for caramelization. Raised on the pan caliente popularized by panaderías that bake off half-frozen industrial bread throughout the day, they wanted warm bread. So Alberto communicated with his customers, explained his bread, and even gave it away for free.

"Try and let me know," he told them. They tried and they came back.

By 9am, Alberto's bake is finished and he's ready to divide his dough for shaping. Madrid is already just a bit too hot in the sun, and signs of the sweltering May day to come are leaking into the bakery. He cuts off large masses of dough and pushes them into a round preshape, while the line of customers peek past the pastries and through the window to watch him work. His movements

are almost impossibly fast, so much so that you might expect him to stumble or drop something. He doesn't.

Alberto works, framed floor-to-ceiling by bannetons, proofing baskets for resting shaped bread. He guesses there's more than 400 baskets. Normally they come from France, which produces the gold standard of bannetons. But when Alberto was opening his bakery, he knew French baskets would be too expensive. Alberto also knew that Spain had its own basket weavers, so he traveled, working his way through the willow-growing regions, until he found two basket weavers, a husband and wife. They'd never made bread baskets before, but Alberto told them what he was looking for and they started weaving them, making one round model and one oval.

Basket making is slow, and starts when the willow is harvested in winter, when the plant is in hibernation and no sap flows through the branches. The branches are selected by size and the cut ends are set in a water bath. By spring, the plant wakes up, sap begins to flow again, and the branches can be peeled, then dried for storage. When Alberto's basket makers are ready to make a basket, they soak the dried willow again, then weave the softened material. When the

basket is woven and dry, they sew in couches — the cloth linings — using French linen.

Basket making is not entirely different from Alberto's craft. Like baskets, bread begins with a plant, which has its own growing season and harvest, before the grain falls into the hands of a miller and then a baker. It's these craftsmen who work the raw materials and turn it into something useful. It's all part of a world of patient handwork.

But Spain has a shortage of certain skilled tradespeople, and as with basket weavers, good bakers are rare. Unlike most of Europe, where trade schools provide a constant stream of artisans into the workforce, in the post-Franco period in which Alberto was born, Spain did away

from the Basque country and an Italian father. The two cultures met around the table — everything was made from scratch and everyone cooked, even from a young age.

"You did what you were capable of," Alberto says. If you were old enough to cut an onion, you did that. His mother always said that when he started to cook, she could see his breathing relax.

At seventeen, Alberto tried to translate his love of cooking to the professional world. He worked in catering briefly and learned that cooking in a restaurant changed his perspective — in a bad way. The tense atmosphere turned him off. He'll smile and tell you that you can feel the bad energy a stressed chef puts into their food — he didn't want to be that chef. So he put

> " *Alberto is building a network of farmers, he wants to know how the grain is grown.*

with baking programs in professional high schools. In the transition from dictatorship to democracy, educational priorities shifted towards university preparation, and bakers and pastry chefs of any ambition went abroad to learn their craft.

Alberto spent his first twenty-one years in Madrid, born to a mother

food aside and went to study art history at university. From there he found a career in cinema, working in everything from costumes to production. When the 2008 financial crisis hit, overnight the Spanish film industry went from producing 130 films a year to forty. Yet for Alberto, it wasn't the tragedy it was for others in the industry. He was at a moment of professional and personal dissatisfaction and wanted to get away. Far away.

Alberto left Europe altogether and went to California to study at the San Francisco Baking Institute. There his French chef told him, "Here you're free." What the chef meant is that Alberto was free from the orthodoxy of the trade school system, the system that Spain abolished but which remains the base of European baking. This trade system has a tendency to tell bakers there's only one way to do things. In America, however, there's no such weight of tradition.

After a year in San Francisco, Alberto moved to London, where he spent three years honing his skills at Balthazar and Pavilion Bakery. Next he went to Belgium to make bread for De Superette in Ghent. There he learned to work with a wood-fired oven and to play with new mixing techniques, working with stone-ground flours grown within twenty km (about twelve and a half miles) of the restaurant. He was back in a restaurant for the first time in years, but it was a different experience. As the baker, he was able to make his own rhythm within the restaurant's pacing.

These years of work and travel were formative for Alberto and exposed him to different ways of approaching his trade. "You learn that there is no unique method," he says. "You adapt — to the bakery, to the needs, to the equipment."

But Alberto didn't want to travel forever. He'd always wanted to open a business with his older brother, so he came back to Madrid to open Ciento Treinta Grados. Now, four years in, they also sell at a market stand and have plans to open a second location next year. But for Alberto, it isn't about expansion. If anything he wishes he had more time to walk his sausage dog and hunt mushrooms in the countryside — things a growing business gets in the way of. But really, what Alberto wants most is to push himself to make better bread. He says this with the modesty and gentle self-doubt that truly great bakers tend to have.

Changes are afoot already. Alberto has brought in a stone mill to begin grinding his own flours, and he's building a network of farmers for sourcing grains. "Would you rather have your coffee ground fresh today, or a month ago?" he asks. It's the same with flour.

Because the uptick in good bread making is new to the area, bakers are a bit on their own when it comes to figuring out sourcing. Local mills haven't had a chance to adapt yet; they're on their way, but these changes take time. Alberto wants a direct connection with his growers. He wants to know how the grain is grown, that it's not just getting an organic stamp slapped on the packaging, but that it's made with good soil management. "Grain is too often thought of as a commodity rather than an ingredient," he says.

For the future, Alberto wants to look beyond the loaves he's making and experiment. While that chef in San Francisco told him he's free from the old European bread guard, in a way, parts of the new artisan world have fallen into the same strict patterns, just with a different kind of product.

"Working with fresh flours isn't a business model," he admits. "It's an urge to break away to play with a more intellectual approach, even if it's just for myself. At the end of the day, what we're doing is feeding people. Being proud of what you do and looking with a critical eye to think of better ways of doing things is great — but just thinking how to be unique is ego."

Alberto Miragoli's Maritozzi con la Panna

May we all eat whipped cream by the bowlful. And when we can't do that, a maritozzo will do. This Roman breakfast bread is simply a soft milk bun that is split and filled with fresh whipped cream. Alberto Miragoli's bakery in Madrid, makes these every day — a nod to his Italian heritage and time spent studying in Rome — and they're an airy and cool pastry to enjoy on a scorching Southern European morning. Eat standing up with an espresso for the full effect.

Tip: On a hot day, put the stand mixer bowl and whisk attachment in the freezer for 20 minutes. Cream whips best when very cold.

YIELD: 12 MARITOZZI

For the dough
· Ingredients for Basic Milk Dough (p. 92)

For the egg wash
· 1 large egg, plus 3 tbsp whole milk, whisked

For the filling
· 400g (1¾ cups) heavy whipping cream
· 50g (⅓ cup plus 2 tbsp) confectioners' sugar
· 1 tsp pure vanilla extract

For the decoration
· 50g (⅓ cup plus 2 tbsp) confectioners' sugar
· Chopped nuts (optional)

Follow the recipe for Basic Milk Dough, including cold bulk proofing (p. 92, A–B).

After the bulk proof, divide the dough into 12 equal portions, about 90g (3¼ ounces) each. Preshape into tight balls (p. 88), then arrange so the balls are smooth-side up, cover with a damp towel, and let rest at room temperature for 20 minutes.

After 20 minutes, flip the balls so they are smooth-side down and flatten, then shape into fat navettes (p. 88). Place the navettes, 5cm (2 inches) apart, on a parchment paper-lined baking tray, brush with the egg wash, and let rest at room temperature for 2 to 2½ hours, or until they are puffed and light and spring back slowly when pressed with a finger.

Preheat the oven to 170°C (340°F) (preferably convection setting).

Brush the buns with egg wash a second time, sprinkle with chopped nuts, if using, and bake for 10 minutes, or until golden brown. Remove from the oven and let cool completely.

Once the buns are completely cool, in the chilled bowl of a stand mixer fitted with a whisk attachment, whip the heavy whipping cream, confectioners' sugar, and vanilla on high until thick and stiff.

Slice each bun through the middle, almost to the bottom, and spoon in the whipped cream. Smooth the tops with a knife or spoon. Using a small sieve, dust with confectioners' sugar before serving.

Elderflower Maritozzi

In late spring and early summer, before the best summer fruits ripen, parks and the edges of fields across the continent fill with the heavy heads of elderflower blossoms. Their citrusy, floral scent is everywhere — yes, I might be romanticizing, but I'm definitely not exaggerating. And all that abundance makes for some grade-A foraging. Indulge in the season and infuse whipped cream with elderflower and use it to fancy-up your Maritozzi con la Panna (p. 114).

Note: *For a similar effect during other seasons, use the same method to infuse cream with fig leaf, coffee beans, bergamot peel, orange blossoms, or whatever you like. The fat in the cream is a sponge for flavor.*

YIELD: 12 MARITOZZI

For the dough
· Ingredients for Citrus Milk Dough (p. 93)

For the filling
· 400g (1 ¾ cups) heavy whipping cream
· 60g (1 ½ cups) elderflower blossoms, washed and stemmed, plus a few blossoms for serving
· 50g (½ cup) confectioners' sugar
· 1 tsp pure vanilla extract

For the egg wash
· 1 egg, plus 3 tbsp whole milk, whisked

For the glaze
· Simple Syrup (p. 266)

Day 1

Follow the recipe for the Basic Milk Dough, using the Citrus Milk Dough variation (p. 93) and including cold bulk proofing (p. 92, A–B).

While the dough is cold bulk proofing, make your filling: In an airtight container, combine the heavy whipping cream and elderflower blossoms, cover, and refrigerate overnight.

Day 2

After the bulk proof, divide the dough into 12 equal portions, about 90g (3 ¼ ounces) each. Preshape into tight balls (p. 88), then arrange so the balls are smooth-side up, cover with a damp towel, and let rest at room temperature for 20 minutes.

After 20 minutes, flip the balls so they are smooth-side down and flatten, then shape into fat navettes (p. 88). Place the navettes, 5cm (2 inches) apart, on a parchment paper-lined baking tray, brush with the egg wash, and let rest at room temperature for 2 to 2 ½ hours, or until they are puffed and light and spring back slowly when pressed with a finger.

Preheat the oven to 170°C (340°F) (preferably convection setting).

Brush the buns with egg wash a second time and bake for 10 minutes, or until golden brown. Remove the buns from the oven but leave the oven on.

Brush the hot buns with Simple Syrup (p. 266) and immediately return to the oven. Bake for 1 more minute to set the shine. Remove from the oven and let cool completely.

When the buns are completely cool, strain the elderflower-infused cream through a fine sieve; discard the elderflower blossoms. Transfer the cream to the chilled bowl of a stand mixer fitted with the whisk attachment, add the confectioners' sugar and vanilla, and whip on high until thick and stiff.

Slice each bun through the middle, almost to the bottom, and spoon in the whipped cream. Smooth with a knife or a spoon. Garnish with a few elderflower blossoms and serve.

Shattered Sugar Rosinenbrötchen · German Raisin Buns

Rosinenbrötchen, sweet German raisin buns, always bring to mind a little postwar anecdote about German-American cultural differences. It goes like this: During the postwar years of the Soviet blockade of Berlin, American and English airlift pilots flew supplies into partitioned West Berlin. In a gesture of goodwill and propaganda, as they landed at the Tempelhof Airport, these pilots threw candy and gum rations out their windows to waiting local children. In English, these pilots came to be known as Candy Bombers. In German, they were called Rosinenbomber, or Raisin Bombers. But the translation doesn't work, because everyone knows that raisins aren't candy. In the spirit of extra sweetness though, why not meet halfway and dress up an otherwise simple German raisin bun with candied orange and a flaky sugar crust and suppose we aren't all so different after all?

YIELD: 10-11 BUNS

For the dough
· Ingredients for Raisin and Candied Orange Peel Milk Dough (p. 93)

For the egg wash
· 1 large egg, plus 3 tbsp whole milk, whisked

For the glaze
· 70g (½ cup plus 2 tbsp cup) confectioners' sugar
· 1 tbsp plus 1 tsp hot water

Day 1
Follow the recipe for the Basic Milk Dough, using the Raisin and Candied Orange Peel variation (p. 93) and including cold bulk proofing overnight in the fridge (p. 92, A–B).

Day 2
Divide the dough into 12 equal portions, about 100g (3 ½ ounces) each. Preshape into balls (p. 87), arrange smooth-side up, and let rest, covered, at room temperature for 20 minutes.

After 20 minutes, flip the balls of dough so they are smooth-side down then flatten and reshape into tight balls. Place the balls of dough, smooth-side up and 5cm (2 inches) apart, on a parchment paper–lined baking tray. Lightly brush with the egg wash and let rest at room temperature for 2–2 ½ hours, or until the dough is puffed and light and springs back slowly when pressed with a finger.

Preheat the oven to 170°C (340°F) (preferably convection setting).

Brush the buns with egg wash for a second time. Bake for 10 minutes, or until golden brown.

While the buns are baking, prepare the glaze: In a small bowl, whisk together the confectioners' sugar and hot water until smooth.

When the buns are fully baked, remove from the oven. Leave the oven on. Brush the hot buns all over with a thick coat of glaze, then return to the oven for 1 minute. In the heat of the oven, the glaze will crackle, giving your buns a sparkly and flaky effect that melts on the tongue. Serve hot or cool the same day.

Paula Gouveia & George Andreadis

On a residential street corner, in Berlin's Prenzlauer Berg neighborhood, is a place they used to call the Stasi Bakery. This is a part of the former East Berlin where, even decades after the wall came down, it's not entirely uncommon to pull forgotten surveillance wires out of apartment walls during renovations, so as a nickname, it's more than a little sinister. But the bakery where secretaries from the Stasi headquarters used to line up to buy bread for the office is cheerful and warm. The scent of yeast buns and custard trickles out the front door. Rather than the communist bureaucrats of yore searching for stodgy Splitterbrötchen, happy young families lean heavy Dutch bicycles against trees and pop in to grab bags of Portuguese bolas de Berlim, or Greek spanakopita. Save the perfectly preserved vintage interior, the bakery has nothing to do with its former incarnation.

And that makes sense. Because really, Bekarei — as the bakery is now called — is rooted in a love story from a very different Berlin, the Berlin of the Nineties. That's where Paula and George, the owners and visionaries, met. She was a visiting student from Portugal, and he was a transplant from a Greek family in Western Germany.

To hear Paula and George tell their story, it's clear the magical post-wall years were a you-had-to-be-there kind of time. The city was so cheap and open that when George arrived from his small town, within a day he had found a job and a flat and, he says, a new life. He could work three nights a week in a bar and make enough money to spend the rest of his time in clubs. Paula, meanwhile, was studying abroad and, in love with the city, kept putting off her

return to Portugal. She'd say, "just one more winter," "just one more summer," "just one more winter," until she never left.

The two of them were neighbors, introduced by friends over coffee — "We always had time for coffee in those days. Endless coffees," Paula says. George was smitten. "I'm not this guy — I never was this guy before," he insists. "But I said to myself, 'This is the woman of my life. And I thought, ok, I have to do something." So he invited her to a dinner party. The only problem was that there was no dinner party. So he called all his friends and begged them to come. They came, and Paula was none the wiser. At the party, over a large communal table, Paula got to know George and his cooking. And George had been right: Twenty years later, it's clear Paula is the woman of his life.

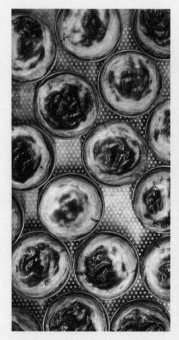

After they fell in love, they moved in together a block from where Bekarei now stands, in an apartment above a kneipe, a shabby local bar. It was a rough place — the neighborhood used to be filled with them — the kind of place to buy cigarettes while old alcoholics drank their morning beers with shots of grain alcohol. One day Paula and George noticed the kneipe was closed. The owner was gone and didn't appear to be coming back. Paula ran to the local office in charge and begged to have the rental contract. It was there that they started Eka, a small café and bar.

"Back then you could open a business with very little money," Paula remembers. "When we started, we didn't even have a coffee machine."

For the first year and a half, both Paula and George worked in other cafés and bars just to sustain it. But

they found their rhythm, and so did the neighborhood. "There were a lot of parties in those days."

By the time they had their son several years later, the bar had found its footing and they found themselves in the rituals of parenthood. Every day they walked the same route, back-and-forth to his kindergarten, and every day, they passed the old Stasi bakery. Paula coveted it. The space had so much charisma and vintage charm.

Then one day the old baker who had been running it for the last forty years wanted to retire. He put a sign in the window. The bakery would be closing. And so, again, Paula ran to the landlords and begged and charmed and got her way. At first, the pair's intention was just to run the bakery as a café, bringing in some pastry and bread from elsewhere and serving coffee.

"It was kind of a disaster from the beginning," Paula says. "After a year like that and almost going bankrupt

— it wasn't going well — our debts got higher, we decided we have to close the place or do it differently and bake ourselves," adds George.

They chose the former, and George, a skilled cook but not a baker, started to train himself. He began with his Greek favorite, spanakopita, then added Portuguese pastries he knew from Paula. He worked at a recipe — a cinnamon bun, a doughnut

for. He asked a passerby to help him bring it inside, then offered the man a bit of money to help him clean it up. The passerby stayed and, years later, is still one of George's bakers. When George looked up what the dough sheeter was used for, he started making croissants and pain au chocolat. "We started making them because I had the machine, not the other way around."

> " *Paula and George continue to carve their niche: full of tradition, yet tethered to none.*

— until he had it exactly right, then he would move on to start perfecting something else. The neighborhood responded to George's homemade baking and the business picked up.

George, still learning as he went, started buying used equipment. "[They] should have been in a museum, these things," says Paula. He bought a dough sheeter for a euro but didn't even know what it was

At this point, George was hooked on his new craft. "I was working twelve, sixteen hour days, seven days a week. I would wake up in a sweat with an idea and have to run to the bakery in the middle of the night to try it."

In 2014, several years into the bakery and by then working with a small team of Portuguese bakers, George got a phone call. The voice on

the other end invited the bakery to participate in a television contest for Germany's Best Baker.

"I thought it was a joke — maybe the tax office was playing a trick. How could they invite us to a best bakery contest? I said, 'We are not German. We don't even bake German.' But then we thought ok, why not? Just to participate would be cool."

The first day of competition was in Dresden, about two hours south of Berlin. It was the same day as the Portugal-Germany match in the World Cup and Paula and George had to be back that evening to show the game at their bar. With low expectations, Paula, George, and their head baker arrived in Dresden. While the other teams — five or six people on each — appeared in sharp kitchen jackets, they wore t-shirts and aprons. The competition was Berliner Schrippen, a local split yeast bun.

"Ok, so there's no way we're going to win," George recalls saying. "We're going against all these traditional bakeries." But to their surprise, they won. George and Paula quickly thanked the jury, then ran back to Berlin to screen the game and spend a long night in the bar. "Portugal lost," Paula remembers.

By the next day, they were back at the competition. This time, they were competing against all of East Germany. The item they had to bake was a German version of a Swiss roll. They didn't even know what it was — the jury had to show George photos. "But it was ok," George says. "We said, 'Yeah, we can do this.'" And so they went to work, finishing their Swiss rolls in an hour. Meanwhile, the other teams all took more than the allotted two hours. It was a big upset — no one had been expecting it — but the scrappy Greek-Portuguese team beat all these traditional bakers and Bekarei won the title for all of East Germany in a landslide.

The competition continued and though Bekarei didn't win for all of Germany — a nation renowned for its baking — they came in sixth, an enormous feat. They weren't prepared for what came next: Overnight the business exploded,

with people lining up to taste their products and ask for signatures. "From that day, it confirmed for people that we had good quality, that we were making everything ourselves," Paula says. "It was a validation."

"We thought it was a show for old people — I mean, they aired it in the middle of the afternoon," George says.

Since the competition, Paula and George have continued to carve their niche. Full of tradition — Greek, German, and Portuguese — yet tethered to none, they're now the bakery that restaurateurs come to when they want a special bread,

that burger shops ask to create a bun to exacting specifications, and where Israeli restaurants order their pitas. They're open to anything. But through all of it, they're a local spot where the neighborhood comes for their coffees and kourambiedes, Greek almond shortbreads. Or bolos de Arroz, fluffy rice cakes. Or Guardanapos, soft folded sugar cream cakes. Or Bougatsa, filo pastries with semolina. Because even these days, when rents are high and the squats of the Nineties are gone, Berliners still have time for a coffee. And in this neighborhood, this is where the coffees happen. Because this bakery has the most Berlin of love stories.

George and Paula's Pão de Deus · Portuguese Sweet Breads

There are hot Portuguese Pão de Deus every day at George and Paula's Berlin bakery Bekarei. Literally "bread of god," this is a soft milk bun baked with a sweet coconut topping. It sticks to your ribs like nothing else. Eat it as is or serve it like they do for a Portuguese treat at Bekarei — hot with slices of ham.

YIELD: 10 BUNS

For the dough
· Ingredients for Basic Milk Dough (p. 92)

For the egg wash
· 1 large egg, plus 1 large egg yolk, whisked

For the coconut topping
· 100g (2 cups) unsweetened grated coconut
· 100g (½ cup) granulated sugar
· 30g (¼ cup) all-purpose flour
· 90g (⅓ cup plus 1 tbsp) whole milk

For dusting
· Confectioners' sugar

Follow the recipe for Basic Milk Dough, including bulk proofing (p. 92, A–B).

Divide the dough into 10 equal portions, about 100g (3 ½ ounces) each. Preshape into balls (p. 87) and let rest, smooth-side up, at room temperature for 20 minutes.

After 20 minutes, flip the balls of dough so they are smooth-side down, then flatten and reshape into tight balls. Place the balls of dough, 5-7cm (2-2 ¾ inches) apart, on a parchment paper–lined baking tray. Brush with the egg wash and let rest at room temperature for 2-2 ½ hours, or until the dough is puffed and light and springs back slowly when pressed with a finger.

While the dough is resting, make the coconut topping: In a medium bowl, whisk together the coconut, granulated sugar, all-purpose flour, and milk.

Preheat the oven to 170°C (340°F) (preferably convection setting).

When the dough is ready, gently place a handful of the coconut mixture on top of each bun. Bake for 20 minutes, or until golden brown. Dust with powdered sugar and enjoy!

Gooey Chocolate Rugelach

Ten years ago, when I opened Fine Bagels, I only served American-style rugelach — cookie-like crescents stuffed with fruit and nuts. The complaints started immediately: "You call this a rugelach? Do you even know what rugelach is?" And so on and so on. If you can't see the controversy, here it goes: My bakery is in Berlin, but half my customers are Israeli. And rugelach in Israel is entirely different from rugelach in America. Israeli rugelach is what happens when an Eastern European pastry meets a syrup-soaked Middle Eastern sweet. The end result is yeasted and sticky, and oozing with gooey chocolate and cinnamon. In short, these rugelach attract bees. And so, I changed my recipe — because I had to concede that this style of rugelach really is The Best. Here is the exact recipe we serve at Fine Bagels — enjoy!

Notes: Add a twist to the chocolate filling with cardamom or espresso powder — or both — added along with the cinnamon.

Keep in mind that you're in for hell if you try to make these without chilled dough, so make the dough in advance!

YIELD: 22-26 RUGELACH

For the dough
· Ingredients for ½ Basic Brioche Dough (p. 90)

For the filling
· 125g (9 tbsp plus 1 tsp) unsalted butter, room temperature
· 160g (¾ cup plus 1 tbsp) granulated sugar
· 70g (¾ cup plus 1 tbsp) cacao powder
· ½ tsp ground cinnamon
· ¼ tsp ground cardamom (optional)
· 1 tsp espresso powder (optional)

For the egg wash
· 1 large egg, plus 3 tbsp whole milk, whisked

For the topping
· 3 tbsp sesame seeds

For the glaze
· Simple Syrup (p. 266)

Follow the recipe for Basic Brioche Dough, including cold bulk proofing for at least 8 hours (p. 90, A–B).

After the bulk proof, when your dough is ready to start shaping, prepare your filling: In the bowl of a stand mixer fitted with the paddle attachment, beat the butter and granulated sugar on high until pale and fluffy. Reduce the speed to low, cover the bowl with a towel to prevent a chocolate cloud, and gradually add the cacao powder and cinnamon in 4 batches. Beat until the cacao and cinnamon are fully incorporated, then increase the speed to high and beat for 1 more minute. Set aside.

Shape your dough: On a lightly floured work surface, press and then hand roll the chilled dough into a log shape. Dust the dough with flour, then use a rolling pin to roll out into a rectangle that is 3mm (⅛ inch) thick and measures 44 x 15cm (17 ½ x 6 inches) with the long sides horizontal and the short sides vertical. Use a knife or a spoon to spread the chocolate filling evenly across the dough. Neatly trim the sides of the rectangle. Mark each long side of the rectangle at 4cm (1 ½ inches) intervals, then cut with a pizza roller to join these marks and make 11 rectangles. Cut each rectangle diagonally to make 2 triangles. On the short end of each triangle — the base — fold both pointed ends in by 1 cm (⅓ inch), then roll up like a croissant. Place the rugelach, with their tails tucked underneath, on a parchment paper–lined baking tray. Brush with the egg wash and let rest at room temperature for 2 hours, or until the dough is puffed and light and springs back slowly when pressed with a finger. *Note: These rugelach proof for less time than other brioche recipes to give them a slightly denser final texture.*

Preheat the oven to 170°C (340°F) (preferably convection setting).

Brush the rugelach with egg wash a second time and sprinkle with sesame seeds. Bake for 10 minutes, or until golden brown and puffed. Brush very, very generously with the Simple Syrup and serve warm or at room temperature.

Julie Bouland

If you get up early enough and walk up the hill to the main square of Châtillon-en-Diois, you'll see the nighttime fog starting to burn off the deep green Vercors mountains. Echoing off the walls of medieval stone houses, spring water splashes from fountains, and everywhere — everywhere — it smells of warm cinnamon. In this village of nearly six hundred people, you have to queue in front of a modest wooden bakery if you want to taste Julie Bouland's breads and pastries.

Though she opened Boulangerie du Haut in a formerly abandoned bakery only recently, the customers speak affectionately of Julie and her baking, as though she is a lost neighbor that's finally come home. And in a way, it's true. She was born in the mountains, raised in this region, and she's come home to do her best work, living above her workspace.

Behind the bread racks and the cash register, Julie slides a flat wooden peel into her oven and pulls out her goods, products that began their lives as dough twenty-four hours earlier. There are yellow einkorn loaves, nutty grain breads, and airy but rich miches that she cuts and sells by weight. Under her glass counter are lines of pure butter croissants, pain au chocolats, cinnamon buns, and roasted hazelnut frangipane snails. It's a deceptively simple range of products but Julie wants simplicity. And though bread is very simple, it takes a lot to achieve a certain kind of quality.

If Julie ever pauses her work, it's only to remind a customer to let their bread cool outside in the open air if they want the crust to stay crisp, or to explain that no, it isn't too dark, it's just caramelized, as it should be. In terms of shape, Julie's breads are rough and rectangular — something that raises people's interest. It's a quirk of her large bulk ferments and her tendency to bypass fussy shaping techniques, an uncommon approach that sets her breads apart. Sometimes she has to gently tell someone that no, there are no baguettes in her bakery — yes, a bakery without baguettes in France. Other customers will often chime in, telling the inquiring party that they don't need baguettes — just try Julie's bread and they'll see.

But Julie wasn't always a baker. Though she spent her young adulthood wrecking her mother's kitchen making cookies and cakes, she started out studying at the prestigious Paris Institute of Political Studies — the "Science Po," as it's commonly known — despite knowing political science wasn't really for her. Still, it wasn't an opportunity one easily turns down in France, and it took her to Boston and New York, where she interned at the French consulate and the UN respectively. Sometime during that period in New York, she was also scouted as a model, though she's reticent to go into detail. Modesty takes over. "I only did it for a few months," she'll tell you, suddenly shy.

Once the UN gig ran out, Julie stayed on in North America and waited tables, which is how she wound up working in a pizzeria in

> ## " When customers exit the bakery, they put their noses to the paper bags and inhale deeply.

Montreal, where they stuck her on prep work. It was new, it was tactile, and she loved it.

Julie set aside politics for good and enrolled at Paris' Ferrandi culinary school to get her pastry license.

At Ferrandi, Julie found herself to be something of a black sheep. Immediately, she noticed they were teaching the aspiring patissiers that there was only one way to make things and that any variation in their method was wrong. She wasn't interested in the traditional pastries she was learning to make, disliking both their taste and their aesthetic. And it was all made with the cheapest ingredients — frozen fruits, chemicals, and gelatins.

"How can you make a good product without good ingredients?" Julie asked herself. She had a sense that things could be done differently.

After graduation, Julie knew she wasn't going to work in any of the classic Paris pastry houses like Ladurée or Cyril Lignac's famed Le Chardenoux — they were too traditional, too military-like. Instead, she was attracted to rustic coffee shop pastries and cakes, and she looked for liberty and creative freedom in the new wave of Parisienne cafés.

For several years, she made a living baking her own style of pastry, elevating the offerings of the grateful coffee scene.

In 2015, however, Julie started to feel bored. She wanted to know more. And in a move that is both radical and telling of both the toppling of pedestals and the cross-pollination of European baking, Julie left Paris for Copenhagen to learn how to bake bread. Sometimes leaving the cradle of orthodoxy is the best way to do things one's own way.

In Copenhagen, Julie spent a year and a half at the renowned Mirabelle Bakery, working under chef Carol Choi, whose bread making she admired enormously. Learning to master sourdough, Julie once again felt drawn to have her own project. Some people are fine working for others, but "I've never been that kind of person," she admits.

Back in Paris, Julie started making simple apple galettes and her own version of Danish kanelbullar. Cinnamon and cardamom aren't common spices in France, and word soon traveled in the coffee shop world about a girl who was making something divine. Overnight, it was as if the entire country had been converted to the joys of cinnamon buns. Copycat kanelbullar unsurprisingly sprung up around town, but none were as moist and lush as Julie's, the result of slowly fermented dough and particularly punchy Indonesian cinnamon.

On the heels of this success, Julie had her first opportunity to create her own business, crafting the bread and pastry of the then soon-to-open Circus Bakery in Paris. The establishment rapidly became famous for Julie's cinnamon buns and apple pies, while her hand in the bakery's creation was largely ignored

by the press that flowed in. "The more you grow up," Julie says, "the more you know what you want. Or rather, what you don't want." And what she didn't want was a business based on social media and food writers.

"I wanted a business that's necessary, that serves a function to a community. Not a bakery in Paris, where practically every street offers choice after choice." No — what Julie wanted was a small place, a village, where she could do everything herself. She wanted nature. And so she looked back to where she started, in a corner of the Vercors, surrounded by mountains, a place where she could jump into a Caribbean-colored river every day after work.

In Châtillon-en-Diois, Julie's customers don't know that the twisted cinnamon knots they buy

have a reputation among the Paris elite. They don't know that people used to line up on the Left Bank, just as they now do in their small mountain town. Here, Julie can source flour from a small farm one village away. She can work with local products and keep things seasonal and simple. When happy customers exit her bakery, they put their noses to the paper bags wrapping their warm purchases and inhale deeply.

Julie's bread has a chew — it's flavorful but not acidic. It's a bread the region has never seen before, a product of Julie's time abroad. To taste it is to understand the demands Julie places on herself. But once all the bread is sold for the day and she looks around, she allows herself to be a little bit pleased. At home, at last, with her model of simplicity embraced. "I didn't think I could do it, but I did," she says with a sly smile.

Julie Bouland's Kanelbullar · Danish Cinnamon Buns

This is a home adaptation of the Danish cinnamon buns that made Julie Bouland a household name in Paris. There are many copies, though they rarely measure up to Julie's. In general, Kanelbullar are no ordinary cinnamon buns and set themselves apart with a very Scandinavian touch of cardamom in the dough. The recipe features a shocking amount of cinnamon, but don't be afraid — it's for the best.

YIELD: 12 BUNS

For the dough
· Ingredients for Cardamom Milk Dough (p. 93)

For the cinnamon butter
· 200g (¾ cup plus 2 tbsp) unsalted butter, room temperature
· 200g (1 cup) granulated sugar
· 3 tbsp ground cinnamon

For the egg wash
· 1 large egg, plus 3 tbsp whole milk, whisked

For finishing
· Simple Syrup (p. 266)

Day 1
Follow the recipe for the Basic Milk Dough, using the Cardamom Milk Dough variation (p. 93) and including mixing and kneading your dough (p. 92, A). Ball up the mixed dough and place in a lightly oiled bowl with room for expansion. Cover with a damp towel and let rise at room temperature for 1 hour, or until the dough is puffed and springs back slowly when pressed with a finger.

After 1 hour, flatten the dough into a thick rectangle that measures about 20 x 15cm (8 x 6 inches). Transfer to a parchment paper-lined baking tray, wrap airtight, and refrigerate overnight.

Day 2
Make your cinnamon butter: In the bowl of a stand mixer fitted with the paddle attachment, beat the butter and granulated sugar on high until light and fluffy. With the mixer off, add the cinnamon, cover the bowl with a towel to prevent a cinnamon cloud, and mix on low until uniform.

Shape your dough: On a lightly floured work surface, use a rolling pin to roll out into a rectangle that measures about 45 x 30cm (18 x 12 inches), with the long sides vertical and the short sides horizontal. Use a knife or spoon to spread the cinnamon butter in a thick even layer across the rolled dough. Fold the top third of the rectangle towards the middle, then fold the bottom third over the top. Roll the dough in the direction of both open sides into a rectangle that measures about 36 x 25cm (14 ½ x 10 inch). Cut the rectangle top to bottom into 3cm (1 ¼ inch) wide, 25cm (10 inch) long strips. You'll see the layers of cinnamon butter now! Twist each strip, then wrap twice around your fingers in the opposite direction you initially twisted the dough. Wrap the tail of the dough over, under, and through to form a knot. Place the buns, 5cm (2 inches) apart, on a parchment paper-lined baking tray, brush with the egg wash, and let rest at room temperature for 2 ½ hours, or until the dough is light and puffed and springs back slowly when pressed with a finger.

Preheat the oven to 170°C (340°F) (preferably convection setting).

Brush the buns with egg wash a second time and bake for 14 minutes, or until golden brown. Brush with the Simple Syrup and serve.

Twice-Baked Almond Pain Perdu

This is one of my favorite ways to use up day-old bread. Ok, this is one of my favorite ways to eat day-old bread. Or five-day old bread. Or forgotten-in-the-freezer-for-the-last-three-months bread. I borrowed this technique from classic almond croissants which are just day-old croissants slathered in almond cream and given a second bake. In this spin-off, the almond cream crisps up in the oven and seals in the vanilla-infused custardiness of the French toast, or pain perdu. Serve for brunch or dessert — it doesn't matter. This recipe will make you forget pancakes for good.

Note: This almond cream recipe is the same as that in Chapter 5 (p. 267), but it uses some hazelnut meal for extra flavor. If it isn't your thing, just use the original recipe.

Tip: Be sure to use room temperature eggs and butter for the almond cream; otherwise, the mixture can separate. You can make the French toast and almond cream the night before, then assemble and bake when it's time to serve. Keep in mind that if you refrigerate the almond cream, you'll have to beat it in your mixer to make it soft and spreadable before using.

YIELD: 10-12 SLICES

For the pain perdu
· 450g (2 cups) whole milk
· 4 large eggs
· 2 tbsp (25g) granulated sugar
· 2 tsp pure vanilla extract
· ½ tsp table salt
· 1 loaf brioche, challah, or milk bread, sliced
· 28g (2 tbsp) unsalted butter, for frying

For the almond cream
· 100g (7 tbsp) unsalted butter, room temperature
· 100g (½ cup) granulated sugar
· 70g (¾ cup plus 1 tbsp) ground almonds
· 30g (⅓ cup) ground hazelnuts
· 1¼ tsp cornstarch
· 2 large eggs, room temperature
· 1 tsp pure vanilla extract

For serving
· Slivered almonds
· Confectioners' sugar
· Maple syrup, honey, or vanilla ice cream

Make your pain perdu: In a wide-bottomed medium bowl, whisk together the milk, eggs, granulated sugar, vanilla, and salt until smooth. Dip slices of the bread in the egg mixture until completely covered and let soak for a couple of minutes.

Heat a large skillet over medium-low heat, then add a small pat of butter to grease the pan. Once the butter melts and gently sizzles, working in batches, fry the bread, flipping, for 2–3 minutes on each side, or until golden brown. Set on a wire rack to cool and repeat to fry the remaining bread, adding more butter to the skillet as needed.

When the pain perdu is cool, make your almond cream: In the bowl of a stand mixer fitted with the paddle attachment, beat the butter and granulated sugar on medium-high until light and fluffy. Reduce the speed to low, add the ground almonds and hazelnuts and the cornstarch and mix until smooth. Add the eggs, 1 at a time, followed by the vanilla, and mix until fully combined. Increase the speed to high and beat for 3 minutes, or until fluffy and smooth.

Preheat the oven to 170°C (340°F) (preferably convection setting).

Place the cooled slices of pain perdu on a parchment paper-lined baking tray. Spread a thick layer of almond cream on top of each slice, then sprinkle generously with slivered almonds. Bake for 10 minutes, or until the almond cream has puffed and turned golden. Sprinkle with confectioners' sugar and serve warm with maple syrup, honey, or vanilla ice cream.

Brioche Bread Pudding

Bread pudding is the kind of cake that fits in just as easily for breakfast as it does a midmorning snack, a road trip bite, or a dessert. Part loaf cake, part egg custard, it's an easy vehicle to stretch the life of a forgotten loaf of brioche or challah. It was invented as such, purportedly as far back as eleventh century England, and to this day you can find versions adapted to local traditions the world over. Of course, it's hardly necessity that has kept bread pudding popular for nearly half a millennium — it's delicious and adaptable. Today, bread pudding is having a new moment, as bakers look for ways to reduce food waste and gussy up unsellable bread.

Note: The low baking temperature helps create a puddingy texture — don't try to speed this up with a higher temperature or the pudding will be much less creamy.

Tip: Throw in apples or any fruit just past its prime for a bit of extra texture and sweetness.

YIELD: 1 LOAF

For the bread pudding
- 40g (¼ cup) raisins
- 3 tbsp dark rum
- 200g (¾ cup plus 2 tbsp) water
- 1 apple, peeled and diced
- 30g (¼ cup) slivered almonds
- 1 loaf stale challah or brioche, cut into 2.5cm (1 inch) cubes
- 560g (2 ½ cups) whole milk
- 120g (½ cup plus ½ tbsp) heavy whipping cream
- 50g (¼ cup) granulated sugar
- 2 large eggs
- 2 tsp pure vanilla extract
- ½ tbsp fleur de sel
- Unsalted butter, for greasing the pan

For serving
- 3 tbsp cinnamon sugar
- 1 tbsp unsalted butter, cut into small pieces
- Honey, sweet molasses, sweetened condensed milk, or maple syrup

In a small bowl, combine the raisins, 1 tbsp of the rum, and the water. Let soak overnight.

Once soaked, drain off and discard any excess liquid from the raisins. In a large bowl, toss the raisins with the diced apple, slivered almonds, and cubed bread.

In a large bowl, combine the milk, heavy whipping cream, granulated sugar, eggs, vanilla, salt, and the remaining 2 tbsp of rum and whisk until smooth. Pour over the bread mixture and toss until no dry bread remains. Let soak for 30 minutes.

Preheat the oven to 150°C (300°F) (preferably convection setting). Butter a loaf pan.

Pour the bread mixture and any extra milk into the loaf pan. Sprinkle with the cinnamon sugar and butter pieces and bake for 25 minutes, or until barely wobbly. If the top becomes too dark, cover loosely with aluminum foil until the end of the bake. Allow the bread pudding to cool completely then turn out onto a serving dish, slice, and serve with a drizzle of honey, sweet molasses, sweetened condensed milk, or maple syrup. Keep refrigerated for up to 4 days.

Poppy and Sweet Cheese Koláčky

Like the Prime Meridian Line that runs through Greenwich, England, a similar demarcation runs top to bottom through Central Europe. It marks the boundary between people who take poppy seeds seriously and those who don't. Should you undertake to cross The International Poppy Seed Line, make your first stop a Czech koláček. Koláčky are sweet round milk breads that are filled with poppy seeds, sweetened tvaroh (or tvarog, a fresh cheese that's also called quark and can be swapped for cream cheese), Povidla (plum butter; p. 263) — or a combination of all three — and then topped with streusel. They're one of the most popular pastries in the Czech Republic and there's even a variation for marriages and a large, pie-sized version called frgál that's made in the mountains bordering Poland.

Notes: If you can't find ground poppy seeds, use a coffee grinder or food processor to grind whole seeds into a rough powder.

If the poppy seed filling isn't to your taste, but tasty little cakes are, replace it with Povidla (p. 263) or any jam of your choosing (p. 260).

YIELD: 14 KOLÁČKY

For the dough
· Ingredients for Basic Milk Dough (p. 92)

For the poppy seed filling
· Poppy Seed Filling (p. 265)

For the sweet cheese filling
· Sweet Cheese Filling (p. 265)

For the egg wash
· 1 large egg, plus 3 tbsp whole milk, whisked

For the topping
· Streusel (p. 266)

Day 1
Follow the recipe for Basic Milk Dough, including cold bulk proofing overnight (p. 92, A–B).

While the dough is bulk proofing, make your Poppy Seed Filling (p. 265) and Sweet Cheese Filling (p. 265) and refrigerate overnight.

Day 2
To shape your koláčky, divide the chilled dough into 14 equal portions, about 70g (2.5 ounces) each. Preshape into balls (p. 87) and arrange smooth-side up. Cover loosely with a damp towel and let rest at room temperature for 20 minutes.

After 20 minutes, reshape the koláčky by pressing out the center of each ball with your thumbs and flattening the middles until each koláček is about 10cm (4 inches) across with a 1.25cm (½ inch) lip around each flattened center. Place the shaped koláčky, 4cm (1½ inches) apart, on a parchment paper–lined baking tray, brush with the egg wash, and let rest at room temperature for 2–2½ hours, or until the dough is puffed and light and springs back slowly when pressed with a finger.

While the dough is resting, make your Streusel (p. 266).

Preheat the oven to 170°C (340°F) (preferably convection setting).

When the dough is ready, brush your koláčky with egg wash a second time. Use a fork to gently poke holes in the flattened centers of each bun, being careful not to deflate the puffed rims. Spoon a generous amount of the Sweet Cheese Filling in the middle of each bun, followed by a large spoonful of the Poppy Seed Filling. Sprinkle all over with the Streusel, then bake for 10–12 minutes, or until golden brown.

Spiced Plum Koláčky

This recipe is close to, but not quite, a strictly traditional Czech koláček. It is, however, a tasty way to use whole seasonal fruit, while not completely departing from Czech baking tradition. After all, plums are the most beloved of Czech fruits, used in everything from plum brandy (slivovice) to streusel cake to steamed dumplings. Macerating the plums overnight in sugar and spices will soften them and extract some of their juice, making them jammy and pink when baked.

Note: The plums most commonly used in Czech baking are the small blue oval-shaped Damson or prune plums, but this recipe works beautifully with any stone fruit you can get your hands on — apricots, mirabelles, peaches, cherries, etc.

YIELD: 14 KOLÁČKY

For the dough
· Ingredients for Basic Milk Dough (p. 92)

For the sweet cheese filling
· Sweet Cheese Filling (p. 265)

For the macerated plums
· 7 large round plums or 21 small blue Damson plums
· 66g (⅓ cup) granulated sugar
· 4 juniper berries, chopped (optional)
· ½ tsp ground cinnamon
· ¼ tsp freshly grated nutmeg

For the egg wash
· 1 large egg, plus 3 tbsp whole milk, whisked

For the topping
· Streusel (p. 266)

To finish (optional)
· Simple Syrup (p. 266) or apricot jam

Day 1

Follow the recipe for the Basic Milk Dough, including cold bulk proofing overnight (p. 92, A–B).

While the dough is proofing, make your Sweet Cheese Filling (p. 265).

Make your plums: Halve the plums and remove their stones. In a large bowl, toss the granulated sugar, juniper berries, cinnamon, and nutmeg. Add the plums and toss until evenly coated. Cover and refrigerate overnight.

Day 2

Shape your koláčky: Divide the dough into 14 equal portions, about 70g (2.5 ounces) each. Preshape into balls (p. 87) and arrange seam-side down. Cover loosely with a damp towel, and let rest at room temperature for 20 minutes.

After 20 minutes, reshape the koláčky by pressing out the center of each ball with your thumbs and flattening the middles until each koláčky is about 10cm (4 inches) across with only a 1.25cm (½ inch) wide lip around each flattened center. Place the shaped koláčky, 4cm (1 ½ inches) apart, on a parchment paper–lined baking tray, brush with the egg wash, and let rest at room temperature for 2–2 ½ hours, or until the dough is puffed and light and springs back slowly when pressed with a finger.

While the dough is resting, make your Streusel (p. 266).

Preheat the oven to 170°C (340°F) (preferably convection setting).

When the dough is ready, brush your koláčky with egg wash a second time. Use a fork to gently poke holes in the flattened centers of each bun, being careful not to deflate the puffed rims. Spoon a generous amount of the Sweet Cheese Filling into the middle of each bun, then sprinkle the whole bun with the Streusel. Press 1 large plum half or 3 small plum halves, cut-side up, in the center of the Sweet Cheese Filling and bake for 10–12 minutes, or until golden brown.

For extra shine, brush the plums with Simple Syrup (p. 266) or melted apricot jam when you remove them from the oven.

Jagodzianki · Polish Blueberry Buns

As a born-and-raised blueberry-picking New Englander, I feel more than a little disloyal to the state of Maine saying there's really nothing that compares to blueberry season in Eastern Poland. The floors of pine forests get so thick with wild berries that you can stain your legs just walking through. Foragers unfold lawn chairs along wooded roads and display glass jars of berries to sell to passersby. Meanwhile, bakeries embrace the abundance with jagodzianki, soft milk buns stuffed with jammy blueberries and topped with streusel. It's a good reason to spend the month of July in Warsaw.

YIELD: 12 BUNS

For the dough
· Ingredients for Basic Milk Dough (p. 92)

For the blueberry filling
· 150g (1⅓ cups) confectioners' sugar
· 30g (¼ cup) cornstarch
· 700g (4½ cups) fresh or frozen blueberries

For the topping
· Streusel (p. 266)

For the egg wash
· 1 large egg, plus 3 tbsp whole milk, whisked

For the glaze
· 60g (½ cup plus 1 tbsp) confectioners' sugar
· 2 tsp hot water
· 1 tsp fresh lemon juice (optional)

Day 1
Follow the recipe for the Basic Milk Dough, including cold bulk proofing overnight (p. 92, A–B).

Day 2
Divide the dough into 12 equal portions, about 84g (3 ounces) each. Preshape into balls (p. 87), cover loosely with a damp towel, and let rest at room temperature for 20 minutes.

While the dough is resting, make your blueberry filling: In a medium bowl, sift together the confectioners' sugar and cornstarch. Add the blueberries and carefully toss to coat without bursting the berries. Set aside.

After 20 minutes, shape your dough: On a lightly floured work surface, use a rolling pin to roll out each ball of dough into a large circle about 5mm (⅕ inch) thick. Pile a generous amount of the blueberry mixture on one half of each circle, leaving a 1.25cm (½ inch) border around the edge. In your bowl of blueberry filling there will be a lot of loose sugar mixture; spoon an extra spoonful or so of this on top of the blueberry pile. Fold the unfilled side of the dough up and over the berries like a turnover. Using the heel of your hand, press to seal the top half of the dough to the bottom. Make sure it's tightly sealed and pinch any open spots, so the berries and juices won't escape while baking.

Arrange the shaped buns, seam-side down and 5cm (2 inches) apart, on a parchment paper–lined baking tray. Gently press the top of each bun to slightly flatten and turn it into an oval shape. Brush each bun with the egg wash and let rest at room temperature for 2-2½ hours, or until puffed and light.

While the buns rise, make your Streusel (p. 266).

Preheat the oven to 170°C (340°F) (preferably convection setting).

When the dough is ready, brush the buns with egg wash a second time, sprinkle with the Streusel, and bake for 14 minutes, or until browned.

While the buns bake, make your glaze: In a small bowl, combine the confectioners' sugar, water, and lemon juice, if using, and whisk until smooth.

Remove the finished buns from the oven and drizzle with the glaze.

Florian Domberger

"I have three passions in life," Florian Domberger says. "Bread, beer, and trucks." They have little to do with one another, he admits, but they've brought him to where he is now. Domberger Brot-Werk is a sunny corner bakery on a residential street in Berlin's Moabit neighborhood, where bread is mixed by gentle old machines and classic Beutebrot, white sourdough bread, sits on the shelves next to sturdy rye tourtes. Dwarfing the other loaves is the enormous spiced Brandenburg Schusterjunge, a classic pull-apart loaf from East Germany that found its way to Florian's hometown in Bavaria — his mother used to buy the whole loaf for the family.

Now it's Florian who's found his way from Bavaria to the former East Germany. Every day, he arrives at the bakery, dressed in hiking boots and his signature "Motörbread" shirt — a play on Motörhead — looking like he's ready to go walking in the Swiss Alps. He's tall and enthusiastic and doesn't waste any time, peeking through oven doors and into mixers, shouting happy "guten tags" to familiar customers. His rolling Southern accent makes it clear he wasn't born a Berliner. Nor was he born a baker, for that matter. Florian was born in Augsburg, Bavaria, to a family of truckers. He's a fourth generation trucker, to be exact.

"It's what a Domberger does," he says. His great grandfather started a coach transport company in the Nineteenth century, with his grandfather taking it over in the Twenties, his father in the Sixties, and Florian's planned handover scheduled for the Nineties. But while he was happy to stay in trucking, he was not happy to stay in Augsburg.

"I thought it was too provincial, so I decided to go to Hong Kong." And just like that, Florian left the family business and went to work in Asia for Kuehne+Nagel, another transportation firm.

"It was the best job you could ever have, regional manager [for] customer information services. I was responsible for integrating tracking and tracing systems right at the time when the internet became the internet. I had a triangle of seventeen countries, from Korea to New Zealand up to Pakistan. I had an unlimited traveling budget and could go wherever I wanted." Florian smiles sheepishly before adding, "I was not so much into climate change at the time."

It was in Hong Kong where Florian met his wife Vanessa. He also learned some Cantonese and developed a love of the island's cuisine. Though he was living his best life, one thing was missing: his beloved German bread.

"I was in Hong Kong for three years and I couldn't get good sausages or bread" says Florian During his childhood in Augsburg, such was the importance of bread that the family would go to different bakeries for each kind of bread —

always to the baker who did things the best, never the same baker for Bretzeln as for Roggenbrot. The same went for sausages.

"So, I started to import, every three to four months, sausages and bread. A whole pallet. We'd keep it in the freezer," explains Florian. "I ate all Asian food, but once or twice a week, I needed good German bread and Wurst."

Eventually the Dombergers moved to Jakarta, where they spent another three years and where their first daughter, Franziska, was born. From there, they relocated to Melbourne, where Florian studied for his MBA and where Charlotte, their second daughter, spent her first months. But again, Florian missed the hearty breads on which he was raised. So the idea came to him: He would get out of trucking and open a bakery.

The family moved back to Europe, but Florian found he no longer had a network in Germany. Playing it safe, he stayed in the supply chain industry, working in Switzerland for years, all the while imagining his future bakery, taking stock of all the good and the bad bread he'd

market and gained a reputation. The whole city was talking about the guy baking bread in a truck. And in 2016, satisfied that he had a market, he established his brick-and-mortar and set up a permanent shop.

As he recounts this story, Florian interrupts himself several times to taste the day's leavened cakes — Zuckerkuchen (sugar cake) and Pflaumenkuchen (plum cake) — and compliment his bakers.

"Laura, these are so, so good, the Schnecken (cinnamon snails), they're moist and perfect, really, really good." And, ever the logistics man, Florian organizes. "How many Mohnkuchen (poppy seed cakes) for next week? We should decide this!"

In the shop, Florian's team of bakers, hailing from around the world, mix, shape, and bake dough in full view of customers. They maintain sturdy rye leavens and don gloves and goggles to dip hand-shaped pretzels into vats of lye water.

"It's really not pleasant, especially when you get it in the eyes," Florian notes. While they work, the bakers, unbothered, lift their heads to say hello and talk about the bread they're making. None of this is a coincidence: Communication is a tenet of Florian's business philosophy.

"I've come to realize one thing, which we did intuitively. But it's proven to be one of the best ideas I've had. Which is to explain everything you do. A conversation with a customer should take as long as the customer wants it to last. If it takes half an hour, let it take half an hour. Two minutes, so two minutes. Sometimes people come back again and again and ask the same question. And that's fine. I'm willing to give people that time. I enjoy it. You may have noticed, I'm not an introvert. That's what I try to teach everybody, I find a good comparison. You're running for Bundestag Election. You go from door to door and tell people what you do until you've made your point. And people — they might not agree with you, but they trust you. I want to make sure the business is done credibly."

eaten in his life. "What I sensed but didn't know was the importance of sourdough," says Florian.

Finally, Florian decided he was ready. He had had enough of corporate life and wanted to be his own boss. The family moved to Berlin, and Florian went into an internship with the Wiese Bakery in Eberswalde, a small town outside the city. For six months, Florian learned to bake with traditional sourdough and shape loaves by hand. To this day, Björn Wiese remains his most strategic partner.

"We speak every day, once or twice. We exchange so much. He taught me baking and I think I taught him a lot about supply chains. We buy and procure together, grow and professionalize."

When he was ready to go out on his own, Florian did it in the most "Domberger" way possible. He bought a truck. Not an ordinary truck though. It was a vintage Swiss army mobile bakery trailer. Built in 1968, the mobile bakery has a gas-heated oven and was designed to bake two and half tonnes (two and three-quarter tons) of handcrafted bread in twenty-four hours — enough to feed a battalion.

Driving the truck around Berlin and surrounding Brandenburg, Florian tested his recipes and the

It's through this philosophy that Florian has created a unique business model. At his bakery, it's the bakers who sell the bread — along with his wife, Vanessa, and their daughters, Charlotte and Franziska, who all work at the shop.

"It's that we put a lot of effort on how we sell, it's why we have bakers selling. They sell from the heart because it's their bread they're selling. They know the product better than anyone."

Though Florian started his bakery working with a trained baker — a bäckermeister — he now employs almost exclusively untrained bakers, creating a unique educational system within the production structure.

"We employ people who don't have a bakery background, which meant that we had to create our own concept of training, because I disagree with how the German system is done," explains Florian. "I think it's overregulated and yields some results, but not the best." At any time, on the floor of his bakery, there are bakers ranging from interns to those who Florian calls "B4 level," the highest grade of trainee in his establishment. As the bakers train, he administers exams and benchmarks for them to reach, giving them raises as they acquire and master skills.

> **On each site, the bread is baked fresh rather than being transferred from the main bakery.**

And though Domberger Brot-Werk has been on its corner in Moabit for five years already, the mobile bakery is still in use, baking and selling 150 days a year, as well as serving as an integrated part of the training system. Florian uses it as a site where bakers can hone their manual baking skills.

A second truck container, stationed at Berlin's Markthalle Neun, and a third one in Tegel, round out Florian's bakery setup. On each site, the bread is baked fresh rather than being transferred from the main bakery. It's a unique approach and the opposite of what most businesses do as they expand. But this is how Florian takes care of his quality and his bakery-to-client approach. In the future, he would like to open more of these container bakeries around the city. But he won't be doing it forever.

"It's like when you drive through desert plains and you see a thunderstorm on the horizon," he explains. "It's not there yet, but you can see it. This is my relationship with Berlin. At the moment, it's fantastic. All sunny. But I can see in the future Berlin is going to get on my nerves like no one's business. Then I'll go home. And I hope it will be the people who work for me now who will take over the shop."

When Florian reflects on the long route he took to owning his own company and becoming a baker, he says, "My father says, 'You could have had that all easier if you had just taken over the company in Augsburg.' But the fact of the matter is, if I had not taken that journey, I would probably not have been a happy entrepreneur. I simply needed to make my journey — there was no other way."

Sometimes, journeys can find their way back to the places they started, just like a Bavarian Bretzel.

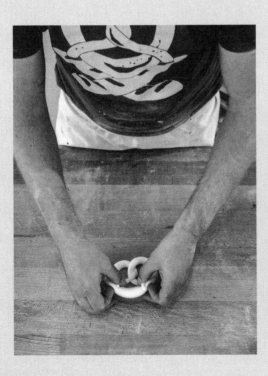

Florian Domberger's Zuckerkuchen · German Sugar Cake

Zuckerkuchen, which translates to "sugar cake," is a yeasted German milk bread, dripping in a golden buttery sugar crust and cut into thick squares for tea time snacking. Yeasted cakes are common in Germany, and are often topped with fruit and streusel, but Zuckerkuchen is the simplest and, I think, most delicious version. This is Florian Domberger's ultra-soft version that he makes at Domberger Brot-Werk in Berlin. It's extra moist because Florian includes a sourdough starter in the dough.

Note: This recipe can also be made with any of the base recipes at the beginning of the chapter.

YIELD: ONE 23 X 33CM (9 X 13 ¼ INCH) CAKE (ABOUT 12 SERVINGS)

For the leaven
· 25g (3 tbsp plus 1 tsp) all-purpose flour
· 25g (1 tbsp plus 2 tsp) cool water
· 5g (1 tsp) ripe sourdough starter

For the dough
· 460g (3 ¾ cups plus 1 tbsp) all-purpose flour
· 66g (⅓ cup) granulated sugar
· 10g (1 tbsp plus ¼ tsp) instant yeast
· 5g (¾ tsp) table salt
· 250g (1 cup plus 2 tbsp) whole milk
· 120g (9 tbsp) unsalted butter, cold and cubed
· 48 g (3 tbsp plus 1 tsp) ripe sourdough starter (leaven)
· 1 large egg

For the topping
· 150g (10 tbsp plus 2 tsp) unsalted butter, cut into small pieces
· 125g (½ cup plus 2 tbsp) granulated sugar

For the glaze
· 114g (½ cup) heavy whipping cream

Morning: Make your leaven
Build your leaven and let it rest, loosely covered, for 8-9 hours (p. 26, A).

Afternoon/Evening (8-9 hours later): Start making your dough
If your leaven is ready (p. 26, B), in the bowl of a stand mixer fitted with the dough hook attachment, combine the all-purpose flour, granulated sugar, yeast, salt, milk, butter, leaven, and egg and mix on low for 6-8 minutes, or until smooth. Increase the speed to high and knead for 2-3 minutes, or until the dough is glossy and pulls away from the sides of the bowl. Form the dough into a ball and place in a lightly oiled bowl with room for expansion. Cover with a damp towel and let rest at room temperature for 1 hour.

After 1 hour, press the dough to degas it, then reshape into a ball and let rest at room temperature for 30 minutes.

After 30 minutes, butter a large brownie tin or casserole dish.

On a lightly floured work surface, use a rolling pin to roll out the ball of dough to fit the pan, then set the dough in the pan, cover with a damp towel, and let rest at room temperature for 1 hour, or until the dough is puffed and light and springs back slowly when pressed with a finger.

Preheat the oven to 170°C (340°F) (preferably convection setting).

After the final proof, press your fingertips into the dough all the way to the bottom of the tray like you would for focaccia (p. 58). In each of the finger holes you made, place a small piece of butter, then sprinkle all over with the granulated sugar. Bake for about 20 minutes, or until the top is golden brown and a knife inserted in the middle comes out clean. Brush the top with heavy whipping cream, then let cool slightly before slicing and serving.

Honey and Fig Tropézienne

Tarte tropézienne, a layered brioche cake that is filled with cream and topped with pearl sugar, is so much a part of the classic French bakery repertoire that you'd hardly guess it was invented as recently as the 1950s and by a Polish pastry chef named Alexandre Micka. This recipe plays with the Tropézienne and gives it an update with a mascarpone and honey-infused cream that is extra delicious with fresh figs. If figs are out of season, try strawberries, raspberries, poached pears, or any other soft, sweet fruit.

YIELD: 1 CAKE

For the dough
· Ingredients for ½ Basic Brioche Dough (p. 90)

For the egg wash
· 1 large egg, plus 3 tbsp whole milk, whisked

For the decoration
· 50g (¼ cup) pearl sugar

For the honey and mascarpone cream
· 227g (1 cup) heavy whipping cream
· 40g (⅓ cup plus 1 tsp) confectioners' sugar
· 1 tsp pure vanilla extract
· 1 tsp fleur d'oranger (orange blossom water)
· 225g (1 cup) mascarpone
· 30g (1 ½ tbsp) honey

For the filling
· 255g (¾ cup) fig jam

For the fruit
· 10–12 ripe figs, halved
· Simple Syrup (p. 266)

Follow the recipe for the Basic Brioche Dough, including cold bulk proofing (p. 90, A–B).

Preshape the brioche into a large ball, cover with a towel, and let rest at room temperature for 20 minutes.

After 20 minutes, lightly flour the brioche and use a rolling pin to roll it into a wide, flat disk, about 1.25cm (½ inch) thick. Brush with the egg wash and let rest at room temperature for 2 ½ hours, or until the dough is puffed and light and springs back slowly when pressed with a finger.

Preheat the oven to 170°C (340°F) (preferably convection setting).

After 2 ½ hours, brush the brioche with egg wash a second time, then sprinkle generously with the pearl sugar. Bake for 25 minutes, or until the top is golden brown and a knife inserted comes out clean. Let cool completely.

Once the brioche is completely cool, make your honey and mascarpone cream: In the chilled bowl of a stand mixer fitted with the whisk attachment, whip the heavy whipping cream, confectioners' sugar, vanilla, and fleur d'oranger on high until starting to thicken. Add the mascarpone and whip on high until stiff and thick. Add the honey and gently fold to incorporate.

Assemble your tropezienne: Slice the brioche horizontally in half to create 2 even layers. Spread fig jam on both halves of the cut brioche, as though you were making a jam sandwich. Spread a thick layer of the honey and mascarpone cream on the bottom half. Add a layer of cut figs, arranging the ones around the edges with the cut side facing out. Spoon or pipe the rest of the cream between and on top of the figs, then top with the other half of the brioche. To finish, brush any visible figs with Simple Syrup for a bit of shine. Chill in the refrigerator until ready to serve. Cut into triangular slices as you would a cake.

Semla

If Swedish bakeries know how to do anything, it's how to bake with cardamom. Semla, or fastlagsbulle, are no exception. The towering holiday buns eaten in the lead-up to Lent are made with a soft cardamom milk dough and stuffed with almond paste and stiff whipped cream. Without being overpowering, the cardamom hits the nose in the most pleasing way imaginable. My friend Hampus says that his mother remembers being served these in a bowl of warm milk. These days they're eaten out of hand straight from the bakery or with a gathering of friends for fika, the Swedish afternoon coffee and cake break.

Pro tip from Hampus: The little cut-out bread cap can double as a spoon if your mouth can't make it around the mountain of cream.

YIELD: 12 SEMLA

For the dough
· Ingredients for Cardamom Milk Dough (p. 93)

For the egg wash
· 1 large egg, plus 3 tbsp whole milk, whisked

For the marzipan filling
· 150g (1 ¾ cups) ground almonds
· 150g (1 ⅓ cups) confectioners' sugar
· 2 large egg whites
· 2 tbsp whole milk
· ½ tbsp almond extract

For the whipped cream
· 600g (2 ⅔ cups) heavy whipping cream
· 75g (⅔ cup) confectioners' sugar
· 2 tsp pure vanilla extract

For the decoration
· Confectioners' sugar

Day 1
Follow the recipe for the Basic Milk Dough, using the Cardamom Milk Dough variation (p. 93) and including cold bulk proofing (p. 92, A–B).

Day 2
Divide dough into 12 equal portions, about 84g (3 ounces) each. Preshape into balls (p. 87) and arrange smooth-side up. Cover with a towel and let rest at room temperature for 20 minutes.

After 20 minutes, flip the balls so they are smooth-side down, flatten, and reshape into tight balls. Place the balls, smooth-side up and 4cm (1 ½ inches) apart, on a parchment paper–lined baking tray, brush with the egg wash, and let rest at room temperature for 2– 2 ½ hours, or until the dough is puffed and light and springs back slowly when pressed with a finger.

Preheat the oven to 170°C (340°F) (preferably convection setting).

After 2–2 ½ hours, brush the balls with egg wash a second time and bake for 12 minutes, or until light golden. Remove from the oven and let cool completely.

When the buns are completely cooled, use a small sharp serrated paring knife, angled steeply into the bun, to make 3 deep cuts to create the triangular cap for each semla, and at the same time create a cavity for the filling. Trim the inner fluff off the lids so they're only about 3cm (1 ¼ inches) deep. Set aside.

Make your marzipan filling: In the bowl of a stand mixer fitted with the paddle attachment, beat the ground almonds, confectioners' sugar, and egg whites on high for about 3 minutes, or until a sticky paste forms. Reduce the speed to low, then add the milk and almond extract and beat to loosen the paste slightly. Set aside.

Make your whipped cream: In the chilled bowl of a stand mixer fitted with the whisk attachment, whip the heavy whipping cream, confectioners' sugar, and vanilla on high until very stiff.

Assemble your buns: Spoon a generous portion of the marzipan filling in the cavity of each bun. Add an even more excessive portion of whipped cream on top of that — you can use a piping bag fitted with a large star pastry tip for a traditional bakery look, or a spoon for a more rustic look. Put the triangular hat on top of each bun, use a small sieve to dust with confectioners' sugar, and serve.

CHAPTER 3

Laminated Pastries and Viennoiseries

Layers and Layers: Working with Laminated Pastry

Laminated pastry is one of the most elegant signatures of European baking. In the traditional bakery world, it's a tourier who specializes in this sophisticated treat. Laminated pastry is considered a baker's pastry — something you'd pick up at a bread shop rather than a pastry shop. These days the lines are more blurred, but what you need to know is that these flaky, buttery layers make the base of croissants, danishes, and infinite pastry incarnations that are as delicate as teacups. Lamination is a versatile technique and suitable for all your pastry fantasies, whether sweet, salty, or somewhere in between.

But how do these layers come to be? Laminating dough is a technical exercise in wall building — walls of butter, that is. The basic principle of lamination is folding and rolling chilled dough — the détrempe — around carefully shaped butter — the beurrage — to create alternating layers of dough and butter, and takes advantage of the melting point of butter, 28°C (84°F). At temperatures cooler than that, butter is solid and nicely partitions the dough, allowing it to rise in thin, individual layers. Once the pastry is in the oven though, the heat melts the butter, and the wall falls away, but not before the layers have baked enough to remain separate.

Risen Laminated Dough (Croissants!) Versus Puff Pastry Dough

There are two kinds of laminated doughs, one with leaven (yeast or sourdough) and one without. Those with leaven (yeast or sourdough) — risen laminated doughs — form the soft, voluminous base of croissants. Treat these doughs like any other bread dough. They require a proof, a shape, and a final rise. Meanwhile, unleavened laminated doughs, more commonly known as puff pastry, have no such rise. Though they are also laminated with butter to create layers, the dough portion of the pastry isn't yeasted, so it doesn't rise. Thus, it is only the melting of butter and released steam that creates the desired flaky gaps. Puff pastry may not expand as much as risen laminated dough, but it forms excellent crispy bases for pies and turnovers.

The Components of Risen Laminated Pastry

The Détrempe: The détrempe is the base dough of a risen laminated pastry — the stuff we want to keep separated by those walls of butter. Though the détrempe is similar to any of the enriched doughs from Chapter 2, it's stiffer.

Why stiffer? Well, part of making the perfect layers means keeping the butter and dough at the same temperature and texture. Chilling the détrempe and keeping the dough at low hydration ensures the correct texture for lamination. If the dough is too soft and the butter is too cold, the butter will crack rather than flatten smoothly as you roll it out, and though you'll still have some layers, the pastry will leak butter as it bakes. On the other hand, if the butter is too warm, it will melt into the dough, and you'll have no layers at all, just a tasty brioche in the shape of a croissant. In other words, messing this one up will hardly result in culinary tragedy — it'll all be delicious.

The Beurrage: The beurrage is the thin square of butter you'll use to laminate your dough. Since butter doesn't arrive on the supermarket shelves in thin squares, we have to do this part ourselves through a bit of pounding and rolling. Pounding enhances the elasticity of the butter and elongates it into the desired dimensions for shaping. This step should be done shortly before laminating. Don't cheat and do it in advance — too long in the fridge and the butter will crack during rolling and leak during baking, and too long at room temperature and it will be too soft and turn your layers into brioche.

Choosing your Butter

There are two kinds of butter you can use for lamination — a high quality European or European-style unsalted butter with at least an 82 percent fat content, or special lamination butter. There are several important elements to keep in mind when it comes to the butter for making laminated pastry: elasticity, flavor, and melting point. For elasticity and flavor, European butter and lamination butter are your best bet. (I'm giving you the side-eye, American butter.)

If you choose to use European butter, know that it has a melting point of 28°C (84 °F). Even if you keep your house colder, all kinds of things can bring your butter to a higher temperature, whether it's rolling the dough or the heat from your own hands. As such, you want to start your process with cold butter and cold dough, and ideally work in a cold room. If you have stone or marble work surfaces, these are the best as they hold cold.

If you want to get a real edge on laminated pastries, lamination butter is your best friend. In Europe, it's available at specialty shops and trade stores; in the U.S., it can be ordered on the internet. Also called dry butter or beurre de tourage, it's a special professional butter that melts at 32°C (90 °F), giving you an advantage on hot days or with overworked dough. It comes in thick sheets, which makes the division and flattening much easier. I cannot overemphasize this: Lamination butter is magic.

Making a Beurrage

(Photos p. 158) To make a beurrage, start with a square of very cold butter (2). The Basic Laminated Dough recipe in this chapter uses 250g (9 ounces) of butter. Most

European butter already comes in 250g (9 ounce) squares, and lamination butter comes in easily divided 1-2 kilo (2 ¼-4 ½ pound) sheets. Oftentimes in the U.S., this butter will come in a 227g (8 ounces) block, as that approximates a cup. If that's the case, simply cut off a thin rectangle of about 23g (¾ ounce) and press onto your block before pounding. If using American-style sticks of butter, allow the butter to come to room temperature, then press it together into an approximate square and return it to the refrigerator to chill completely.

Next, generously flour both a stable work surface and your square of butter. Using a rolling pin, pound the butter bit by bit along its length (3), then rotate the butter 90 degrees and do the same progressive pounding along the new length (4) until you have a rough square — about 15cm (6 inches) long. Fold a square of parchment paper around the butter, like an envelope, into a 25cm (10 inch) square (5). The square of parchment paper will be larger than the butter. Use the rolling pin to roll out the butter until it fills the entire paper envelope (6-7). Now you have a 25cm (10 inch) beurrage. The pounding and rolling process will have warmed up the butter considerably, so return it to the fridge to chill for 20 minutes.

Placing

(Photos p. 158) Once your beurrage is chilled, remove both the beurrage and the détrempe from the refrigerator. Place your détrempe on a lightly floured work surface. With your beurrage still in its paper, set it in the middle of the circle and check that it fits perfectly inside. If the détrempe is a bit smaller than your beurrage, give the détrempe a tiny roll to make it a bit bigger. When you're satisfied that the butter fits exactly in the détrempe, with the corners of the butter square just reaching the edge of the circle, peel off the parchment paper from the beurrage and set it in the middle (8). Next, fold each side of the circle around the butter, meeting in the middle (9-10). Stretch the dough gently, being careful to not rip it. Pinch along each seam to seal the dough (11), then press an X along these seams with your rolling pin (12). This will set the butter inside so it doesn't move around.

Rolling

(Photo p. 159) Laminating dough requires a nice, even roll. One of the best ways to do this is to prep your dough by pressing your rolling pin bit by bit along the length of your dough, making a speed-bumped surface (13). When you roll, you'll find it goes much easier and stays much straighter. Because rolling heats your dough and butter, you want to use as few rolls as possible.

Turning

Turns are the process of folding and rolling your dough to create butter layers. There are two kinds of turns, single and double, each making a different number of layers. For practical instructions, see the Basic Laminated Dough recipe (p. 159, D-E), for visuals, see photos 15-22 on p. 159.

Chilling

The most critical aspect of homemade laminated dough is to keep your ingredients cold. This is why the dough is always chilled between turns, rather than laminated all the way through without chilling. Respect temperature and your patience will be rewarded with gorgeous pastry.

Making Ahead

I could lie, but I won't: Laminated pastry is a project! The good news is that if you want to go through the effort in advance — on your own time — to serve at a later time, you can freeze your shaped pastries before their final rise. Just be sure they're in an airtight container, so they don't get freezer burn. The night before you want to bake, take your pastries out of the freezer and defrost them overnight in the fridge. In the morning, place them on a parchment paper-lined baking tray, brush with egg wash, and allow to proof fully at room temperature.

Troubleshooting Laminated Dough

Butter cracks when rolled, and the final pastry leaks butter: This means the dough was too warm or soft and the butter too cold. Make sure your butter and dough are the same temperature and texture.
No layers: This means the butter was too warm and melted before it could make "walls."

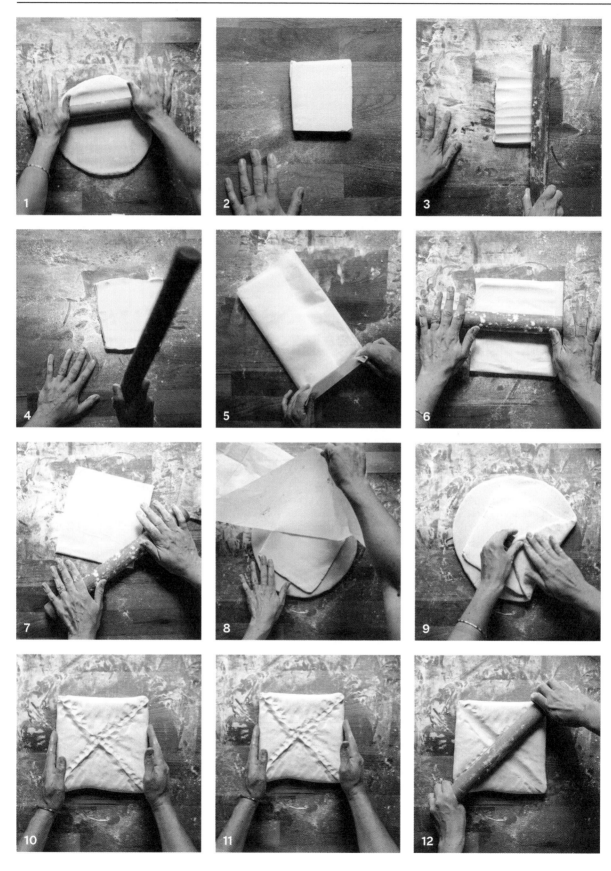

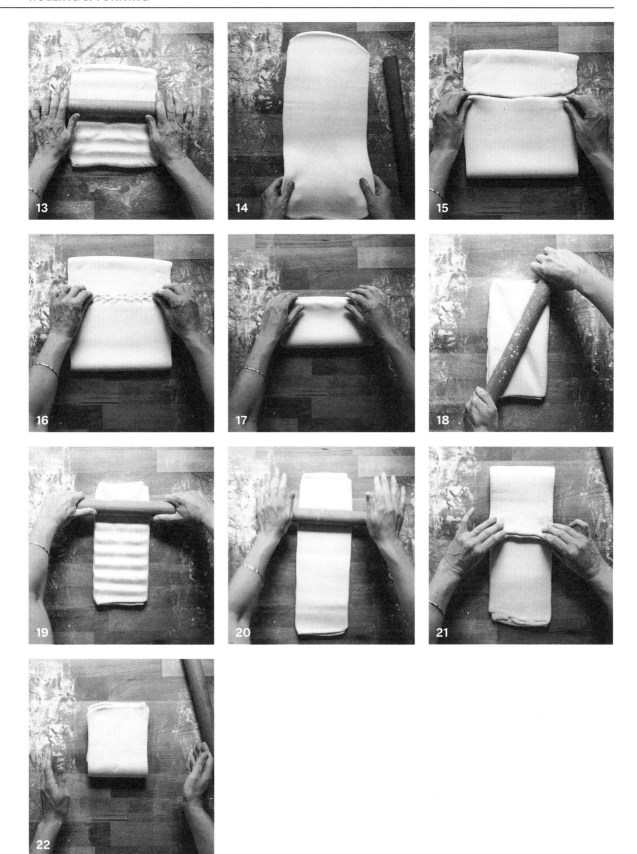

Base Recipe: Basic Laminated Dough · Pâte Feuilletée Levée

This is your base for croissants, danishes, and more. The not-so-secret secret to any laminated pastry is using texture and temperature to your advantage. It's important to rest and chill the dough and butter throughout the lamination process. If you want to create perfect layers, the butter can neither melt nor be softer or harder than the détrempe. Control this — and your patience — and your layers will be the stuff of pastry dreams.

Note: *The détrempe calls for an overnight rest. This is crucial as it will help relax the dough, so that it doesn't retract when it comes time to laminate and shape.*

For visuals, see photos on pp. 158-159.

YIELD: ABOUT 1170G DOUGH (2 ⅔ POUNDS) OR 10-12 INDIVIDUAL PASTRIES

For the détrempe
- 520g (4 ⅓ cups) all-purpose or pastry flour 100%
- 60g (¼ cup plus 1 tbsp) granulated sugar 11.5%
- 10g (1 tbsp plus ¼ tsp) instant yeast 2%
- 10g (heaping ½ tbsp) table salt 2%
- 160g (⅔ cup plus 2 tsp) cold water 31%
- 100g (⅓ cup plus 1 tbsp) whole milk 20%
- 60g (4 tbsp plus 1 tsp) unsalted butter, room temperature 11.5%

For the beurrage
- 250g (9 ounces) unsalted butter (European or European-style 82% fat butter or dry lamination butter), very cold

TIMELINE
24 h, start to finish
Day 1:
Mix détrempe, bulk proof, 1 h
Preshape, refrigerate 8-48 h
Day 2:
Prepare beurrage, refrigerate 20 min
Laminate, 40 min
Final proof, 2 ½ h

Day 1

A - Make your détrempe
In the bowl of a stand mixer fitted with the dough hook attachment, combine the all-purpose or pastry flour, granulated sugar, yeast, salt, cold water, milk, and butter and mix on low for 5 minutes. Increase the speed to medium-high and knead for about 4 minutes, or until the dough is glossy and passes the windowpane test (p. 86). Shape the dough into a ball and place it on a lightly floured work surface. Cover loosely and let bulk proof at room temperature for about 1 hour, or until nearly doubled in size and very light.

After 1 hour, flour the dough and use a rolling pin to roll out into a thick disk, about 25cm (10 inches) in diameter (1). Place on a parchment paper-lined baking tray, wrap airtight, and refrigerate overnight or for up to 48 hours.

Day 2

B - Make your beurrage and set it in the détrempe
Pound and shape the very cold butter into a 25-cm (10-inch) square beurrage (2-7 and pp. 156-157). Wrap airtight, then refrigerate for 20 minutes.

After 20 minutes, remove your détrempe from the fridge and place on a lightly floured work surface. Place your chilled beurrage on top. It should fit precisely inside the détrempe (8); if it doesn't, give your détrempe a little roll so it does. Fold the circle of dough around the butter like an envelope (9-10), stretching the dough as needed. If the dough tears, simply press it back together. Join the dough along the seams and pinch to seal (11), so that the butter is completely enclosed in the dough and no longer visible — a nice little package!

C - Roll and laminate your dough
Your dough is now ready to be rolled out and given its turns — laminated! Using a rolling pin, firmly press an X across the diagonals of the dough to anchor the butter inside (12). Roll the dough out vertically until about 75cm (30 inches) long (13-14). Do this with plenty of pressure and as few rolls as possible — the more you work the dough, the more the butter will heat up and compromise those gorgeous layers. When rolling, run your hands along the underside to help the dough relax.

D - Give your dough a double turn

Brush away any excess flour on the dough. Fold the top quarter down to the middle then fold the bottom up to meet it (15), pinching the seam (16). Fold the top down to meet the bottom (17). This is called a double turn. Wrap the dough airtight and refrigerate for 20 minutes — this keeps the butter and dough cold and helps relax the dough so it's easier to roll for your next turn.

E - Give your dough a single turn

After 20 minutes, place the dough on the floured work surface, but arrange it with a 90-degree rotation from the direction you rolled it previously. The fold should be on the left side, like the spine of a book. Firmly press another X across the dough (18), then roll it out vertically until about 75cm (30 inches) long (19-20). Brush away any excess flour. Fold the top third of the dough down by one-third (21) then fold the bottom up and over to meet the top (22). This is called a single turn. Wrap the dough airtight and refrigerate for 20 minutes.

F - Use your dough

After 20 minutes, your dough is ready to roll out and use. Place the dough on a lightly floured work surface and use a rolling pin to roll out to a 2.5-3mm (1/10–1/8 inch) thickness before cutting and shaping. The final proof is 2 ½ hours.

Base Recipe: Basic Laminated Challah

Challah dough makes an incredible, though not traditional, base for viennoiseries. Its eggy richness stays soft, while its distinct challah flavor isn't overpowered by the butter with which it's laminated. Because challah is made with oil rather than butter or milk, it's a fast rising dough, making this the closest you can get to instant gratification with laminated dough. As with all laminated dough, the secret to success is temperature control. Because challah dough is a bit softer and more elastic than a typical croissant détrempe, chilling the dough to stiffen it is even more important for a successful final product.

Note: This recipe is the base for making Challah Croissants (p. 168), Boureka Croissants (p. 174), and Asparagus Manchego Twists (p. 178), but you can sub it anywhere that calls for basic croissant dough.

For visuals, see photos on pp. 158-159.

YIELD: ABOUT 1KG (2 ¼ POUNDS) DOUGH OR 10-12 INDIVIDUAL PASTRIES

For the dough
· 235g (1 cup plus 2 tsp) cold water 39%
· 6 large egg yolks 18%
· 35g (3 tbsp) neutral oil (or olive oil) 5.8%
· 10g (2 tsp) pure vanilla extract 1.7%
· 600g (5 cups) all-purpose flour 100%
· 66g (⅓ cup) granulated sugar 10%
· 10g (heaping ½ tbsp) table salt 1.7%
· 8g (2 ½ tsp) instant yeast 1.3%

For the beurrage
· 170g (6 ounces) unsalted butter (European or European-style 82% fat butter or dry lamination butter), very cold

TIMELINE
24 h, start to finish
Day 1:
Mix détrempe, bulk proof, 1 h
Preshape, refrigerate 8-24 h
Day 2:
Prepare beurrage, refrigerate 20 min
Laminate, 40 min
Final proof, 2 h

Day 1

A - Make your détrempe
In the bowl of a stand mixer fitted with the whisk attachment, combine the cold water, egg yolks, oil, and vanilla. Add the all-purpose flour, granulated sugar, salt, and yeast, then switch to the dough hook attachment, and knead on low for about 9 minutes, or until the mixture forms a smooth, medium-stiff mass that doesn't stick to the sides of the bowl. Increase the speed to medium-high and knead for about 1 minute. Remove the dough from the bowl and form it into a tight ball. When formed into a ball, the texture will be smooth and a bit stiff but not glossy like the Basic Laminated Dough. *Note: If mixing and kneading by hand, give the dough 12-15 minutes of slaps and folds until smooth (p. 84, Hand Mixing and Kneading).*

Place the ball of dough in a lightly oiled bowl with room for expansion, cover with a damp towel, and let rest at room temperature for about 50 minutes. Once properly risen, the dough will have almost doubled in size and when pressed with a finger, the dough will spring back slowly. *Note: If the dough collapses under your finger with no spring back, it's been over-proofed, and your final loaf will be flatter and lose its shape easily.*

After 50 minutes, turn out the dough onto a lightly floured work surface and use a rolling pin to roll out into a disk, about 25cm (10 inches) across and 2 cm (¾ inch) thick (1). Place on a parchment paper-lined and floured baking tray, then wrap airtight and refrigerate overnight.

Day 2

B - Make your beurrage and set it in the détrempe
Pound and shape the very cold butter into a 25-cm (10-inch) square beurrage (2-7 and pp. 156-157). Wrap airtight, then refrigerate for 20 minutes.

While the butter chills, transfer your détrempe from the fridge to the freezer and let chill for 20 minutes to stiffen further.

After 20 minutes, remove your détrempe from the freezer and place on a lightly floured work surface. Place your chilled beurrage on top. It should fit precisely inside the détrempe (8); if it doesn't, give your détrempe a little roll so it does. Fold the circle of dough around the butter like an envelope (9-10), stretching the dough as needed. If the dough tears, simply press it back together. Join the dough along the seams and pinch to seal (11), so that the butter is completely enclosed in the dough and no longer visible — a nice little package!

C - Roll and laminate your dough

Your dough is now ready to be rolled out and given its turns — laminated! Using a rolling pin, firmly press an X across the diagonals of the dough to anchor the butter inside (12). Roll the dough out vertically until about 75cm (30 inches) long (13-14). Do this with plenty of pressure and as few rolls as possible — the more you work the dough, the more the butter will heat up and compromise those gorgeous layers. When rolling, run your hands along the underside to help the dough relax.

D - Give your dough a double turn

Brush away any excess flour on the dough. Fold the top quarter down to the middle then fold the bottom up to meet it (15), pinching the seam (16). Fold the top down to meet the bottom (17). This is called a double turn. Wrap the dough airtight and refrigerate for 20 minutes — this keeps the butter and dough cold and helps relax the dough so it's easier to roll for your next turn.

E - Give your dough a single turn

After 20 minutes, place the dough on the floured work surface, but arrange it with a 90-degree rotation from the direction you rolled it previously. The fold should be on the left side, like the spine of a book. Firmly press another X across the dough (18), then roll it out vertically until about 75cm (30 inches) long (19-20). Brush away any excess flour. Fold the top third of the dough down by one-third (21) then fold the bottom up and over to meet the top (22). This is called a single turn. Wrap the dough airtight and refrigerate for 20 minutes.

F - Use your dough

After 20 minutes, your dough is ready to roll out and use. Place the dough on a lightly floured work surface and use a rolling pin to roll out to a 3-5mm ($\frac{1}{8}$ – $\frac{1}{5}$ inch) thickness before cutting and shaping. The final proof is 2 hours.

Base Recipe: Rough Puff · Pâte Feuilletée

This recipe is a simplified puff pastry, based on the laminating principle of creating butter pockets that expand, then melt, during baking. Unlike yeasted laminated doughs, here it is only the butter that creates the rise, which means a crisper pastry. This isn't the pastry school kosher method, but it's less fussy and yields marvelous results. Use everywhere — sweet or savory — that you need a good flake.

Note: Make the dough ahead and keep in the freezer, defrosting it overnight in the fridge before using.

YIELD: ABOUT 1 KG (2 ½ POUNDS) DOUGH OR 10–12 INDIVIDUAL PASTRIES

- 500g (4 cups plus 2 tbsp) all-purpose or pastry flour 100%
- 10g (1 tbsp) fleur de sel or large flaky sea salt 2%
- 400g (1 ¾ cups) unsalted butter (European or European-style 82% fat butter or dry lamination butter), cut into 2.5cm (1 inch) cubes and frozen for 20 minutes
- 125g (½ cup plus 2 tsp) cold water 25%
- A few drops fresh lemon juice

In a large bowl, whisk together the all-purpose or pastry flour and salt. Add the frozen butter and toss well to coat. Turn the mixture out onto a clean work surface (1) and use a rolling pin to carefully roll it in all directions (2), using a bench knife to bring the mixture back together as it flattens and spreads. This step helps recoat the butter with flour, so it doesn't stick to the rolling pin. Continue rolling until you have a rough mixture of flour and long, flat, ragged strips of butter (3).

Create a well in the middle of the mixture and pour the cold water and lemon juice into the center of the well (4). Using your hands and a bench knife, gently bring the flour mixture in from the sides, bit by bit, and mix it with the water (5–6). When there is no more dry flour, shape the dough into a thick square (7), wrap it airtight, and refrigerate for 20 minutes.

After 20 minutes, place the dough on a floured work surface and use a rolling pin to roll out vertically (8–9) until about 50cm (20 inches). Give the dough a double turn (10–12 and p. 161, D) then wrap airtight and refrigerate for 20 minutes. Roll the dough out again and give it another double turn, then wrap airtight and refrigerate for at least 30 minutes and for up to 3 days.

When using this puff pastry, roll it out very thin, no more than 3mm (⅛ inch). Any scraps can be chilled, rerolled, and used again.

Base Recipe: Dairy Dough

This easy dough has its origins in Eastern Europe, where fresh farmer's cheeses like tvaroh and quark are abundant, and is typically a base for flaky Jewish dairy pastries like rugelach and potato knishes. Use it anywhere you'd use puff pastry — it has a very similar texture yet requires much less work.

YIELD: ABOUT 900G DOUGH (2 POUNDS) OR 10–12 INDIVIDUAL PASTRIES

- 300g (2 ½ cups) all-purpose or pastry flour 100%
- 300g (1 ½ cups) unsalted butter, cubed and cold 100%
- 300g (1 ⅓ cups) cream cheese 100%
- 7g (2 ¼ tsp) fleur de sel or flaky sea salt 2.3%
- 5g (1 tsp) fresh lemon juice 1.6%
- 5g (1 tsp) pure vanilla extract 1.6% (optional)

In a stand mixer fitted with the paddle attachment, combine the all-purpose flour and butter and beat on low until sandy. Add the cream cheese, salt, lemon juice, and vanilla, if using. Mix on low until just combined — over-mixing will develop too much stretch in the dough. Form the dough into a flat round, wrap airtight, and refrigerate for at least 2 hours or for up to 3 days.

Croissants

A good croissant can make you wonder: How can something be so heavy on butter yet float out of the oven as weightless as a leaf? The real deal guarantees shiny fingers and a lap of crumbs, but oh, to sit in a Paris café on a sunny autumn morning and slowly peel one apart — you might start to feel as lovely as the pastry itself. This is your first step to mastering laminated pastry.

YIELD: 12 CROISSANTS

For the dough
· Ingredients for Basic Laminated Dough (p. 160)

For the egg wash
· 1 large egg, plus 1 large egg yolk, whisked

Keep in mind: You need to start this recipe the day before you want to bake.

Follow the recipe for Basic Laminated Dough until you've given your dough all of its folds and then rested it for 20 minutes (pp. 160-161, A-E).

On a lightly floured work surface, arrange your laminated dough so the folded seam is along the top, farthest from you. Holding a rolling pin horizontally in line with the top seam, press the rolling pin, bit by bit, down the length of the laminated dough — this will help guide an even roll. Next, roll quickly and with a strong hand — the fewer passes with a rolling pin in the shortest amount of time, the cooler the dough will stay. As you roll, occasionally pause to gently run your hands along the underside of the dough to help it contract and relax. Roll out the dough to a rectangle that is 3mm (⅛ inch) thick and measures 50 x 30cm (20 x 12 inches), with the long sides horizontal and the short sides vertical. *Note: If the dough resists rolling, don't force it; put it in the refrigerator for 10 minutes to chill and relax it.*

Once the dough is the right size and you can run your hands underneath without it contracting, brush away any excess flour and trim 1cm (⅓ inch) off each side. Use a ruler to measure 8cm (3¼ inch) intervals along the top and bottom, then join the markings to cut long rectangles that measure 28 x 8cm (11 x 3¼ inches) — a pizza cutter is best for this, but if using a knife, press rather than saw the dough. Cut each rectangle on the diagonal, from the top left corner to the bottom right corner, to make 12 triangles. In the middle of the base of each triangle, cut a 1cm (⅓ inch) notch. Roll up each croissant from base to tip, using one hand to roll and one hand to hold the end, and stretching a bit to give the croissant some tension.

Place the croissants, 5cm (2 inches) apart and with their tails tucked underneath, on a parchment paper-lined baking tray. Tucking the tails underneath is essential; it prevents unrolling while baking. Brush away any excess flour, then brush with the egg wash. Avoid brushing egg wash on the cut sides where the butter layers are visible — we want these to open up while they bake, and egg wash can seal them shut. Let proof at room temperature for 2½ hours, or until the dough is light and puffed and the layers start to visibly separate.

Preheat the oven to 170°C (340°F) (preferably convection setting).

After 2½ hours, brush with egg wash a second time. Bake for about 15 minutes, or until golden brown.

Challah Croissants

Of all the loveable things about challah, it's the way it pulls apart in long peels that I love the most. Laminating challah dough with butter takes that effect for a trip to the moon. Though challah with butter isn't really challah, that's not what this recipe is about. This recipe is about having the best of all worlds.

Note: *Freeze any leftovers and use for toasty egg and cheese breakfast sandwiches.*

YIELD: 12 CROISSANTS

For the dough
· Ingredients for Basic Laminated Challah (p. 162)

For the topping
· 3 tbsp sesame seeds

For the egg wash
· 1 large egg, plus 1 large egg yolk, whisked

Keep in mind: You need to start this recipe the day before you want to bake.

Follow the recipe for Basic Laminated Challah until you've given your dough all of its folds and then rested it for 20 minutes (pp. 162-163, A-E).

On a lightly floured work surface, arrange your laminated dough so the folded seam is along the top, farthest from you. Holding a rolling pin horizontally in line with the top seam, press the rolling pin, bit by bit, down the length of the laminated dough — this will help guide an even roll. Working quickly and with a strong hand — the fewer passes with a rolling pin in the shortest amount of time, the cooler the dough will stay — roll out the dough to a rectangle that is 3mm (⅛ inch) thick and measures 56 x 30cm (22 ½ x 12 inches), with the long sides horizontal and the short sides vertical. As you roll, occasionally pause to gently run your hands along the underside of the dough to help it contract and relax. *Note: If the dough resists rolling, don't force it; put it in the refrigerator for 10 minutes to chill and relax it.*

Once the dough is the right size and you can run your hands underneath without it contracting, brush away any excess flour and trim 1cm (⅓ inch) off each side. Use a ruler to measure 9cm (3 ½ inch) intervals along the top and bottom, then join these markings to cut long rectangles — a pizza cutter is best for this, but if using a knife, press rather than saw the dough. Once cut, you will have six rectangles that measure 28 x 9cm (11 x 3 ½ inches). Cut each rectangle on the diagonal, from the top left corner to the bottom right corner, to make 12 triangles. In the middle of the base of each triangle, cut a 1cm (⅓ inch) notch. Roll up each croissant from base to tip, using one hand to roll and one hand to hold the end, and stretching a bit to give the croissant some tension.

Place the croissants, 5cm (2 inches) apart and with their tails tucked underneath, on a parchment paper-lined baking tray. Tucking the tails underneath is essential; it prevents unrolling while baking. Brush away any excess flour, then brush with the egg wash. Avoid brushing egg wash on the cut sides where the butter layers are visible — we want these to open up while they bake, and egg wash can seal them shut. Let the croissants proof at room temperature for 2 hours, or until the dough is light and puffed and the layers start to visibly separate.

Preheat the oven to 170°C (340°F) (preferably convection setting).

After 2 hours, brush with egg wash a second time, sprinkle with sesame seeds, and bake for 12 minutes, or until rich golden brown.

Hazelnut Chocolatines

Here's a recipe for pain au chocolat with a rich ganache-like filling. Ordinary pain au chocolat, or chocolatine, is filled with two little sticks of chocolate made special for the pastry, bâtons boulangers — I can't tell you how many of those little bars I've snuck. But why use those industrial chocolate sticks at all when you can make the chocolate filling extra thick and melty and from scratch? Here we make a chocolate and roasted hazelnut spread that's a bit like gianduja (read: homemade Nutella) but with some crunch. It will stay soft and won't spread out as it bakes. Magic.

YIELD: 10 CHOCOLATINES

Keep in mind: You need to start this recipe the day before you want to bake.

For the dough
· Ingredients for Basic Laminated Dough (p. 160)

For the chocolate filling
· 200g (1 ½ cups) whole skinless hazelnuts, plus chopped hazelnuts for sprinkling (optional)
· 225g (1 ⅓ cups) chopped bittersweet chocolate
· 180g (¾ cup plus 1 tbsp) unsalted butter
· 75g (⅔ cup) confectioners' sugar
· 40g (½ cup) cacao powder
· 2 tsp pure vanilla extract

Make your dough
Follow the recipe for Basic Laminated Dough until you've given your dough all of its folds and then rested it for 20 minutes (pp. 160-161, A-E).

While the laminated dough rests in the fridge, make your chocolate filling
Preheat the oven to 150°C (300°F) (preferably convection setting). Spread the hazelnuts on a rimmed baking tray and roast for 10-15 minutes, or until tanned and fragrant. Remove from the oven and set aside too cool.

Using a double boiler or the microwave, melt the chocolate and butter together. Add the confectioners' sugar, cacao powder, and vanilla, and stir until smooth. As soon as the hazelnuts are cool, chop finely or run through the food processor for a smoother texture, then mix with the chocolate spread. Set aside to cool.

On a lightly floured work surface, arrange your laminated dough so the folded seam is along the top, farthest from you. Holding a rolling pin horizontally in line with the top seam, press the rolling pin, bit by bit, down the length of the laminated dough — this will help guide an even roll. Working quickly and with a strong hand — the fewer passes with a rolling pin in the shortest amount of time, the cooler the dough will stay — roll out the dough into a rectangle that is 3mm (⅛ inch) thick and measures 50 x 38cm (20 x 15 inches), with the long sides horizontal and the short sides vertical. As you roll, occasionally pause to gently run your hands along the underside of the dough to help it contract and relax. *Note: If the dough resists rolling, don't force it; put it in the refrigerator for 10 minutes to chill and relax it.*

Spread a thick layer of the chocolate filling across the entire rectangle then trim 1cm (⅓ inch) off each side. Use a ruler to measure 9cm (3 ½ inch) intervals along the top and bottom, then join these markings to create 5 long rectangles that measure 36 x 9cm (14 ½ x 3 ½ inches). Cut each rectangle horizontally in half to make 10 smaller rectangles that measure 18 x 9cm (7 x 3 ½ inches). Roll up each chocolatine tightly from top to bottom.

Place the chocolatines, 4cm (1 ½ inches) apart, on a parchment paper-lined baking tray with the end of each roll touching the paper. Brush away any excess flour on the chocolatines, then brush with the egg wash. Avoid brushing egg wash on the cut sides where the butter layers are visible — we want these to open up while they bake, and egg wash can seal them shut. Let proof at room temperature for 2 ½ hours, or until the dough is light and puffed and the layers start to visibly separate.

Preheat the oven to 170°C (340°F) (preferably convection setting).

Brush the chocolatines with egg wash a second time and sprinkle with chopped hazelnuts, if using. Bake for 15 minutes, or until golden brown and fully baked.

Marzipan Poppy Snails

I used to work in a café that got a daily delivery of pastry from a Dutch bakery — these big folds of laminated pastry with a sticky layer of baked marzipan inside. At the end of each shift, I got to take home any of the day's leftovers — it was my dinner, breakfast, and then some. All that marzipan and pastry more than made up for the minimum wage and lack of benefits. In my opinion, the abundance of marzipan is one of the sweetest things about European baking — or, at least I feel that way since I could start to afford dental care. Marzipan arrived from the Middle East five hundred or so years ago, and it's hard to imagine European pastry culture without it. Whether it's shaped and painted into bright lemons, plums, and cherries for Frutta di Martorana in Sicily, dyed teal and draped over an airy sponge for Swedish Prinzessinnentorte, or simply stuffed into a bun, this sweet almond paste is just about everywhere. Here, a homemade marzipan poppy seed filling is rolled up in croissant dough and baked like a cinnamon roll for a sugary almondy bite.

Note: If you find marzipan too cloying, sprinkle a few flakes of Maldon sea salt on top of your baked pastry. It will balance the sweetness.

YIELD: ABOUT 15 SNAILS

For the dough
· Ingredients for Basic Laminated Dough (p. 160)

For the marzipan poppy seed filling
· 100g (1 cup plus 3 tbsp) ground almonds
· 100g (¾ cup plus 2 tbsp) confectioners' sugar
· 1 large egg white
· 100g (7 tbsp) unsalted butter, room temperature
· 100g (½ cup) granulated sugar
· 20g (3 tbsp) all-purpose flour
· 3 tbsp poppy seeds

For the egg wash
· 1 large egg, plus 1 large egg yolk, whisked

To finish
· Simple Syrup (p. 266)

Keep in mind: You need to start this recipe the day before you want to bake.

Make your dough

Follow the recipe for the Basic Laminated Dough until you've given your dough all of its folds and then rested it for 20 minutes in the refrigerator (pp. 160-161, A-E).

While the laminated dough rests in the fridge, make your marzipan poppy seed filling

In the bowl of a stand mixer fitted with the paddle attachment, combine the ground almonds, confectioners' sugar, and egg white and beat on medium-high until a thick paste forms, about 2 minutes. Reduce the speed to low, then add the butter, granulated sugar, all-purpose flour, and poppy seeds and mix until well-incorporated. Increase the speed to medium-high and beat until fluffy, about 2 minutes. Cover and set aside until ready to use.

On a lightly floured work surface, arrange your laminated dough so the folded seam is along the top, farthest from you. Holding a rolling pin horizontally in line with the top seam, press the rolling pin, bit by bit, down the length of the laminated dough — this will help guide an even roll. Next, roll quickly and with a strong hand — the fewer passes with a rolling pin in the shortest amount of time, the cooler the dough will stay. As you roll, occasionally pause to gently run your hands along the underside of the dough to help it contract and relax. *Note: If the dough resists rolling, don't force it; put it in the refrigerator for 10 minutes to chill and relax it.* Roll out the dough into a rectangle about 3mm (⅛ inch) thick that measures 42 x 32cm (17 x 13 inches), with the long sides vertical and the short sides horizontal, then trim 1cm (⅓ inch) off each side. *Note: If the dough has warmed up considerably, let it chill in the fridge for 15 minutes.*

On the same lightly floured work surface, make sure the rectangle of dough is arranged so that the long sides are vertical and the short sides are horizontal. Spread an even layer of the marzipan poppy seed filling over the surface of the dough, leaving a 2cm (¾ inch) border along the very bottom. To shape, start with the short side furthest from you and roll the rectangle of dough from the top to the bottom stretching as you go to create a tight roll that's about 30cm (12 inch) long. Place the roll on a parchment paper–lined baking tray, seam-side down, and chill in the freezer for 15 minutes — this will make it easier to slice.

After 15 minutes, use a sharp knife to slice the roll at 2cm (¾ inch) intervals. Arrange the snails, about 4cm (1½ inches) apart, on the same papered baking tray. Gently reshape the snails so they are perfectly round, then tuck the unfilled tail of each roll underneath — this will keep the snails from falling apart while baking. Brush the sides but not the top of each snail with the egg wash, then let proof at room temperature for 2½ hours, or until the dough is light and puffed and the layers start to visibly separate.

Preheat the oven to 170°C (340°F) (preferably convection setting).

When the snails are ready to bake, brush the sides with egg wash a second time. Bake for 15 minutes, or until the pastry is golden brown and the marzipan is puffed. Remove from the oven and brush the tops with Simple Syrup (p. 266), then return to the oven for 1 minute to set the shine.

Boureka Croissants

If the east coast of the United States has a borscht belt, then Southeastern Europe has a burek belt. In the region stretching from the countries of former Yugoslavia, through Greece and Turkey, and into Central Asia and even the Middle East via Lebanon and Israel, a variation on this baked savory bun is everywhere. Depending on the region, it's burek, borek, boureka — or a host of other names — but it's nearly always some form of pastry stuffed with salty white cheese and greens or meats. The doughs vary — from filo to puff pastry to buttery enriched dough — as does the shaping. This is my non-traditional twist with light and flaky laminated challah dough. As for the greens, use what's in season and available locally. Mixing any combination of spinach, mustard greens, chard, collards, radish greens, arugula, and broccolini will add flavor and nuance.

YIELD: 10 BOUREKA CROISSANTS

For the dough
· Ingredients for Basic Laminated Challah (p. 162)

For the filling
· 350g (12 ½ oz) chopped hearty greens (about 10 cups)
· 2 ½ tbsp olive oil
· 1 medium yellow onion, finely diced
· 3 cloves garlic, crushed
· 125g (1 ¼ cups) crumbled feta or other white salty cheese
· 60g (¼ cup) ricotta cheese
· Heaping ½ tsp table salt
· 1 tsp freshly ground black pepper
· 1 tsp red pepper flakes
· ¼ tsp freshly ground nutmeg

For the egg wash
· 1 large egg, plus 1 large egg yolk, whisked

For the garnish
· Sesame seeds

Keep in mind: You need to start this recipe the day before you want to bake.

Start making your dough
Follow the recipe for the Basic Laminated Challah until the détrempe has chilled overnight (p. 162, A).

Before you laminate your dough, make your filling
Your filling needs time to cool before you assemble the croissants. (The filling can also be made the night before.)

Use a steamer or a skillet to wilt the greens until reduced to about a quarter of their original bulk — you should have about 2 ½ cups of wilted greens. Strain any excess water, place the greens in a large bowl, and set aside.

Heat the olive oil in a frying pan over medium heat then add the onion and garlic and sauté until fragrant and translucent. Add the onions and garlic to the wilted greens, along with the feta, ricotta, salt, black pepper, red pepper flakes, and nutmeg. Set aside to cool completely.

Once the filling is cool, finish making your dough
Prepare your beurrage and laminate the chilled dough, then give it a 20 minute rest in the refrigerator (pp. 162-163, B-E).

Once the dough is chilled, place it on a lightly floured work surface. Use a rolling pin to roll out into a rectangle that is 3mm (⅛ inch) thick and measures 50 x 26cm (20 x 10 ½ inches), with the long sides horizontal and the short sides vertical. Trim 1cm (⅓ inch) off each side. Use a ruler to measure 9cm (3 ½ inch) intervals along the top and bottom, then join these markings to create five 24 x 9cm (9 ½ x 3 ½ inch) rectangles. Divide these each in half to make ten 12 x 9cm (5 x 3 ½ inch) rectangles.

To fill and shape your bourekas, spoon a generous portion of filling at the top of each rectangle. Starting from the top, roll up each rectangle to form a roll. Arrange the bourekas, 5cm (2 inches) apart, on a parchment paper-lined baking tray with the tail of each roll touching the paper. Brush each boureka with the egg wash and let proof at room temperature for 2 ½ hours, or until the dough is light and puffed and the layers start to visibly separate.

Preheat the oven to 170°C (340°F) (preferably convection setting).

When the bourekas are ready to bake, brush them with egg wash a second time, then use a razor blade or small knife to decoratively score the tops — use a strong hand to make fast, shallow slices all the way across top of the pastry. If the blade sticks, dip it into egg wash before scoring. Sprinkle with sesame seeds and bake for 17 minutes, or until golden brown.

Quince and Melty Cheese Danishes

Dulce de membrillo in Spain, pâte aux coings in France — whatever it's called, quince paste is divine stuff, especially when paired with cheese. Here, we stuff rolled danishes with quince paste and soft cheese that melts and browns during the bake. While you'd usually pair quince paste with a hard cheese, I like to use the almost drippingly soft Saint-Félicien for this pastry — it's a texture thing. Brie, Camembert, Brillat-Savarin, a goat cheese log, or whatever you have on hand, will also be delicious. Quince paste is sold by the slice in cheese shops around Europe, but if baking in North or South America, guava paste makes a perfect substitute and is easier to find.

Note: The division and rolling of this dough is identical to that of Croissants (p. 166), but for small cocktail hour-friendly versions, divide the dough into 24 half-sized triangles. If you want to serve these hot from the oven, begin your lamination and shaping about three hours before you want to serve the danishes.

YIELD: 12 DANISHES

For the dough
· Ingredients for Basic Laminated Dough (p. 160)

For the filling
· 150g (¾ cup) Quince Paste (p. 264)
· 250g (9 ounces) Saint-Félicien cheese or any other soft, meltable cow or goat's milk cheese
· Freshly ground black pepper

For the egg wash
· 1 large egg, plus 1 large yolk, whisked

For the topping
· Poppy seeds or freshly ground black pepper

Keep in mind: You need to start this recipe the day before you want to bake.

Make your dough
Follow the recipe for the Basic Laminated Dough until you've given your dough all of its folds and then rested it for 20 minutes in the refrigerator (pp. 160-161, A-E).

Put your laminated and chilled dough on a lightly floured work surface and use a rolling pin to roll out into a rectangle that is 3mm (⅛ inch) thick and measures 50 x 30cm (20 x 12 inches), with the long sides horizontal and the short sides vertical. Trim 1cm (⅓ inch) off each side of the dough. Use a ruler to measure 8cm (3 ¼ inch) intervals along the top and bottom, then join these markings to create 6 rectangles, each measuring 28 x 8cm (11 x 3 ¼ inch). Cut each rectangle on the diagonal, from the top left corner to the bottom right corner to create 12 triangles.

Fill and shape your danishes
Spread about 1 tbsp of quince paste in an even layer on each triangle then spoon about 2 tbsp (20g) of cheese at the wide base of each triangle. Starting from the base, roll up each danish, then arrange, 5cm (2 inches) apart and with the tails tucked underneath, on a parchment paper-lined baking tray. Brush with the egg wash and let proof at room temperature for 2 ½ hours, or until the dough is light and puffed and the layers start to visibly separate.

Preheat the oven to 170°C (340°F) (preferably convection setting).

When the danishes are ready to bake, brush with egg wash a second time, sprinkle with poppy seeds or black pepper, and bake for 15 minutes, or until deep golden brown.

Asparagus Manchego Twists

Spring is the most wonderful time of year. It comes in many ways — lilacs in France, snowdrops in Scandinavia, bluebells in England. And in Germany — asparagus. It's Spargelzeit — asparagus time — to be precise. Restaurants devote entire menus to the stuff. To an outsider, the national enthusiasm is, frankly, surprising, especially since the favored variety is woody, colorless asparagus. But, if you can't beat 'em…eat asparagus, too. Consider this recipe a foreigner's submission to Spargelzeit, but we skip the classic white spargel and go for the snappier, more flavorful green. Serve these as a starter course for a sit-down spring dinner or as finger food with the sauce for dipping.

Notes: This recipe calls for Manchego, but any hard cheese will do. Pecorino, aged cheddar, or Comté are all excellent options.

If you don't have the time to fuss with laminated dough and don't mind a crunchier effect, use the Rough Puff (p. 164) or Dairy Dough (p. 164) instead.

For the asparagus, use young, tender stalks for better texture and taste. The blanching process will help keep these qualities intact.

YIELD: 12-14 TWISTS

For the dough
· Ingredients for Basic Laminated Challah (p. 162) or Basic Laminated Dough (p. 160)

For the filling
· 36–42 stalks green asparagus 150g (5 ½ ounces) Manchego or other hard cheese, cut into 12-14 batons

For the manchego white pepper sauce
· 50g (3 ½ tbsp) unsalted butter
· 40g (⅓ cup) all-purpose flour
· 550g (2 ½ cups) whole milk
· 1 tsp freshly ground white pepper
· 1 tsp freshly ground black pepper
· 1 tsp mustard powder
· 100g (1 cup) shredded Manchego cheese
· 1 tsp table salt

For the egg wash
· 1 large egg, plus 1 large egg yolk, whisked

Keep in mind: You need to start this recipe the day before you want to bake and you should begin the laminating and shaping process 3 hours before you want to serve your twists.

Make your dough
Follow the recipe for the Basic Laminated Challah (pp. 162-163, A-E) or Basic Laminated Dough (pp. 160-161, A-E) until you've given your dough all of its folds and then rested it for 20 minutes in the refrigerator.

While the laminated dough rests in the fridge, make your filling
Trim and discard the hard, light bottoms of the asparagus, leaving only the bright green stalks. Bring 1 liter (4 ½ cups) of water and 20g (heaping 1 tbsp) of table salt to a boil. Fill a large bowl with ice water and set aside. Add the asparagus to the boiling water and boil for 2 minutes, then remove from the boiling water, and immediately plunge into the ice water. As soon as the asparagus is cool, remove it from the ice water and set aside in a colander while you roll the dough.

Put your laminated and chilled dough on a lightly floured work surface and use a rolling pin to roll out to a 36cm (14 ½ inch) square. Trim 1cm (⅓ inch) from each side, then cut long strips, about 2cm (¾ inch) wide, from top to bottom.

To fill and shape your twists, bundle 3 stalks of poached asparagus with a strip of cheese, then wrap a strip of dough in a spiral three times around the bundle, leaving space between the dough for expansion. Arrange the twists, about 4cm (1 ½ inches) apart and with the ends of dough tucked underneath, on a parchment paper-lined baking tray. Brush the dough with the egg wash and let proof at room temperature for 2-2 ½ hours, or until the dough is light and puffed and the layers start to visibly separate.

Preheat the oven to 170°C (340°F) (preferably convection setting).

When the twists are ready to bake, brush with egg wash a second time, sprinkle with sesame seeds, and bake for 15 minutes, or until the pastry is golden brown.

While the asparagus twists bake, make your white pepper sauce
In a medium saucepan, melt the butter over low heat. Add the flour. This will create a loose paste. Cook, stirring to prevent burning, for about 5 minutes, or until a thick paste forms — this is your roux. Add the milk, white pepper, black pepper, and mustard powder, whisking until smooth. With the heat still on low, add the shredded Manchego and the salt. Continue cooking, whisking gently to melt the cheese, then raise the heat to medium and cook for 5 minutes, or until the sauce bubbles and thickens. Remove from the heat and keep warm.

Serve the asparagus twists hot from the oven, either on a plate spread with a generous puddle of the white pepper sauce or with the sauce in a small bowl for dipping.

Baklava Danishes

There isn't a scented candle in the world that rivals the smells of a Greek or Turkish bakery when the baklava is hot. There are whole streets in Berlin that I walk down for no other reason than that smell. The same nutty, warm, vanilla aroma will hang around the house all day after you bake these simple nut-loaded danishes. This pastry is literally dripping in hot honey syrup, combining the flavor of fresh baklava with the lightness of a croissant.

YIELD: 14 DANISHES

For the dough
· Ingredients for Basic Laminated Dough (p. 160)

For the nut topping
· 150g (1⅓ cups) salted pistachios
· 150g (1⅓ cups) walnuts or almonds
· ¼ tsp ground cinnamon
· 100g (7 tbsp) butter, melted

For the syrup
· 150g (¾ cup) granulated sugar
· 180g (¾ cup) water
· 170g (½ cup) honey
· 2 tsp pure vanilla extract
· ¼ tsp table salt or a pinch of fleur de sel

For the egg wash
· 1 large egg, plus 1 large egg yolk, whisked

Keep in mind: You need to start this recipe the day before you want to bake.

Make your dough
Follow the recipe for the Basic Laminated Dough until you've given your dough all of its folds and then rested it for 20 minutes in the refrigerator (pp. 160–161, A–E).

On a lightly floured work surface, roll out the laminated dough into a rectangle that is 3mm (⅛ inch) thick and measures 52 x 32cm (21 x 13 inches), with the long sides vertical and the short sides horizontal. Trim 1cm (⅓ inch) off each side, then cut lengthwise into 14 long strips.

To fill and shape your danishes, place a palm on each end of a strip of dough, then roll each end in opposite directions to twist the strip of dough — you want to create a lot of twists but not twist the dough super tightly. Next, wrap the twisted dough in a spiral, forming the spiral in the opposite direction that it was twisted to prevent the twist from coming undone. Tuck the end of dough under the spiral, then place on a parchment paper–lined baking tray. Repeat with the remaining strips of dough to create 13 more danishes. Add to the parchment paper-lined baking tray, leaving 5cm (2 inches) between each. Brush with the egg wash and let proof at room temperature for 2 hours, or until the dough is light and puffed and the layers start to visibly separate.

While the danishes are resting, make your nut topping and syrup
For the nut topping, finely chop the pistachios and walnuts, then toss with the cinnamon and melted butter and set aside.

For the syrup, combine the granulated sugar, water, and honey in a saucepan over low heat. Once the sugar melts and no granules are visible, bring to a low boil and continue gently boiling for 5 minutes, or until just thickened. Remove from the heat and stir in the vanilla and salt.

Preheat the oven to 170°C (340°F) (preferably convection setting).

Once the danishes are ready to bake, brush with egg wash a second time, then pile each with a handful of the nut topping. Bake for 12 minutes, or until golden brown. Remove from the oven and generously drizzle the syrup over each danish. Return the tray to the oven for 1 minute to set the syrup.

Lemon Meringue Danishes

We made my grandfather's favorite dessert — lemon meringue pie — from a box. The lemon filling was mixed from a packet and tasted not-so-subtly of Joy dish soap. Let's not even get started on the powdered meringue. It wasn't until deep into my twenties that I tasted the real thing — a tarte citron meringuée — a ubiquitous dessert in French bistros. It was so tart, so silky, so lemony. This is what I'd been missing all those years? Here, using laminated pastry as a shell, each one of these danishes is its own perfect little lemon meringue pie. Serve in place of cakes, pies, or cupcakes.

Note: For ease and organization, I like to make the lemon curd in advance, at the same time that I make the détrempe for the pastry, but you can also make it while the danishes proof as instructed below. To make a classic tarte citron meringuée, follow the directions for the Lemon Curd (p. 263) and Italian Meringue (p. 267) and throw it in a Basic Tarte Dough shell (p. 216).

YIELD: 12 DANISHES

For the dough
· Ingredients for Basic Laminated Dough (p. 160)

For the filling
· Lemon Curd (p. 263)

For the topping
· Italian Meringue (p. 267)

Keep in mind: You need to start this recipe the day before you want to bake.

Make your dough

Follow the recipe for the Basic Laminated Dough until you've given your dough all of its folds and then rested it for 20 minutes in the refrigerator (pp. 160–161, A–E).

With a rolling pin, roll out your laminated dough into a rectangle that is 3mm (⅛ inch) thick and measures 50 x 34cm (20 x 13 ½ inches). Trim 1cm (⅓ inch) off each side of the dough. Use a ruler to measure 8cm (3 ¼ inch) intervals along each side of the rectangle. Join the markings to cut 24 (8-cm / 3 ¼-inch) squares — a pizza cutter is best for this, but if using a knife, press rather than saw the dough. Arrange 12 of the squares, 5cm (2 inches) apart, on a parchment paper-lined baking tray and brush the tops with egg wash.

Use a small round cookie cutter or shot glass to cut a circle in the middle of the rest of the squares of dough. Place the squares with the cut out holes neatly on top of the whole squares, brush the tops with egg wash, and let rest at room temperature for 2 ½ hours, or until the dough is puffed and the layers start to visibly separate.

While the danishes proof, make your Lemon Curd (p. 263)

Preheat the oven to 170°C (340°F) (preferably convection setting).

Once the danishes are ready to bake, brush the tops with egg wash a second time and score the middle of each danish with a fork to prevent the middle from puffing up. Bake for 15 minutes, or until deep golden. Set aside to cool.

While the danish shells cool, make your Italian Meringue (p. 267)

To assemble, spoon Lemon Curd into the center of each danish. Using a piping bag or spoon, pipe or dollop a generous circle of Italian Meringue around the Lemon Curd. If you're feeling wild, hit the meringue with a kitchen torch, then serve.

Franzbrötchen

The city of Hamburg has many claims to fame: wind, rain, some excellent dim sum — and a very special German cinnamon bun, the Franzbrötchen. This pastry was allegedly brought to the city by Napoleon's army, which helps explain its name. The Franz in Franzbrötchen isn't Franz like Franz Kafka or Franz Joseph — here it means French. So is this German pastry French? Who cares? It's delicious. What makes the Franzbroetchen unique is its butterfly shape and ultra-simple cinnamon filling. It's just cinnamon and sugar and, as such, caramelizes in a way that butter-based fillings simply don't. Franzbrötchen pastry is flaky and layered, and while the original version is often a bit more rustic, here we use the same dough we use to make croissants.

YIELD: 10 FRANZBRÖTCHEN

For the dough
· Ingredients for Basic Laminated Dough (p. 160)

For the filling
· 150g (¾ cup) granulated sugar
· 1 tbsp plus 1 tsp ground cinnamon

For the egg wash
· 1 large egg, plus 1 large egg yolk, whisked

To finish
· Simple Syrup (p. 266)

Keep in mind: You need to start this recipe the day before you want to bake.

Make your dough
Follow the recipe for the Basic Laminated Dough until you've given your dough all of its folds and then rested it for 20 minutes in the refrigerator (pp. 160–161, A-E).

Once the dough is laminated and chilled, use a rolling pin to roll out the dough into a rectangle that is 3mm (⅛ inch) thick and measures 52 x 32cm (21 x 13 inches), with the long sides horizontal and the short sides vertical. Trim 1cm (⅓ inch) off the long and short sides, then let the dough rest, refrigerated, for 20 minutes to relax.

While the laminated dough rests in the fridge, make your filling
In a small bowl, combine the granulated sugar and cinnamon.

Once the dough has rested, lightly brush with water, then spread the cinnamon sugar evenly across the top, leaving a 2cm (¾ inch) border along the bottom — that's where you'll seal the roll. Brush egg wash along the unfilled border, then roll up the dough, from top to bottom, stretching the dough as you roll to create tension. Put the log of dough on a baking tray and put in the freezer for 10–20 minutes to firm it up.

Once the dough is firm, cut the log at 5cm (2 inch) intervals to create 10 Franzbrötchen. Place the rolls, upright like a bicycle wheel with the seal on the bottom and 5cm (2 inches) apart, on a parchment paper-lined baking tray. Using the flat of your hand or a wooden board, press the top of each roll firmly until the rolls are at half their original height and stay put — they should resemble flat tires. Let rest at room temperature for 20 minutes.

Once the rolls are rested, firmly press a clean pencil or smooth chopstick lengthwise into each roll, pressing nearly all the way to the tray below so the spirals flare out and create the pastry's signature butterfly shape. Brush the top of each Franzbrötchen with egg wash and let proof at room temperature for 2 more hours, or until the dough is light and puffed and the layers start to visibly separate.

Preheat the oven to 170°C (340°F) (preferably convection setting).

When the Franzbrötchen are ready to bake, brush them with egg wash a second time, then bake for 15 minutes, or until the pastry is golden brown and the sugar filling is caramelized. Remove from the oven, brush with Simple Syrup (p. 266), and return to the oven for 1 minute to set.

Kouign Amann

The richest, most buttery pastry in France comes from the richest, most buttery region: Brittany. Kouign Amann (pronounced queen ah-mahn) came about in the 19th century as a way to cope with a flour shortage and a butter surplus. Today, it's having a surge in popularity, as bakeries look for creative ways to cope with food waste and repurpose dough trimmings into kouign amann. Slightly different from standard croissant dough, the dough for kouign amann is laminated in sugar rather than flour, and the final product is baked with a weighted top to ensure a dense, caramelized texture. My favorite way to serve kouign amann is hot from the oven with a scoop of vanilla ice cream on top for a plated caramel sundae.

Beware: There are lots of imposters out there that skimp on the sugar and butter. And remember — it's not supposed to be good for you. It's just supposed to taste good. So if it isn't gooey, it isn't a kouign amann.

Notes: This recipe starts from scratch, but if you have leftover trimmings of laminated dough, you can roll them out in sugar and bake according to this recipe for a similar effect.

If you only have a standard muffin tin available, change the dimensions of your rolled out dough to be longer horizontally and shorter vertically to create smaller spirals for each muffin cup.

YIELD: 12 KOUIGN AMANN

For the dough
· Ingredients for a détrempe, see Basic Laminated Dough (p. 160)
· 250g (9 ounces) unsalted butter (European or European-style 82% fat butter or dry lamination butter), very cold

For the lamination
· 500g (2 ¼ cups) Demerara or granulated sugar

For the muffin cups
· 120g (½ cup plus 1 tbsp) unsalted butter
· 50g (¼ cup) granulated sugar

For the topping
· Sesame seeds, halved peanuts, slivered almonds, or chopped pistachios (optional)
· Flaky sea salt

Day 1: Start making your dough
Follow the recipe for Basic Laminated Dough to make the détrempe and refrigerate overnight (pp. 160–161, A).

Day 2, About 3 hours before baking: Laminate your kouign amann
Pound and shape the very cold butter into a 25-cm (10-inch) square beurrage (p. 156–157). Wrap airtight, then refrigerate for 20 minutes.

After 20 minutes, remove your détrempe from the fridge and place on a lightly floured work surface. Place your chilled beurrage on top. It should fit precisely inside the détrempe; if it doesn't, give your détrempe a little roll so it does. Fold the circle of dough around the butter like an envelope, stretching the dough as needed. If the dough tears, simply press it back together. Join the dough along the seams and pinch to seal, so that the butter is completely enclosed in the dough and no longer visible — a nice little package.

Now take note! This is where things take a small departure from our usual laminated pastry!

Your dough is now ready to be rolled out and given its turns — laminated! Brush away any excess flour from your dough and work surface, then coat your work surface in a thick layer of Demerara or granulated sugar. Lay the dough on the sugar, then heavily dust the top of the dough with sugar as well. Using a rolling pin, roll out the dough, giving it 1 double turn, followed immediately by 1 single turn and replenishing the sugar on the work surface as needed. *Note: Unlike ordinary laminated dough, which needs a chill between each step, this dough must be rolled and turned straight through with no pauses in the fridge. This is because a rest in the cold fridge causes the sugared dough to become sticky and wet.*

Once the dough is fully laminated, roll it out into a rectangle that is 3mm (⅛ inch) thick and measures 32 x 30cm (13 x 12 inches). Trim 1cm (⅓ inch) off each side. Next, starting with 1 of the shorter sides, roll the rectangle tightly into a log. Cut the roll into 12 even, roughly 2.5cm (1 inch) thick, pieces.

Generously grease an extra-large muffin tray or pastry rings, ideally nonstick, with butter. In the center of each cup, place a pat of butter and a teaspoon of sugar. If adding nuts or seeds, now add a thin layer in each muffin cup. Place each kouign amann in a sugared muffin cup then let proof at room temperature for 2 ½ hours, or until the dough is light and puffed and the layers start to visibly separate.

Preheat the oven to 170°C (340°F) (preferably convection setting).

When the kouign amanns are ready to bake, cover the tray with a sheet of parchment paper, followed by a baking tray, and finally something heavy and oven-safe like a casserole to weigh it down. Bake for 30 minutes, then remove the weights, baking tray, and parchment paper to check that the pastry is honey colored. If it isn't, cover with the tray again and return to the oven for another 3 minutes and check again. Once the pastry is baked, remove the muffin tin from the oven, then set the baking tray back on top. Carefully flip the whole thing over to release the kouign amann and reveal their shiny caramelized undersides. Sprinkle with flaky sea salt for a salted caramel flavor.

Chaussons aux Pommes · French Apple Turnovers

My husband Roman's only ask when I ditched him for France to study bakery was that I promised to learn how to make chaussons aux pommes. Something between a handheld strudel and a pie, these French apple turnovers are as much a boulangerie staple as croissants. The key to keeping chaussons aux pommes plump with filling is to cook down the apples in advance. Follow this recipe and your apple-to-pastry ratio will be on point for this perfect autumn snack.

Note: The decorative leaf pattern scored into the pastry is traditional, but the design is up to you!

YIELD: 10 CHAUSSONS AUX POMMES

For the dough
· Ingredients for Puff Pastry (p. 164)

For the apple filling
· 1kg (2 ¼ pounds) Granny Smith or other tart baking apples (about 10 medium apples), thinly sliced or cut into 1cm (⅓ inch) chunks
· 100g (7 tbsp) unsalted butter
· 3 tbsp Demerara sugar
· ½ lemon, juiced
· 1 tsp pure vanilla extract
· 2 tsp ground cinnamon (optional)
· ¼ tsp table salt

For the egg wash
· 1 large egg, plus 1 large egg yolk, whisked

Make your dough
Follow the recipe for Puff Pastry (p. 164) and chill for at least 2 hours or for up to 3 days.

While the dough is chilling, make your apple filling
In a large pot, combine the apples, butter, Demerara sugar, lemon juice, vanilla, cinnamon, if using, and salt. Cover and bring to a simmer over low heat. Once simmering, uncover the pot and continue simmering until all the water has come out of the apples, about 20 minutes. Remove from the heat and let cool completely. This will make soft apple slices or chunks rather than sauce.

Once the filling is completely cool, prepare your pastry
On a lightly floured surface, use a rolling pin to roll out the dough into a rectangle that is 3mm (⅛ inch) thick and measures 57 x 40cm (23 x 16 inches), with the long sides horizontal and the short sides vertical. Trim the sides just enough to make straight edges. Fold the top down to meet the bottom, then unfold, to create a middle seam to guide your cuts. Use a ruler to measure 11cm (4 ½ inch) intervals along the top, bottom, and middle seam. Cut to join the intervals and create five 38 x 11cm (15 x 4 ½ inch) rectangles. Then cut each of these rectangles in half along the middle seam to create ten 19 x 11cm (7 ½ x 4 ½ inch) rectangles. Use a pizza cutter or pie crimper to round out the edges of each rectangle to create ovals. Set the dough ovals on parchment paper–lined baking tray and chill in the fridge for 20 minutes.

After 20 minutes, remove the dough ovals from the fridge and assemble your turnovers. Put a generous mound of the apple filling on one half of a dough oval, leaving a 1cm (⅓ inch) border around the edge of the pastry. Brush this border with water, then fold the uncovered half of the dough oval up and over the apple filling to create a pocket. Use a fork to press and seal the edges, then flip the pocket over to hide the fork marks. Repeat to create 9 more turnovers. Brush the tops of each turnover with the egg wash, then chill in the fridge for 20 minutes.

Preheat the oven 170°C (340°F) (preferably convection setting).

After 20 minutes, brush the turnovers with egg wash a second time. Use a fine knife or a razor blade to carve fine decorative lines into the surface of the turnovers, barely grazing the dough. Use the tip of the knife to poke a very discrete hole in 1 of your decorative lines (this will conceal the hole) to allow steam to vent during the bake. Bake for 40 minutes, or until puffed and golden brown.

Roasted Apricot Turnovers

Apples are not the only fruit — at least when it comes to puff pastry turnovers. For a more avant garde chausson, try roasting apricots to create a quick sour compote that isn't overly sweet. When stuffed into a turnover or hand pie, the technicolor orange filling makes for a bright surprise that remains hidden until the first bite.

YIELD: 10 LARGE OR 15-20 SMALL TURNOVERS

For the dough
· Ingredients for Puff Pastry (p. 164)

For the apricot filling
· 1kg (2 ¼ pounds) apricots, halved and pitted
· 2 tbsp honey
· 1 tsp fresh lemon juice

For the egg wash
· 1 large egg, plus 1 egg yolk, whisked

To finish
· Demerara or cinnamon sugar

Make your dough
Follow the recipe for Puff Pastry (p. 164), wrap airtight, and chill for at least 2 hours or for up to 3 days.

While the dough is chilling, make your apricot filling
Preheat the oven to 165°C (325°F) (preferably convection setting).

In a large bowl, toss the halved apricots with the honey and lemon juice. Spread evenly on a rimmed roasting pan or casserole dish greased with butter and bake for 30 minutes, or until the apricots are very soft and surrounded by their own juices. Drain the apricots in a fine mesh sieve (the juice can be saved to use in seltzers or cocktails) and cool completely before using. *Note: The apricots can be prepared in advance and stored in the refrigerator for up to 5 days; drain a second time before using.*

Once the filling is completely cool, prepare your pastry
On a lightly floured work surface, use a rolling pin to roll out the dough into a rectangle that is 3mm (⅛ inch) thick and that measures about 57 x 40cm (23 x 16 inches) with the long sides vertical and the short sides horizontal. You can cut and fill these like the Chaussons aux Pommes (p. 188) or use a small round cookie cutter or water glass to cut the dough into circles. The size is up to you — the circles can be very small and fit only 1 apricot half or they can be slightly larger to fit more apricots — but you will use 2 rounds of dough for each turnover and there needs to be enough room to seal the pastry around the edges.

Once you've cut your pastry, place it on a parchment paper-lined baking tray and chill in the fridge for about 20 minutes.

After 20 minutes, put a small mound of filling in the center of half of the dough circles, leaving a 1.25cm (½ inch) border around the edges. Brush the uncovered borders with water, then place the unfilled pastry circles on top. Use a fork to press and seal the edges. You can flip these over to conceal the fork marks, or leave them as they are for a more rustic look. Brush the tops of each turnover with the egg wash, then chill in the fridge for 20 minutes.

Preheat the oven 170°C (340°F) (preferably convection setting).

After 20 minutes, brush the turnovers with egg wash a second time. Use a fine knife or a razor blade to score the top of each turnover all the way through with an X to release steam. Sprinkle with Demerara or cinnamon sugar and bake for 40 minutes, or until golden brown.

Heymische Rugelekh · Homestyle Rugelach

With their roots in the Jewish bakeries of Poland, these heymische rugelekh — Yiddish for homestyle rugelach — have more in common with the glazed and nut-stuffed rogale found in modern Polish bakeries than they do with yeasted Israeli rugelach (p. 126). What these little cookies lack in shine, they make up for in flavor and texture. Made with a traditional dairy dough, they're flaky and tender and taste somewhere between sunshine and cinnamon toast.

YIELD: 24 RUGELACH

For the dough
· Ingredients for ½ Dairy Dough
  (p. 164)

For the walnut and raisin filling
· 160g (¾ cup) packed brown sugar
· 100g (7 tbsp) unsalted butter, room temperature
· 50g (½ cup plus 2 tbsp) walnut meal
· 50g (½ cup) finely chopped walnuts
· 50g (⅓ cup) finely chopped golden raisins
· 3 tbsp all-purpose flour
· 2 tsp ground cinnamon

For the egg wash
· 1 large egg, plus 1 large egg yolk, whisked

To finish
· Cinnamon sugar

Make your dough
Follow the recipe for Dairy Dough (p. 164). Divide the dough into 2 equal-sized balls and press into disks. Wrap airtight, then chill in the fridge for at least 1 hour or for up to several days.

While your dough chills, make your walnut and raisin filling
In the bowl of a stand mixer fitted with the paddle attachment, combine the brown sugar, butter, walnut meal, finely chopped walnuts, raisins, all-purpose flour, and cinnamon and beat until there are no visible pieces of butter. Set aside.

Once the dough is chilled, place it on a lightly floured surface. Using a rolling pin, roll out each disk of dough into a circle that measures about 30cm (12 inches) across. Trim the edges. Spread the filling evenly across each circle, then slice each circle like a pizza into 12 triangles. Roll up each triangle like a croissant and place, about 1.25 –2cm (½–¾ inch) apart and with their tails tucked underneath, on a parchment paper–lined baking tray. Chill in the fridge for 20 minutes.

Preheat the oven 170°C (340°F) (preferably convection setting).

After 20 minutes, brush each cookie with egg wash, sprinkle with cinnamon sugar, and bake for 10 minutes, or until golden brown. Let cool completely, then store in a cookie tin and eat all week.

Caramelized Cabbage Braid

Back when I lived in Prague, there was a brutally spartan bodega across the street from my tram stop that sold little more than cigarettes, tram tickets, and some non sequitur heads of cabbage. It was a relic of an era already long gone by, but I have to guess that it wasn't trying very hard even in its heyday. It's been a while now since I saw cabbage as a convenience store impulse item. After all, who wants an old-fashioned winter vegetable when they can have, well, just about anything else?

But wait, not quite! Cabbage is absolutely enchanting! It hides loads of natural sweetness and slow cooking is the best way to harness cabbage's best qualities and prime it for baking. Baking? Indeed: Caramelized cabbage is key to countless Central and Eastern European pastries, kugels, and noodle dishes. Let me finally get to my point: The inspiration for this charming cabbage braid is cabbage strudel, a savory strudel found everywhere from Germany to Hungary to Croatia and Serbia. However, rather than make a true strudel, which features dough so delicate it requires a plate, this recipe uses Dairy Dough for a flaky yet sturdy handheld slice.

YIELD: 1 LARGE CABBAGE BRAID, ABOUT 10 PORTIONS

For the dough
· Ingredients for ½ Dairy Dough (p. 164)

For the cabbage filling
· 2 ½ tbsp olive oil
· ½ medium green cabbage, thinly sliced
· 6 shallots, thinly sliced
· 1 tsp table salt
· 2 tsp freshly ground black pepper
· 20g (1 ½ tbsp) unsalted butter
· 2 ½ tsp granulated sugar
· 1 tsp apple cider vinegar

For the egg wash
· 1 large egg, plus 1 large egg yolk, whisked

For the topping
· Caraway seeds (optional)

For serving
· Sour cream

Make your dough
Follow the recipe for the Dairy Dough (p. 164) and chill for at least 1 hour or for up to several days.

While the dough is chilling, make your cabbage filling
In a large pan, heat the olive oil over low heat. Add the cabbage, shallots, salt, and pepper and cook, stirring occasionally, for about 45 minutes, or until rich brown and reduced to about a quarter of its original volume. Add the butter and granulated sugar and allow it to melt, then raise the heat to medium. Add the vinegar and cook for 5 more minutes. Remove from the heat and let cool completely. *Note: The cabbage can be prepared in advance and refrigerated for up to 3 days or frozen indefinitely.*

Once the filling is completely cool, prepare your pastry
Using a rolling pin and a lightly-floured work surface, roll out the dough into a rectangle that is 3mm (⅛ inch) thick and measures 42 x 28cm (17 x 11 inches), with the long sides vertical and the short sides horizontal. Trim each side just enough to straighten then place on a parchment paper-lined baking tray and chill for 10 minutes.

Preheat the oven to 170°C (340°F) (preferably convection setting).

After 10 minutes, fold the long sides of the dough over the middle like a pamphlet, dividing the rectangle into thirds, then unfold. This will make three even columns. Using the fold lines as your guide, cut 1cm (⅓ inch) horizontal strips along the 2 outer columns. Cut the first 2 strips off the top and bottom of both outer columns, leaving only the middle column of dough. Spoon the cooled cabbage mixture evenly down the middle column of dough, leaving the 2 end portions from which you cut the strips empty. Fold these unfilled top and bottom ends over the column of cabbage to seal the ends — this will prevent leaking. Now you're ready to start braiding. To braid, start at the top and lay the side strips diagonally across the cabbage, alternating each side all the way to the bottom. Brush the pastry with the egg wash, sprinkle with caraway seeds, if using, and bake for 45 minutes, or until the pastry is golden brown and crispy. Serve hot or cold with a dollop of sour cream.

E5 BAKEHOUSE · LONDON, ENGLAND

Ben McKinnon & Eyal Schwartz

In London's Hackney neighborhood, just removed from the tidy brick row houses of the residential streets, the e5 Bakehouse sits tucked into a railway arch. Inside the great curved space of corrugated tin is a little bit of everything. First there are the newspaper-reading breakfasters in peak morning ritual, their eggs and toast steeped in sunlight. They're surrounded by walls of portioned-out sacks of freshly milled flours and shelves with anything and everything for bread making. Across the room there's a cold case of farm-fresh cultured butter, bacon, and cheddar, each neatly labeled with its farm provenance and waiting to be taken home. From there, a coffee counter is filled with the day's spread of pastry and bread. Customers walk off with rhubarb danishes and Cornish pasties in their hands and the signature Hackney Wild loaves under their arms. After that, it's not entirely clear where the workspace begins. Beyond boxes of vegetables and fruit from the e5 farm, the hustle of pastry chefs and bread bakers at production is on full display.

As a visitor to e5, it's hard not to feel that you've entered an old village square from long before supermarket chains and big box stores existed, where a kind of humble economy of specialized merchants and craftspeople can make anything you might need. But Ben McKinnon, who dreamed up e5 twelve years ago, had the vision of a bakery far less bustling than the one he now runs with his partner-in-bread Eyal Schwartz.

Before the bakery, Ben worked in sustainability and like so many change-minded people, he wasn't entirely satisfied. It felt like he was just writing reports and paying lip service. He wanted something with a more direct impact: "Something I could really get my teeth into, get behind — wholeheartedly." It was around this time that he visited a small Spanish mountain village.

"It felt like the end of an era there, but you could see the beauty of the small farming system — how nature and food production can so comfortably overlap." It was there that he got interested in food as a vehicle for social and ecological change and ideas for his future began to ferment.

"The beauty of food is it's a very direct form of change," Ben says. "Depending on the flour we use in our bread, we're literally changing the nature of the fields. The milk that we put in our coffee — we're having a direct impact on an agricultural landscape."

Back in London, and looking for his entry point into food, Ben decided that bread ticked all the boxes. Having little baking experience, he signed up for a short course on breadmaking and, to use his words, just threw himself into it. He rented a little space from a vegan gluten-free bakery — admittedly not the most compatible scenario for a sourdough bakery — in a Hackney archway, not far from the current e5 Bakehouse. Then, in a rare move, he went to work building an oven from foraged and waste materials.

"It was a bit of an artistic project," Ben says. To start, he gathered clay and old bricks off a fallen down building in the Suffolk countryside where he's from. Then a metalworker built the door and heat piping. The end result was a rustic-looking massive incinerator of a thing. But it was that odd homemade oven that helped catalyze the bakery. People wanted to come see the totally illegal wood-fired oven in the middle of

machine, and once every twenty minutes someone would come and order coffee and one of the bakers would make a coffee with their doughy hands. Then, at some point, people started asking, 'Do you have any sandwiches?'" And in that same manner, the bakery kept growing. One person, one product, at a time.

As Eyal tells the story, every step of growth meant a new person coming into the bakery community. Both Ben and Eyal drop name after name — this person who taught them this, this other person who brought this skill. Hannah, John, Franzi, Lewyn, Jessie… it goes on, with each name mentioned in hyperbolic gratitude and excitement.

And so the bakery grew. From bread to coffee to sandwiches to pastries. After that first year in the borrowed space and with a handmade oven, Ben and Eyal rented their own archway nearby. A proper second-hand oven was bought, some tables were made, and that's where e5 really began.

"It just sort of came about," Ben says. "No predesigned vision. But the fundamental basis of it was doing things as ecologically and sustainably as possible. It was a nice framework to work within."

From the beginning, Ben focused on sourcing flour and ingredients from organic whole foods suppliers. About five years into the bakery though, with the business turning a small profit, Ben decided to take things a step further. He wanted to change the supply chain for the bread, so he bought some farmland. "It makes it a bit easier to get out of bed when you really believe in what you're doing."

Ben moved out to the farm, leaving Eyal to manage the bakery. Now, the e5 farm produces half the flour that the bakery mills and the rest comes from neighbors, local organic farmers near the e5 farm. Always in search of a new project, Ben has been playing with market gardening, growing all the vegetables and herbs used at the bakehouse, as well as planting a vineyard to grow biodynamic wines. There's a small wood-fired oven

London — and the guy who built it. For the first year, he worked with a kind of punk crew — people attracted to the bakery but with little baking experience. Just two months into that first year, Eyal, who was newly arrived from Israel, with his wife and baby, walked past and smelled the bread. The small family went in and bought a loaf. They liked what they tasted.

The very next day, Eyal came back and had a chat with Ben. Eyal had just finished his degree in Neuroscience and was planning to get a job as a software engineer. But he'd always loved bread. In Israel, he'd baked his own pitas, but he'd

never worked with sourdough. He told Ben he'd love to learn and help around for free until he found a real job. They agreed to give it a month, but when Eyal came home after that initial meeting he told his wife, "I'm really sorry — we're going to be broke, but we'll have fresh bread for life."

Eleven years later. Ben and Eyal will tell you that it's amazing how a business can evolve without a plan. "One day, a guy came to us and said, 'Look, I have a coffee machine. What if I give it to you, you make and sell coffee? Whenever I come, I get a cup of coffee?'" Eyal recounts. "We said sure. So now we have the free coffee on the farm and Ben makes bread once a week in between broad bean harvests and mulching vines — a bit like the old days when e5 was just him and his homemade oven.

Back in London at the bakehouse, Eyal oversees not just the bakery, but its side projects, of which there are many. Bean-to-bar chocolate, coffee, the sourdough school, season

of creating employment for the graduates of their classes.

The eleven years of e5 has brought enormous changes. The neighborhood where Ben started the bakery — once all joineries and car mechanics and where he was told he was crazy for starting the bakery — now boasts five other artisan sourdough bakeries. Coworking spaces and architectural

Still, there is enormous optimism in Eyal and Ben's voices when they talk about the future. Their next project is always around the corner — there are so many things to plant, to nurture, to grow, to bake.

Once, back when Eyal first started at the bakery, his family, all academics, asked him, "What's the appeal to spending eight hours with two other people making dough?" And he said, "What do you mean? You just said it. I get to spend eight hours, making dough with two other people, chatting about anything and nothing, using my hands, and making bread. It was amazing."

" **Ben, Eyal, and their team have created an ecosystem of good, honest food production.**

pickling and ferments, and just about any other thing imaginable. And while most businesses that find success tend to push into more of the same, Eyal and Ben push laterally to keep things interesting and new.

This doesn't just mean new products — it also means job creation. During the pandemic, they were able to create the Poplar Bakehouse. It's a joint project with the Refugee Council, for whom they'd been running training programs in hospitality and breadmaking for refugees and asylum seekers. They realized they could expand the space into a proper bakery as a way

firms have popped up and property values have skyrocketed. All this rapid gentrification has meant the railway arch system has turned into a suddenly valuable asset. Corporate speculators are increasing rents on long-established small businesses at alarming rates. Community members are being displaced, as are businesses. Put shortly, the fabric of the e5 neighborhood is threatened. Ben is working to unite and advocate for the tenants of the railway arches in support of reasonable yet manageable rent increases that will enable everyone to stay, but no one is sure how it will play out.

"It's an important thing being a baker," Ben says. "It's changed my life — it's brought me everything. From my wife, to my community, to the opportunity to practice this kind of farming. The whole movement of small artisan bakeries is so, so positive."

And, in this village of a bakery, so it is. Ben, Eyal, and their whole team have created something special, a whole ecosystem of good, honest food production tied to its sources. Farm to loaf, in the truest sense.

e5 Bakehouse's Spelt Fruit Galettes

This is the recipe for e5 Bakehouse's cute little spelt fruit galettes, courtesy of their head pastry chef, Louise Lateur. The dough is a great example of how you can incorporate varied and tasty flours into your puff pastry. At e5 Bakehouse in London, they use freshly milled organic flour and suggest sourcing some great local flour for the desired flaky texture, and more importantly, lots of flavor. They use a 50/50 ratio of whole spelt flour and light spelt flour, along with kefir, a cultured fermented milk drink.

This version features fruit, but the folks at e5 suggest using any sweet or savory filling. In summer, use some ripe yellow peaches and tart apricots or marinated zucchini with fresh chiles, oregano, lemon, and olive oil.

YIELD: 10-12 GALETTES

For the spelt puff pastry
· 170g (1 ¾ cups) light spelt flour
· 170g (1 ¾ cups) whole spelt flour
· 5g (¾ tsp) table salt
· 250g cultured butter, cut into 1cm (⅓ inch) pieces and frozen for 1 hour
· 110g (½ cup) kefir

For the peach filling
· 5-6 peaches, halved and thickly sliced
· 2 tbsp superfine sugar
· ½ lemon, juiced

For the topping
· 1 large egg
· 110g (½ cup) Demerara sugar (optional)

Make your dough
On a clean work surface, mix the light and whole spelt flours and the salt. Add the cold butter and with your fingertips, incorporate it into the flour, making sure there are visible flakes of butter. Add the kefir and mix with your fingertips until the dough just comes together and some butter flakes are still visible. Don't worry if there are dry bits of flour; they will get incorporated at a later stage. Wrap the dough airtight and let it rest in the fridge for at least 2 hours or overnight.

When the dough is ready, place it on a floured work surface. Use a rolling pin to roll it out into a long rectangle that is about 6mm (¼ inch) thick. Give the dough a single turn: Fold the top third of the dough down by one-third, then fold the bottom up and over to meet the top. Then rotate the dough by 45 degrees, roll it out again into a long rectangle, and give it a second single turn to complete the lamination. Cover airtight and rest in the fridge for 1 hour to relax the gluten and cool the butter.

While the dough rests, make your peach filling
In a large bowl, toss the sliced peaches with the superfine sugar and lemon juice. Set aside.

Preheat the oven to 170°C (340°F) (preferably convection setting).

To shape and fill your galettes, place the dough on a lightly floured work surface. Use a rolling pin to roll out the dough until about 3mm (⅛ inch) thick, then use a 10cm (4 inch) cookie cutter to cut it into 10-12 rounds. Gather the scraps and put them in the fridge to roll out later.

Place a generous mound of the peach filling in the middle of a round of dough, leaving a 1.25 cm (½ inch) border around the edges. To make the 5-point star shape, starting at the bottom of the round, fold a 4cm (1 ½ inch) wide strip of dough up and over the edge of the filling and press down with your thumbs to seal it on both sides. Rotate the dough to the left and fold over the bottom edge again. Continue rotating, folding, and sealing until you have 5 same-sized edges. Repeat to make more galettes. Whisk your egg and give the pastry an egg wash and if you love a crunchy sweet crust, sprinkle it with Demerara sugar. Arrange the galettes on a parchment paper-lined baking tray and bake for 20 minutes, then rotate the baking tray, and bake for 15-20 more minutes, or until the pastry is crispy with flaky, golden brown edges.

Lamb and Fennel Sausage Rolls

On a side street in Berlin's Neukölln district is Geist im Glas. It's an unassuming place — all dark wood with a touch of dive bar — to house the city's best artisan cocktails but has held its ground for over a decade, despite being shuttered in a pandemic and burned down in a fire. The owner, Aishah Bennett, is the force behind the intelligent infusions and well-made classics. She's a tough bar girl and generous as anything, and if you're really lucky — and you've had enough old fashioneds — she'll anchor your drinks with some of her glorious sausage rolls. Aishah combines her Palestinian and English cooking heritage by subbing lamb in for the pork, as a twist on the classic British pastry.

YIELD: 25-30 SAUSAGE ROLLS

For the dough
· Ingredients for Puff Pastry (p. 164)

For the lamb filling
· 60g (¾ cup) breadcrumbs (¾ cup)
· 100g plain yogurt (⅓ cup plus 2 tbsp), plus more for serving
· 2 ½ tbsp olive oil
· 3 garlic cloves, crushed
· 3 shallots, finely chopped
· 50g (⅓ cup plus 2 tbsp) chopped unsalted pistachios
· 2 tsp green fennel seeds
· ¼ tsp cumin seeds
· 600g (21 ½ ounces) ground lamb
· 2 large eggs
· ½ tbsp table salt
· 1 tbsp sumac
· 1 tsp ground cinnamon
· 1 tsp freshly ground black pepper
· 1 tsp garlic powder
· 1 tsp dried mint
· 3 stems fresh parsley, leaves removed and chopped

For the egg wash
· 1 large egg, plus 1 large egg yolk, whisked

To finish
· Nigella seeds, cumin seeds, or sumac

To serve
· Yogurt and fresh chopped mint

Make your dough
Follow the recipe for the Puff Pastry (p. 164) and chill for at least 2 hours or for up to 3 days.

While the dough is chilling, make your lamb filling
In a large bowl, combine the breadcrumbs and yogurt and mix together. Set aside to soak for 30 minutes.

In a medium frying pan, heat the olive oil over medium heat. Add the garlic, shallots, pistachios, fennel seeds, and cumin seeds and sauté until the shallots are translucent. Remove from the heat and let cool completely.

Add the cooled shallot mixture to the large bowl with the breadcrumb-yogurt mixture. Add the lamb, eggs, salt, sumac, cinnamon, pepper, garlic powder, mint, and parsley.

To shape and fill the sausage rolls, put the pastry on a lightly floured work surface. Use a rolling pin to roll out the dough into a rectangle that is 3mm (⅛ inch) thick and measures 50 x 30cm (20 x 12 inches), with the long sides vertical and the short sides horizontal. Divide the rectangle the long way, so you have two 50 x 15cm (20 x 6 inch) strips. Spoon an even line of the lamb filling along 1 long side of each dough rectangle, leaving a 1cm (⅓ inch) border around the edges. Brush the uncovered borders with the egg wash, then fold the uncovered dough up and over the lamb filling, slightly overlapping the sides and pressing to seal with a fork. Cut each sausage roll into 5cm (2 inch) sections and arrange, 5cm (2 inches) apart, on a parchment paper-lined baking tray. Brush the pastry with the egg wash, then chill in the fridge for 20 minutes.

Preheat the oven to 170°C (340°F) (preferably convection setting).

After 20 minutes, brush the pastry with egg wash a second time, sprinkle with nigella seeds, cumin seeds, or sumac, and bake for 30 minutes, or until the pastry is golden brown and the meat is fully cooked. Serve with yogurt and fresh mint.

Wild Mushroom and Parsley Slab Tarte

As children, my brother and I weren't allowed to pick wild mushrooms. They're right up there with trampolines, diving boards, and hotdogs, in our family's Index of Dangerous Things. So, I got a late start on the most beloved of pastimes in Central and Eastern Europe: mushroom hunting. Every year, my Czech husband, who can't so much as recognize a daisy on a sunny day, turns expert mycologist at the first hint of autumn. Chanterelles, porcinis, morels. It's hard to keep up if you're not born into the tradition, but this free-form tarte makes it worth getting out the guidebook and taking a basket to the forest — or at least the farmer's market.

Note: I use a mixture of chanterelles, porcinis, and morels, but use whatever variety is available to you — even brown button mushrooms will turn out a delicious tarte!

YIELD: 1 LARGE SLAB TARTE

For the dough
- Ingredients for ½ Puff Pastry or ½ Dairy Dough (p. 164)

For the mushroom filling
- 45g (3 ½ tbsp) olive oil
- 2 large shallots, diced
- 3 cloves garlic, crushed
- 600g (21 ½ ounces) mixed mushrooms, roughly chopped (7–8 cups)
- 1 tsp fresh or dried thyme
- Table salt and freshly ground black pepper
- 300g (1 ⅓ cups) thick sour cream
- 100g (⅓ plus 1 tbsp) whole milk
- 30g (¼ cup) all-purpose flour
- 1 tsp mustard powder
- 25g (¼ cup) grated Parmesan
- 40g (1 ½ cups) roughly chopped flat-leaf parsley

For the egg wash
- 1 large egg, plus 1 large egg yolk, whisked

Make your dough
Follow the recipe for Puff Pastry or Dairy Dough (p. 164) and chill for at least 2 hours or for up to 3 days.

While the dough is chilling, make your mushroom filling
In a large frying pan, heat the olive oil over medium heat. Add the shallots and garlic and sauté until translucent and starting to brown. Add the mushrooms and thyme, season with salt and pepper, and sauté, stirring occasionally, until the mushrooms are browned, reduced, and simmering in their own juices, about 10 minutes.

While the mushrooms cook, whisk together the sour cream, milk, all-purpose flour, and mustard powder.

Once the mushrooms are ready, add the sour cream mixture and stir to incorporate. Allow to bubble gently, until the mixture starts to thicken. Remove from the heat, stir in the Parmesan and 25g (1 cup) of the parsley, and let cool completely.

Preheat the oven to 170°C (340°F) (preferably convection setting).

When the filling is completely cool, prepare your pastry
On a lightly floured work surface, use a rolling pin to roll out the dough into a rectangle that is about 3mm (⅛ inch) thick and measures 40 x 30cm (16 x 12 inches). Slide the dough onto a parchment paper-lined baking tray. Spread the mushroom filling evenly across the pastry, leaving a 2.5cm (1 inch) border around the sides. Fold the edges up and over the filling, pressing the corners together tightly. Brush the pastry with the egg wash and bake for about 35 minutes, or until the crust is golden brown and the bottom is fully cooked. Let rest for 15 minutes, then garnish with the remaining parsley and serve.

Potato, Thyme, and Gruyère Hand Pies

The true calling of puff pastry and its ilk are in the salty and savory domain. Cornish pasties in England, empanadas in Spain, and Chebureki in Ukraine are all fine examples of crunchy and flaky pastry encasing meaty stews, veggies, and cheese — it's an ideal format for sneaking food between meals. These potato hand pies, full of fresh thyme and cheese, are my favorite for picnics and just as good hot as cold. Gruyère is a great mild cheese for melting — you might recognize it from its starring role atop French onion soup — but any hard cheese will work.

YIELD: 10-12 HAND PIES

For the dough
· Ingredients for Puff Pastry (p. 164)

For the potato filling
· 300g (11 ounces) new, fingerling, or small red potatoes
· 3 tbsp thick sour cream
· 140g (1 ¼ cups) shredded Gruyère
· 1 small shallot, finely chopped
· Leaves from 5-6 large sprigs fresh thyme
· Table salt and freshly ground black pepper

For the egg wash
· 1 large egg, 1 large egg yolk, whisked

To finish
· 10 fresh thyme sprigs

Make your dough
Follow the recipe for Puff Pastry (p. 164) and chill for at least 2 hours or for up to 3 days.

While the dough is chilling, make your potato filling
Wash then boil the unpeeled potatoes until soft. Drain and let cool, then slice into thin rounds.

In a large bowl, combine the cooled potatoes with the sour cream, Gruyère, shallot, and the thyme leaves. Season with salt and pepper. Set aside.

On a lightly floured work surface, use a rolling pin to roll out the dough into a rectangle that is about 3mm (⅛ inch) thick and measures 55 x 40cm (22 x 16 inches), with the long sides horizontal and the short sides vertical. Fold the top down to meet the bottom, then unfold to create a middle seam to act as a guide line. Using a ruler, mark off intervals of 11cm (4 ½ inches) along the top, bottom, and middle seam. Cut to join these markings, forming 5 long rectangles. Cut each rectangle along the middle seam to divide them in half and create a total of ten 20 x 11cm (8 x 4 ½ inches) rectangles. Spoon a generous amount of the potato mixture on half of each dough rectangle, leaving a 1cm (⅓ inch) border around the edges. Brush the uncovered edges with water, then fold the unfilled half up and over the filling to create turnovers. Press and seal with a fork, then flip the pies over to hide the fork marks. Place, about 2cm (¾ inch) apart, on a parchment paper-lined baking tray, then brush with the egg wash and chill in the fridge for 20 minutes.

Preheat the oven to 170°C (340°F) (preferably convection setting).

After 20 minutes, brush the turnovers with egg wash a second time, then using a sharp knife or razor blade, slice diagonal lines all the way through the top of the pastry. Lay a spring of fresh thyme on top of each, then bake for 40 minutes, or until golden brown.

Tiny Tatins with Tarragon

This recipe is a simplified muffin-tin version of tarte Tatin, the classic French upside-down caramelized apple cake. It's a great use of leftover pastry scraps, and the fresh tarragon adds a distinct sweet vanilla note to the caramel. I use pears here, but if they aren't to your taste, use apples or firm nectarines.

Note: *I like to serve this as a hot dessert, because it can all be prepped up to a day in advance and baked up at the last minute. Fill the muffin tin with caramel and cut and chill the pastry, storing everything wrapped separately in the fridge. When it's time to bake, simply top the caramel with pears and the chilled pastry.*

YIELD: ABOUT 12 TINY TATINS

For the dough
· Ingredients for ½ Puff Pastry or ½ Dairy Dough (p. 164), or dough scraps

For the caramel
· 100g (½ cup) granulated sugar
· 55g water (3 ½ tbsp)
· 25g (2 tbsp) unsalted butter
· 25g (1 ⅔ tbsp) heavy whipping cream, plus more for serving
· 1 tsp pure vanilla extract
· 4 sprigs fresh tarragon, plus more for garnish
· Pinch of table salt

For the fruit
· 8 firm pears, cut into thick slices that will fit the base of your muffin tin

Make your dough
Follow the recipes for Puff Pastry or Dairy Dough (p. 164) and chill for at least 2 hours or for up to 3 days.

When the dough is ready, place it on a lightly floured work surface. Use a rolling pin to roll out the dough to 3mm (⅛ inch) thickness. Using a small round cookie cutter or water glass that is slightly larger than the cups in your muffin tin, cut out 1 circle for each mini tarte. Stack and wrap these dough circles and chill until you're ready to use.

Make your caramel
In a heavy-bottomed small saucepan, melt the granulated sugar and water over low heat, without stirring, until no more sugar granules are visible. Let come to a gentle boil, then continue gently boiling for 3 minutes. Add the butter and let melt, stirring to incorporate, then stop stirring and let come to a boil. Continue boiling, without stirring, for a few minutes, or until the light yellow syrup darkens to a medium honey color. Remove from the heat and immediately add the heavy whipping cream, vanilla, tarragon, and salt. It will splutter and bubble, but just keep stirring until smooth, then set aside to cool and thicken. Let sit for 15 minutes to infuse with the tarragon.

Grease the muffin tin with butter.

Remove the tarragon from the caramel, then spoon about 1 tbsp of the caramel into the base of each cup. Arrange the pear slices on top of the caramel, then set aside and let the caramel cool to room temperature.

Preheat the oven to 170°C (340°F) (preferably convection setting).

Once the muffin tin is cool to the touch, cover each cup with a dough circle, pushing the sides downward slightly around the pears. Score the middle of each pastry with a small X to release steam during the bake. Bake for about 25 minutes, or until the caramel bubbles up a bit and the pastry is browned. Remove from the oven and let sit for several minutes, then place a rimmed baking tray over the muffin tin and invert the whole thing. The tatins will separate easily, thanks to the hot caramel. To serve, plate each tatin, spoon on any extra hot caramel, and garnish with a few leaves of tarragon and some heavy whipping cream.

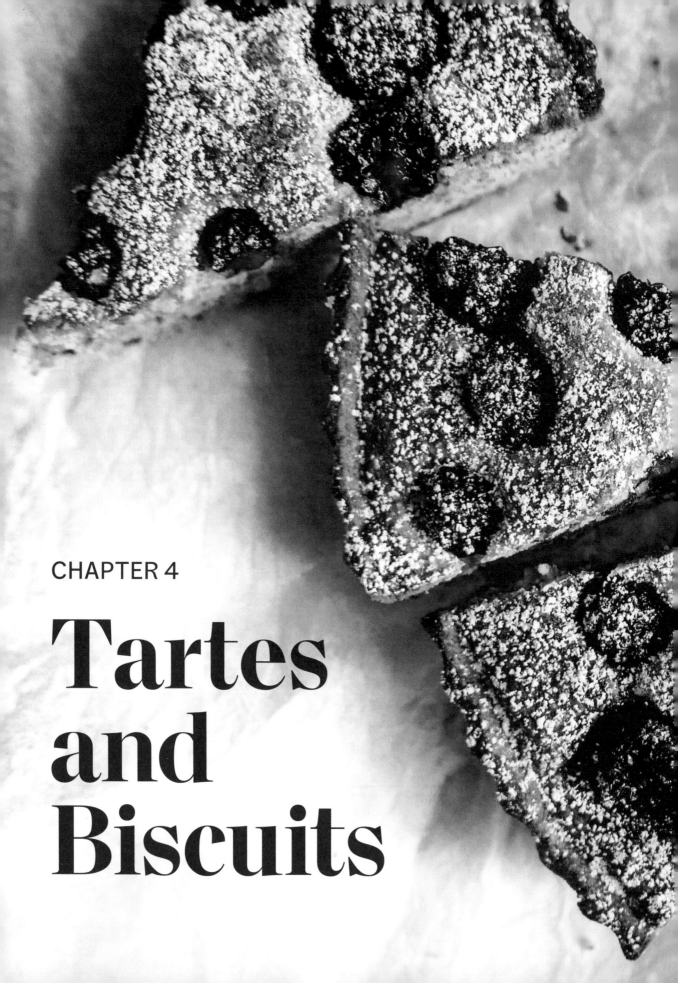

CHAPTER 4

Tartes and Biscuits

I Walk the Line: Working with Shortcrust Pastry

There's a gray area that exists in the bakery world between the baker and the pastry chef. Sometimes we overlap or meet in the middle — that's what laminated pastry is for. But usually, bakers deal in breads, viennoiseries, and enriched doughs, while pastry chefs' work falls into fussier categories like elegant tartes and cakes, choux pastries, and plated desserts. Tartes usually fall squarely in the territory of pastry chefs, but there's a long tradition of something called "baker's pastry." Often more rustic than those of pastry chefs, baker's tartes and biscuits are baked in the residual heat of the ovens after the bread is done and tend toward baked custard tartes, quiches, and sablé cookies. Modern bakers like Monika Walecka use pastry as a way of using up old bread, while Xavier Netry brings pastry techniques into bread making itself. With the old walls now down and bakers jumping around culinary professions and drawing from the experience, there's no harm in playing fast and loose with the definition of baker's pastry.

The base recipes for this chapter are classic pâte sablée and pasta frolla, short doughs from which you can make just about any tartes or biscuits from here to eternity. There's just a few terms and techniques to learn first!

Shortcrust Pastry

For the base of our baker's pastry, we'll use several different types of shortcrust pastry, or short doughs, which are flour-based doughs with a high percentage of fat. These doughs require minimal gluten development — the opposite of the breads and brioches from previous chapters — to stay moldable, not stretchy. The exact components of short doughs vary by country and use. Some contain egg, while some do not and though some are sweet, others are more neutral. You can find infinite incarnations of short dough, but I like to stick to a couple favorites. The recipes here are all for sweet tartes and biscuits, so we'll use a French dough and an Italian dough, both of which are sweet but use slightly different methods and yield subtly different results. The following are the basic steps and methods for mixing and shaping a short dough.

Sablage

(Photos p. 214) Sablage is the process of coating flour with fat and is the most important step in making any short dough. When liquids mix with flour, the gluten in the flour is activated. Gluten development — the stretch and chew we want from our bread doughs — is exactly what we don't want in tarte dough. By rubbing butter and flour into a sablage, a layer of fat protects the flour so that once we add the liquid, only minimal gluten development is possible. Practically speaking, this means your tarte shell won't contract while baking.

To perform sablage by hand, toss flour and cubes of butter until the butter is coated (1), then rub the flour and butter until you have a sandy texture (2), being careful to work quickly so as not to melt the butter. On warm days, chill (but don't freeze) your butter cubes in the freezer before using. Rub the butter and flour until there are no visible bits of butter (3), then add ground nuts and confectioners' sugar. Give this a mix, continuing the rubbing motion with your fingers, until homogenous (4). (You can also do this in a food processor using pulses!) Next, add the egg and vanilla (5), and mix by hand until just incorporated and there are no dry bits (6), being careful not to overwork the dough. Once mixed, form the dough into a flat disk (7) and wrap it airtight (8). Refrigerate for at least two hours or for up to three days, or freeze for up to two months.

Breaking and Rolling the Dough

(Photos pp. 214–215) Once your dough is chilled, it's time to break and roll it using a rolling pin on a lightly floured surface (9–11). At first, the dough should crack and be difficult to roll. It simply needs to be softened or "broken." Do this by pounding the dough, or folding it over itself and rolling it, then repeating until it's supple enough to roll out without cracking. Don't overdo this step! If you take it too far, you'll have built up the gluten and find yourself with stretchy dough. Once your dough is broken, roll it out to the desired thickness (12–13).

Choosing a Tarte Form

Tarte forms or pans are sold by size, which is given as the diameter of the base. The recipes in this chapter work best for a 28–30cm (11–12 inch) form with 3cm–4cm (1¼–1½ inch) sides. Look for a tarte form made of thin, nonstick metal with a push-out bottom and crimped sides.

Setting a Tarte

(Photos p. 215) Slide your rolled out dough onto a nonstick or parchment paper-lined baking tray or a large flat board and chill in the fridge for twenty minutes. This will relax the dough and slightly stiffen it, while keeping it supple. Once chilled, carefully lift and set the round of dough in your tarte form (14–15). Gently press the base and then the sides (16–17), using the fonçage method (see below). If the dough cracks, simply press it back together.

Fonçage

(Photo p. 215) For years, I struggled to set and blind bake a tarte shell until my friend Marion Liard, a talented Paris-based pastry chef, taught me a simple little step called fonçage, which literally means "sinking." Marion will always tell you: "Pastry is all about the tricks." To fonçage your tarte shell, press the sides of the tarte gently downward at the point where the sides meet the base (18). Move methodically around the entire circle, creating a tight corner. That's it! This gentle pressing and pushing down of the sides of the pastry dough into the tarte form will prevent the sides from collapsing during a blind bake and make perfect 90 degree interior pastry edges that look beautiful on cut tarte slices.

Blind Baking Tarte Shells

(Photos p. 215) Blind baking is the process of baking a tarte shell with no filling inside. The advantage is a tarte shell that can be filled with creams and fruits that don't require baking. The disadvantage is there's nothing holding up the sides of the tarte shell while it bakes! That's the challenge of a blind bake — keeping the sides upright. There are two things that will help: a good dough and a good fonçage. When blind baking, bake until the pastry just starts to turn golden like the color of a sugar cookie.

While some people like to use pie weights or dried beans to keep their tarte shells in place while baking, this can still lead to sunken sides or an irregular bottom — not to mention an extra step. I've always had more success with a carefully managed dough and the fonçage technique for setting a tarte.

To blind bake your tarte, after the fonçage step, trim the edges of the dough with a knife (19) and return it to the fridge for twenty minutes. Once chilled, prick holes all over the base of the tarte shell with a fork (20). The technical term for this is "docking" and it prevents the base from puffing up during the bake. Once you've docked the tarte, bake it at 170°C (340°F) for 12 minutes, or until lightly tan. If making individual tartlets, the timing should be reduced to about 8 minutes. Let your tarte shells cool before filling and removing from the tarte form (21).

Note: Unfilled baked tarte shells can be wrapped in plastic and frozen until ready to use. Unwrap and defrost at room temperature.

Partially Blind Baking Tarte Shells

Some tartes like the Tart Berry Frangipane Tarte (p. 224) call for a partial blind bake to start baking the pastry before adding the filling and baking further. This ensures there is no soggy bottom. Note that this is only possible for unleavened dough — that is, dough that doesn't contain baking powder. To do a partial blind bake, simply set the tarte with the fonçage method, then trim, chill, and prick the tarte with a fork exactly as you would for a full blind bake. Bake for 7-8 minutes at 170°C (340°F). The tarte shell should still be pale when it comes out of the oven.

Baking a Filled Tarte

Some tartes like the Crostata Ricotta e Visciole (p. 242) are fully assembled and then baked, which means the fillings are baked along with the tarte shell. The fillings have a stabilizing effect on the tarte dough — they hold up the sides while the whole thing bakes. However, this means you have to be extra careful that the bottom of the pastry is properly cooked, as no one likes a soggy bottom! There's a few tricks to doing this. First, once your tarte shell is set in its form, brush the bottom with egg white, then chill for 10-20 minutes before filling. This will help create a barrier between the pastry and the filling. When it's time to bake, prick the base of the tarte with a fork, then set your tarte form directly on the oven rack, not on a baking tray, and keep the convection or fan settings turned on. This will allow air to circulate and properly bake the pastry from the bottom.

Base Recipe: Basic Tarte Dough · Pâte Sablée

This pâte sablée has a little extra fleur de sel to zip the tongue and ground nuts to add stability and flavor. For a neutral taste, use almond flour and for a more complex, earthy flavor, try almond, walnut, or hazelnut meal, which can all be made by grinding whole nuts in a food processor. One of the advantages to this dough is that it won't spread as it bakes, so it blind bakes easily. Use it as a base for any tarte, cookie, or bar cookie you can dream up.

Note: Once you've mastered the original recipe, tarte dough is a great place to play with different grains. Substitute part of the flour with spelt, einkorn, rye, or whole grain flour for a different flavor and texture.

For visuals, see photos on pp. 214–215.

YIELD: DOUGH FOR ONE 28-30CM (11-12 INCH) TARTE SHELL OR FIVE 7CM (2 ¾ INCH) TARTLET SHELLS

· 120g (½ cup plus 1 tbsp) unsalted butter, cubed and cold
· 220g (1 ¾ cups plus 1 tbsp) all-purpose or pastry flour
· 65g (⅔ cup) almond flour or 65g (¾ cup) almond, walnut, or hazelnut meal
· 60g (½ cup plus 1 tsp) confectioners' sugar, sifted
· 2 g (½ tsp) fleur de sel or flaky sea salt
· 1 large egg, beaten
· 5g (1 tsp) pure vanilla extract

A - Mix your dough
Sablage the butter and flour (p. 212): In a large bowl, toss together the all-purpose or pastry flour and the butter cubes until the butter is coated (1). Rub the butter and flour together between your thumb and fingers until it has a uniform sandy texture and there are no visible bits of butter (2-3). Add the almond flour or nut meal, confectioners' sugar, and salt and mix, continuing the rubbing motion with your fingers until homogenous (4). Add the egg and vanilla (5), and mix by hand until just incorporated and there are no dry bits (6), being careful not to overwork the dough. If making one tarte shell, form the dough into a flattened disk (7) and wrap it airtight (8). If making five tartlet shells, divide the dough into five parts, form into flattened disks, and wrap airtight. Refrigerate the dough for at least 2 hours or for up to 3 days. (This dough can also be frozen for up to 2 months and defrosted overnight in the fridge before using.)

B - Break and roll out your dough
When ready to use, on a lightly floured work surface, use a rolling pin to break the chilled dough (9-11, and p. 212), then roll out to a 2-3mm (¹⁄₁₂-⅛ inch) thickness (12-13). Slide onto a nonstick or parchment paper-lined baking tray and chill in the fridge for 20 minutes.

C - Set your tarte
After 20 minutes, carefully lift and set the chilled round of dough in one 28-30cm (11-12 inch) tarte form (14-15) or five 7cm (2 ¾ inch) tartlet shells. Gently press the base and then the sides (16-17), using the fonçage method (p. 213). If the dough cracks, simply press it back together. Trim the edges of the dough with a knife (19) and return to the fridge for 20 minutes.

D - Bake your tarte shell
After 20 minutes, prick the base of the chilled tarte shell or tartlet shells all over with a fork (20) and blind bake or partially blind bake (p. 213) as required by the individual recipe. Let cool completely (21). Fill and assemble your tarte or tartlets as required by the individual recipe, then remove from the tarte form or tartlet forms.

Base Recipe: Chocolate Tarte Dough

Add a bit of contrast to your tartes with this chocolate version of the Basic Tarte Dough. For a bit of variation, I like to substitute the almond flour or nut meal with finely ground coconut.

For visuals, see photos on pp. 214-215.

YIELD: DOUGH FOR ONE 28-30CM (11-12 INCH) TARTE SHELL OR FIVE 7CM (2 ¾ INCH) TARTLET SHELLS

- 200g (1 ⅔ cups) all-purpose or pastry flour
- 25g (5 tbsp) cacao powder
- 120g (½ cup plus 1 tbsp) unsalted butter, cubed and cold
- 65g (⅔ cup) almond flour or 65g (¾ cup) almond meal
- 70g (½ cup plus 2 tbsp) confectioners' sugar
- 2g (½ tsp) fleur de sel or flaky sea salt
- 1 large egg
- 5g (1 tsp) pure vanilla extract

A - Mix your dough

In a large bowl, toss together the all-purpose or pastry flour and cacao powder until uniform. Add the butter and sablage by tossing the butter and flour mixture until the butter is coated (1). Rub the butter and flour mixture together between your thumb and fingers until it has a uniform sandy texture and there are no visible bits of butter (2-3). Add the almond flour or meal, confectioners' sugar, and salt and mix, continuing the rubbing motion with your fingers until homogenous (4). Add the egg and vanilla (5), and mix by hand until just incorporated and there are no dry bits (6), being careful not to overwork the dough. If making one tarte shell, form the dough into a flattened disk (7) and wrap it airtight (8). If making five tartlet shells, divide the dough into five parts, form into flattened disks, and wrap airtight. Refrigerate the dough for at least 2 hours or for up to 3 days. (This dough can also be frozen for up to 2 months and defrosted overnight in the fridge before using.)

B - Break and roll out your dough

When ready to use, on a lightly floured work surface, use a rolling pin to break the chilled dough (9-11, and p. 212), then roll out to a 2-3mm (¹⁄₁₂-⅛ inch) thickness (12-13). Slide onto a nonstick or parchment paper-lined baking tray and chill in the fridge for 20 minutes.

C - Set your tarte

After 20 minutes, carefully lift and set the chilled round of dough in one 28-30cm (11-12 inch) tarte form (14-15) or five 7cm (2 ¾ inch) tartlet shells. Gently press the base and then the sides (16-17), using the fonçage method (p. 213). If the dough cracks, simply press it back together. Trim the edges of the dough with a knife (19) and return to the fridge for 20 minutes.

D - Bake your tarte shell

After 20 minutes, prick the base of the chilled tarte shell or tartlet shells all over with a fork (20) and blind bake or partially blind bake (p. 213) as required by the individual recipe. Let cool completely (21). Fill and assemble your tarte or tartlets as required by the individual recipe, then remove from the tarte form or tartlet forms.

Base Recipe: Pasta Frolla Dough

Italian pasta frolla is a great base tarte dough. Sweet and cookie-like, you can use it free-form in galettes, or molded in a pan. You can also use it as a base for biscuits, sandwich cookies, and bar cookies. Unlike the Basic Tarte Dough, pasta frolla contains baking powder, which provides lift and softness, but also means it doesn't blind bake as well. It's mostly used for filled tartes, but if you wish to use it for a blind baked tarte shell, simply leave out the baking powder, set, and blind bake (p. 213).

It's important to break pasta frolla — that is, to give it a brief knead or a second roll to smooth out the dough and prevent it from cracking. If the dough does crack, however, holes can be patched, and more dough can be added while it's in the tarte pan. When using it to bake filled tartes, it's often helpful to brush the base of the tarte with egg white before filling. When baking, the tarte form should always sit directly on the oven rack, rather than on a baking tray, so that air can circulate and properly brown the bottom, ensuring the entire crust bakes and there's no soggy bottom.

Note: While the method calls for a stand mixer, it's also possible to do the sablage and mix by hand or in a food processor.

YIELD: DOUGH FOR ONE 28-30CM (11-12 INCH) TARTE SHELL WITH LATTICE OR ABOUT 700G COOKIE DOUGH FOR ROLLING

For the dough
- 314g (2 ½ cups plus 2 tbsp) all-purpose or pastry flour
- 4g (1 tsp) baking powder *(Note: omit the baking powder if your recipe calls for blind baking)*
- 160g (⅔ cup plus 1 tbsp) unsalted butter, cubed and cold
- 130g (1 cup plus 2 tbsp) confectioners' sugar
- 4g (1 tsp) fleur de sel (or 5g (¾ tsp) table salt)
- 1 large egg, plus 1 large egg yolk, beaten

For baking
- 1 large egg white, whisked

For the egg wash (if making a lattice)
- 1 large egg, plus 3 tbsp whole milk, whisked

A - Mix your dough
In the bowl of a stand mixer fitted with the paddle attachment, combine the all-purpose or pastry flour, baking powder, if using, and butter and mix until sandy. Add the confectioners' sugar and salt and beat on low until uniform. Add the egg and egg yolk and beat on low for 2-3 minutes, or until the dough comes together and is smooth, not crumbly. Form the dough into a disk, wrap airtight, and chill in the fridge for at least 2 hours or for up to 3 days. (This dough can also be frozen for up to 2 months and defrosted overnight in the fridge before using.)

Note: If adding a lattice to your tarte, remove a quarter of the dough, wrap it separately, and chill in the fridge.

B - Break and roll out your dough
When ready to use, on a lightly floured work surface, use a rolling pin to break the chilled dough (p. 212), then roll out to a 3mm (⅛ inch) thickness. Slide onto a nonstick or parchment paper-lined baking tray and chill in the fridge for 20 minutes.

C - Set your tarte
After 20 minutes, remove the dough from the fridge and cut a round of dough large enough to fit the base and sides of your tarte form. Save any scraps to reroll for a lattice, if making. Slide the dough onto the form or use a rolling pin to help transfer the dough onto the form. Gently press the dough into the form, using the fonçage method (pp. 212-213). Trim the edges neatly with a knife, then score the bottom of the tarte with a fork. Brush the bottom of the tarte with the egg white then chill in the fridge until stiff, about 20 minutes.

Note: If making a lattice, remove the reserved quarter of the dough from the fridge. On a lightly floured work surface, use a rolling pin to roll out the dough and any scraps to a 3mm (⅛ inch) thickness. Slide onto a baking tray and chill in the fridge for 20 minutes.

D - Fill and bake your tarte
After 20 minutes, fill and bake your tarte shell as desired.

Note: If making a lattice, remove the rolled out dough from the fridge and cut six 2cm (¾ inch) wide strips from the dough. Crisscross over the top of the tarte filling, then press along the edges and trim as needed. Brush with the egg wash before baking.

Base Recipe: Chocolate Pasta Frolla Dough

The chocolate version of pasta frolla is a personal favorite. It's a very dark and rich dough that makes for loads of contrast and flavor. Like the classic Pasta Frolla, this one also contains baking powder and therefore doesn't blind bake well, but if you'd like to use it to make a profoundly chocolatey blind baked tarte shell, simply leave out the baking powder and use the fonçage method (pp. 212-213).

As with the original Pasta Frolla, when using this dough to bake filled tartes, it's often helpful to brush the base of the tarte with egg white before filling. When baking, the tarte form should always sit directly on the oven rack, rather than on a baking tray, so that air can circulate and bake the bottom.

YIELD: DOUGH FOR ONE 28-30CM (11-12 INCH) TARTE SHELL WITH LATTICE OR ABOUT 700G COOKIE DOUGH FOR ROLLING

For the dough
- 280g (2 ⅓ cups) all-purpose or pastry flour
- 60g (¾ cup) cacao powder
- 4g (1 tsp) baking powder *(Note: omit the baking powder if your recipe calls for blind baking)*
- 170g (¾ cup) unsalted butter, cubed and cold
- 130g (1 cup plus 2 tbsp) confectioners' sugar
- 4g (1 tsp) fleur de sel (or 5g (¾ tsp) table salt)
- 1 large egg, plus 1 large egg yolk, beaten

For baking
- 1 large egg white, whisked

For the egg wash (if making a lattice)
- 1 large egg, plus 3 tbsp whole milk, whisked

A - Mix your dough
In the bowl of a stand mixer fitted with the paddle attachment, combine the all-purpose or pastry flour, cacao powder, baking powder, if using, and butter and beat until sandy. Add the confectioners' sugar and salt and beat on low until uniform. Add the egg and egg yolk and beat on low for 2-3 minutes, or until the dough comes together and is smooth, not crumbly. Form the dough into a disk, wrap airtight, and chill in the fridge for at least 2 hours or for up to 3 days. (This dough can also be frozen for up to 2 months and defrosted overnight in the fridge before using.)

Note: If adding a lattice to your tarte, remove a quarter of the dough, wrap it separately, and chill in the fridge.

B - Break and roll out your dough
When ready to use, on a lightly floured work surface, use a rolling pin to break the chilled dough (p. 212), then roll out to a 3mm (⅛ inch) thickness. Slide onto a nonstick or parchment paper-lined baking tray and chill in the fridge for 20 minutes.

C - Set your tarte
After 20 minutes, remove the dough from the fridge and cut a round of dough large enough to fit the base and sides of your tarte form. Save any scraps to reroll for a lattice, if making. Slide the dough onto the form or use a rolling pin to help transfer the dough onto the form. Gently press the dough into the form, using the fonçage method (pp. 212-213). Trim the edges neatly with a knife, then score the bottom of the tarte with a fork. Brush the bottom of the tarte with the egg white then chill in the fridge until stiff, about 20 minutes.

Note: If making a lattice, remove the reserved quarter of the dough from the fridge. On a lightly floured work surface, use a rolling pin to roll out the dough and any scraps to a 3mm (⅛ inch) thickness. Slide onto a baking tray and chill in the fridge for 20 minutes.

D - Fill and bake your tarte
After 20 minutes, fill and bake your tarte shell as desired.

Note: If making a lattice, remove the rolled out dough from the fridge and cut six 2cm (¾ inch) wide strips from the dough. Crisscross over the top of the tarte filling, then press along the edges and trim as needed. Brush with the egg wash before baking.

Tahini Tarte au Chocolat

One of the prettiest — and my favorite — little pastry shops in Paris is the blue-tiled Maison Aleph. There, Levantine flavors — everything from figs to pistachios to rosewater — merge with Parisian patisserie and vice versa. It's a perfect story of culinary traditions magnifying each other into something even more delicious and is the inspiration for this, a classic tarte au chocolat topped with fudgy tahini ganache. The soft chocolate filling balances the slight bitterness of tahini to make a whole that's something, well, even more wonderful than its parts.

YIELD: ONE 28-30CM (11-12 INCH) TARTE OR FIVE 7CM (2 ¾ INCH) TARTLETS

For the tarte shell
· Ingredients for Basic Tarte Dough (p. 216)

For the chocolate filling
· 2 large eggs
· 25g (3 tbsp plus 1 tsp) all-purpose flour
· 25g (3 tbsp plus 1 ½ tsp) cornstarch
· 100g (½ cup) granulated sugar
· 500g (2 cups plus 3 tbsp) whole milk
· 100g (3 ½ ounces) bittersweet chocolate, chopped
· 50g (3 ½ tbsp) unsalted butter, room temperature
· 1 tsp pure vanilla extract

For the tahini ganache
· 200g (7 ounces) bittersweet chocolate, chopped
· 280g (1 cup plus 1 tbsp) tahini

To finish
· Red currants or berries

Make your tarte shell

Follow the recipe for the Basic Tarte Dough (p. 216, A–C), including setting into one 28-30cm (11-12 inch) tarte form or five 7cm (2 ¾ inch) tartlet forms and chilling in the fridge for 20 minutes.

Preheat the oven to 170°C (340°F) (preferably convection setting).

When ready to bake, prick the base of the chilled tarte shell or tartlet shells all over with a fork. If using 1 large form, blind bake for 12 minutes, or until lightly tan. If using 5 tartlet forms, bake for 8 minutes, or until lightly tan. Let cool completely.

Make your chocolate filling

In a heat-proof medium bowl, whisk together the eggs, all-purpose flour, cornstarch, and half of the granulated sugar. Set aside.

In a medium to large saucepan, heat the milk and the remaining granulated sugar over medium heat until steaming. Add the chopped chocolate and melt, stirring constantly. Remove from the heat and gradually pour half of the hot milk into the egg mixture in a slow, fine stream, whisking constantly to temper the eggs. Pour the tempered egg mixture into the saucepan with the rest of the milk, place over medium-low heat, and bring to a gentle boil, whisking constantly. Continue to gently boil, whisking constantly, for 1–2 minutes, or until thick. Remove from the heat, then add the butter and vanilla and whisk until smooth. Pour the filling directly into the cooled tarte shell or tartlet shells, leaving about 6mm (¼ inch) of space at the top of the pastry, and let cool completely.

Once the filled tarte or tartlets are cool, make your tahini ganache

Using a double boiler or the microwave, melt the chocolate, then stir in the tahini. Pour the mixture on top of the chocolate filling in the tarte shell or tartlet shells, filling it just up to the edge of the pastry. Refrigerate to cool for at least 1 hour before sprinkling with red currants or berries, removing from the tarte form or tartlet forms, and serving.

Pistachio Cloud Tarte

Every time I see a green-colored pastry, I hope for pistachio. Usually, it turns out to be matcha. No offense to matcha — I just really love pistachio. Alas, I live in Northern Europe, and the best pistachios come out of Sicily and Greece, as do the best pistachio treats. When I do get my hands on good pistachios, I like to stretch them by grinding them into a butter and making this ultra-light but hugely flavorful tarte. The filling's mousse-like texture comes from whipped mascarpone set with salted pistachio butter. Raspberries brighten and add a sour note.

Notes: *If you're feeling lazy, skip the tarte shell altogether, spoon the filling into jars, and chill for a whipped pistachio dessert.*

If you don't want to make your own pistachio butter, buy it and stir in fleur de sel to taste. Keep in mind that pistachio butter and pistachio cream are not the same.

YIELD: ONE 28-30CM (11-12 INCH) TARTE OR FIVE 7CM (2 ¾ INCH) TARTLETS

For the tarte shell – Option 1
· Ingredients for Basic Tarte Dough (p. 216)

For the tarte shell – Option 2
· Ingredients for Chocolate Tarte Dough (p. 217)

For the pistachio butter
· 250g (2 cups plus 3 tbsp) lightly salted pistachios
· 35g (5 tbsp) confectioners' sugar
· 2 tbsp olive oil

For the mascarpone filling
· 300g (1⅓ cups) mascarpone
· 300g (1⅓ cups) heavy whipping cream
· 75g (⅔ cups) confectioners' sugar
· 1 tsp pure vanilla extract

For the tarte
· 3 tbsp Raspberry Jam (p. 260)
· 240g (2 cups) fresh raspberries
· 40g (⅓ cup) lightly salted pistachios

Option 1: Make your tarte shell with Basic Tarte Dough
Follow the recipe for the Basic Tarte Dough (p. 216, A–C), including setting the dough into one 28–30cm (11–12 inch) tarte form or five 7cm (2 ¾ inch) tartlet forms and chilling in the fridge for 20 minutes.

Preheat the oven to 170°C (340°F) (preferably convection setting).

When ready to bake, prick the base of the chilled tarte shell or tartlet shells all over with a fork. If using 1 large tarte form, blind bake for 12 minutes, or until lightly tan. If using 5 tartlet forms, blind bake for 8 minutes, or until lightly tan. Let cool completely.

Option 2: Make your tarte shell with Chocolate Tarte Dough
Follow the recipe for the Chocolate Tarte Dough (p. 217, A–C), including setting into one 28–30cm (11–12 inch) tarte form of five 7cm (2 ¾ inch) tartlet forms and chilling in the fridge for 20 minutes.

Preheat the oven to 170°C (340°F) (preferably convection setting).

When ready to bake, prick the base of the chilled tarte shell or tartlet shells all over with a fork. If using 1 large tarte form, blind bake for 12 minutes, or until fragrant and dry. If using 5 tartlet forms, blind bake for 8 minutes, or until fragrant and dry. Let cool completely.

Make your pistachio butter
In a food processor, grind the pistachios and confectioners' sugar to a fine powder. While blending, drizzle in the olive oil. Continue blending for a few minutes, or until the mixture comes together as a paste.

Make your mascarpone filling
In a large bowl, use a spatula to fold the pistachio butter into the mascarpone until smooth. Set aside.

In the chilled bowl of a stand mixer fitted with the whisk attachment, whip the heavy whipping cream, confectioners' sugar, and vanilla on high until stiff peaks form, about 5 minutes. Add the whipped cream to the mascarpone-pistachio mixture and gently fold until it's an even green color with no streaks.

Assemble your tarte
Spread a thin layer of raspberry jam on the bottom of the cooled tarte shell or tartlet shells, then spread an even layer of the pistachio-mascarpone cream on top. Sprinkle with raspberries and pistachios, then chill for at least 2 hours or for up to 2 days before removing from the tarte form or tartlet forms and serving.

Tart Berry Frangipane Tarte

This is a simple snacking tarte similar to an English Bakewell Tarte. It's a good way to use summer berries and fruits, and the sweet almond of the frangipane is particularly gorgeous when loaded with tart fruits like gooseberries, wild blackberries, young plums, or sour cherries. For a richer taste, substitute all or part of the ground almonds for hazelnuts. Bring this to a summer picnic for a chic-but-not-trying-too-hard look.

Notes: For a nice crunchy base to contrast the soft frangipane, I give the tarte a partial blind bake (p. 213) before filling and finishing the bake.

If you want to push the flavor to the best kind of limit, toast whole almonds in the oven until fragrant, then use a food processor to blend them into a fine powder for homemade toasted almond meal

YIELD: ONE 28-30CM (11-12 INCH) TARTE

For the tarte shell
· Ingredients for Basic Tarte Dough (p. 216)

For the frangipane
· 150g (1 ¼ cups) all-purpose or pastry flour
· 300g (3 ½ cups plus 1 tbsp) almond meal
· 200g (¾ cup plus 2 tbsp) unsalted butter, room temperature
· 200g (1 cup) granulated sugar
· 4 large eggs, room temperature
· 2 tsp pure vanilla extract
· 2 tsp rum or walnut liqueur

For the filling and topping
· 200g (1 ⅔ cups) gooseberries or blackberries
· 3 tbsp slivered almonds

For serving
· Cold heavy whipping cream or lightly sweetened sour cream

Make your tarte shell
Follow the recipe for the Basic Tarte Dough (p. 216, A–C), including setting into one 28-30cm (11-12 inch) tarte form and chilling in the fridge for 20 minutes.

Preheat the oven to 170°C (340°F) (preferably convection setting).

When ready to bake, prick the base of the chilled tarte shell all over with a fork. Partially blind bake for 12 minutes, or until lightly tan. Let cool completely.

Make your frangipane
Preheat the oven to 170°C (340°F) (preferably convection setting).

Sift together the all-purpose or pastry flour and almond meal. Set aside.

In the bowl of a stand mixer fitted with the paddle attachment, combine the butter and granulated sugar and beat on medium-high until fluffy. Reduce the speed to medium, then add the eggs, 1 at a time, scraping the bowl with a spatula as needed, until smooth. Add the vanilla and rum and mix to incorporate. Reduce the speed to low, then add the flour mixture in 4 batches. Mix until incorporated, then increase the speed to high and beat for 2–3 minutes, or until light, creamy, and uniform.

Assemble and bake your tarte
Pour the frangipane into the cooled tarte shell and spread evenly. Press the berries into the frangipane then scatter the tarte with slivered almonds. Bake for 40 minutes, or until the frangipane is puffed and the center no longer wiggles. If the top starts to brown too much before it's ready, cover with aluminum foil and continue baking. Cool completely, then remove from the tarte form and serve with cold heavy whipping cream or a bit of lightly sweetened sour cream.

Rhubarb Meringue Tarte

When rhubarb hits farmers markets in late spring, bakeries and pastry shops go wild. It's stuffed into danishes, baked into cakes, and churned into sorbets. And because rhubarb has such a sour flavor, it cooks up into a perfect curd for this very pretty meringue tarte.

Notes: Not all rhubarb is the same — in color or flavor. In England, a special variety of deep red rhubarb is grown in dark forcing sheds in a process that yields a sweet, bright stalk. However, in most of continental Europe — and kitchen gardens the world over — rhubarb varieties tend towards light green and pink. For this reason, I add some strawberries to the curd to naturally brighten and sweeten the tarte without compromising the rhubarb flavor.

I like this recipe equally with a plain or chocolate tarte shell. Opting for the chocolate will give you even more contrast and a richer flavor profile.

YIELD: ONE 28-30CM (11-12 INCH) TARTE

For the tarte shell - Option 1
· Ingredients for Basic Tarte Dough (p. 216)

For the tarte shell - Option 2
· Ingredients for Chocolate Pasta Frolla Dough (p. 219), omitting the baking powder

For the rhubarb curd
· 2 large eggs, plus 1 large egg yolk
· 30g (¼ cup) cornstarch
· 200g (1 cup) granulated sugar
· 425g (3 ½ cups) cubed rhubarb (fresh or frozen)
· 200g (1 ⅔ cups) halved strawberries
· 65g (4 ½ tbsp) fresh lemon juice
· 1 tbsp peeled and chopped fresh ginger
· 75g (⅓ cup) unsalted butter, cubed and room temperature

For the tarte
· Italian Meringue (p. 267)

Option 1: Make your tarte shell with Basic Tarte Dough
Follow the recipe for the Basic Tarte Dough (p. 216, A-C), including setting the dough into one 28-30cm (11-12 inch) tarte form and chilling in the fridge for 20 minutes.

Preheat the oven to 170°C (340°F) (preferably convection setting).

When ready to bake, prick the base of the chilled tarte shell all over with a fork. Blind bake for 12 minutes, or until lightly tan. Let cool completely.

Option 2: Make your tarte shell with Chocolate Pasta Frolla Dough
Follow the recipe for the Chocolate Pasta Frolla Dough (p. 219, A-B), omitting the baking powder. Set the dough into one 28-30cm (11-12 inch) tarte form, prick the base all over with a fork, brush the base with egg white, and chill in the fridge for 20 minutes (p. 219, C).

Preheat the oven to 170°C (340°F) (preferably convection setting).

Blind bake for 12 minutes, or until fragrant and dry. Let cool completely.

Make your rhubarb curd
In a heat-proof medium bowl, whisk together the eggs, egg yolk, cornstarch and half of the granulated sugar until smooth. Set aside.

In a medium saucepan, bring the rhubarb, strawberries, lemon juice, ginger, and the rest of the granulated sugar to a simmer over low heat. Continue simmering, stirring occasionally, until the sugar is dissolved and the fruit softens and falls apart. Strain the mixture through a fine-mesh sieve, using a wooden spoon to help extract every last bit of juice. Discard the pulp.

Gradually pour the hot strained juice into the egg mixture in a slow, fine stream, whisking constantly to temper the eggs. Return the mixture to the saucepan and bring to a gentle boil, whisking constantly, over low heat. Continue gently boiling and whisking until the curd starts to thicken. Gently boil and whisk for 2 more minutes, then remove from the heat and immediately stir in the butter. Pour the curd directly into your cooled tarte shell and let cool completely.

Make your Italian Meringue (p. 267)
Spoon the meringue over the curd in big fluffy swoops. If you like, hit the edges with a kitchen torch. Keep refrigerated until ready to serve or for up to 3 days. Remove from the tarte form before serving.

Salted Caramel Mousse Tarte

This tarte hides a gooey layer of salted caramel under dark chocolate mousse, but not just any mousse. It's the simplest and best chocolate mousse I've ever encountered — it's perfectly feathery yet firm enough to always hold its shape. Joelle Courant, a very kind beekeeper in Normandy, taught me this mousse recipe, and I'm forever grateful. You will be, too. Did you know that bees can communicate up to 200 words with their wings? Joelle also taught me that.

YIELD: ONE 28-30CM (11-12 INCH) TARTE

For the tarte shell - Option 1
· Ingredients for Chocolate Tarte Dough (p. 217)

For the tarte shell - Option 2
· Ingredients for Chocolate Pasta Frolla Dough (p. 219), omitting the baking powder

For the salted caramel
· Caramel (p. 264)

For the chocolate mousse
· 300g (11 ounces) dark chocolate, chopped
· 8 large eggs, separated
· 60g (¼ cup) espresso or strong coffee, cooled
· 1 tsp pure vanilla extract
· ¼ tsp fleur de sel

For serving
· Maldon salt

Option 1: Make your tarte shell with Chocolate Tarte Dough
Follow the recipe for the Chocolate Tarte Dough (p. 218, A-C), including setting into one 28-30cm (11-12 inch) tarte form and chilling in the fridge for 20 minutes.

Preheat the oven to 170°C (340°F) (preferably convection setting).

When ready to bake, prick the base of the chilled tarte shell all over with a fork. Blind bake for 12 minutes, or until fragrant and dry. Let cool completely.

Option 2: Make your tarte shell with Chocolate Pasta Frolla Dough
Follow the recipe for the Chocolate Pasta Frolla Dough (p. 219, A-B), omitting the baking powder. Set the dough into one 28-30cm (11-12 inch) tarte form, prick the base all over with a fork, brush the base with egg white, and chill in the fridge for 20 minutes (p. 219, C).

Preheat the oven to 170°C (340°F) (preferably convection setting).

Blind bake for 12 minutes, or until fragrant and dry. Let cool completely.

While the tarte shell cools, make your Caramel (p. 264)

Once the filled tarte is completely cool, make your chocolate mousse
Using a double boiler or the microwave, melt the chocolate.

In a large bowl, whisk together the egg yolks, espresso, vanilla, and salt. Gradually add the melted chocolate in a slow, fine stream, whisking constantly to temper the eggs. Set aside and let cool to room temperature.

Once the chocolate mixture comes to room temperature, in the bowl of a stand mixer fitted with the whisk attachment, whip the egg whites on high until stiff peaks form. Gently fold the whipped egg whites, a quarter at a time, into the chocolate mixture. Continue folding until no egg white is visible.

Assemble your tarte
Spread a thick layer of caramel on the base of the tarte shell, then fill it up to the top with the chocolate mousse, spreading it evenly. Chill in the fridge for 2-3 hours, or until set. Remove from the tarte form and sprinkle with Maldon salt before serving.

Note: For a tidy slice, dip the knife in boiling water between cuts.

Sablés, Plain and Fancy

Sablés are buttery shortbread-adjacent cookies that, depending on who you ask, get their name from either their sandy texture or the town of Sablé-sur-Sarthe. But since a mouthful of sand isn't really appealing, I'm just gonna spoil the surprise and say these cookies really aren't sandy — they're tender with a bit of crunch and crumble. You can transform these to suit any taste with the addition of toasted grains and spices, dried fruits, and chopped nuts.

YIELD: ABOUT 25 SABLÉS

- 220g (1 ¾ cups plus 1 tbsp) all-purpose, light stone-ground wheat, or spelt flour
- 2g (½ tsp) baking powder
- 120g (½ cup plus 1 tbsp) unsalted butter, cubed and cold
- 65g (⅔ cup) almond flour or 65g (¾ cup) almond, walnut, or hazelnut meal
- 60g (½ cup plus 1 tsp) confectioners' sugar
- 2g (½ tsp) fleur de sel
- 1 large egg
- 2 tsp pure vanilla extract
- Granulated sugar, for rolling (optional)

In a medium to large bowl, whisk together the all-purpose, light stone-ground wheat, or spelt flour and the baking powder until combined, then follow the same steps as the Basic Tarte Dough to mix your dough (p. 216, A). Once your dough has come together, turn it out onto a sheet of parchment paper and form it into a long log that's about 3cm (1 ¼ inches) in diameter. Roll up the log in the paper and wrap it tightly to create a firm tube. Chill in the fridge for at least 1 hour or for up to 5 days. (The log of dough can also be frozen for up to 2 months and defrosted overnight in the fridge.)

Preheat the oven to 170°C (340°F) (preferably convection setting).

To add an optional sugar edge to your cookies, spread some granulated sugar on a plate, then roll the log of dough in the sugar.

Slice the log at 1cm (⅓ inch) intervals to create cookies. Place the cookies, 1–2cm (⅓–¾ inch) apart, on a parchment paper-lined baking tray and bake for 10 minutes, or until the bottoms are golden brown.

VARIATIONS:

Chocolate Pistachio Sablés

- 200g (1 ⅔ cups) all-purpose or pastry flour
- 25g (5 tbsp) cacao powder
- 2g (½ tsp) baking powder
- 120g (½ cup plus 1 tbsp) unsalted butter, cubed and cold
- 65g (⅔ cups) almond flour
- 75g (⅔ cups) confectioners' sugar
- 2g (½ tsp) fleur de sel
- 1 large egg
- 5g (1 tsp) pure vanilla extract
- 50g (⅓ cup) chopped unsalted pistachios
- 70g (⅔ cup) ground pistachios for rolling

Follow the base recipe, but add the cacao powder with the all-purpose or pastry flour and add the chopped pistachios after the dough has come together. Roll the log in ground pistachios before cutting and baking.

Buckwheat, Cranberry, and White Chocolate Sablés

- 220g (1 ¾ cups plus 1 tbsp) all-purpose, light stone-ground wheat, or spelt flour
- 50g (⅓ cup plus 1 tbsp) dark buckwheat flour
- 2g (½ tsp) baking powder
- 120g (½ cup plus 1 tbsp) unsalted butter
- 60g (½ cup plus 1 tbsp) confectioners' sugar
- 3g (¾ tsp) fleur de sel
- 1 large egg
- 10g (2 tsp) pure vanilla extract
- 100g (3 ½ ounces) white chocolate chopped into small pieces
- 38g (⅓cup) dried cranberries, chopped

Follow the base recipe, but add the buckwheat flour with the all-purpose, light stone-ground wheat, or spelt flour and add the white chocolate and cranberries after the dough has come together.

Oat, Golden Raisin, and Dark Chocolate Sablés

- 170g (1 ½ cups) all-purpose, light stone-ground wheat, or spelt flour
- 70g (¾cup) finely ground oats or oat flour
- 2g (½ tsp) baking powder
- 120g (½ cup plus 1 tbsp) unsalted butter
- 60g (½ cup plus 1 tbsp) confectioners' sugar
- 3g (¾ tsp) fleur de sel
- 1 large egg
- 10g (2 tsp) pure vanilla extract
- 100g (3 ½ ounces) mini dark chocolate chips
- 75g (½ cup) dried golden raisins, chopped

Follow the base recipe, but add the ground oats with the all-purpose, light stone-ground wheat, or spelt flour and add the mini chocolate chips and golden raisins after the dough has come together.

Lemon Zest and Green Fennel Sablés

- 220g (1 ¾cups) all-purpose, light stone-ground wheat, or spelt flour
- 10g (2 tsp) green fennel seeds, toasted
- Zest of 1 lemon
- 2g (½ tsp) baking powder
- 120g (½ cup) unsalted butter, cubed and cold
- 65g (⅔ cups) almond flour
- 60g (½ cup plus 1 tbsp) confectioners' sugar
- 3g (¾ tsp) fleur de sel
- 1 large egg
- 10g (2 tsp) pure vanilla extract

Follow the base recipe, but add the green fennel seeds and the lemon zest with the all-purpose, light stone-ground wheat, or spelt flour.

Espresso Espresso Biscuits

I'm a little overly affectionate — protective, even — towards the sort of Central European coffee houses and Southern European espresso bars that are as much tied to a sense of place as they are to their clients and the unpretentious coffee they serve. In a world where one bland Scandi-minimal cafe blends into the next, it's the details of the old spots — be it miniature metal trays or strings of local lottery tickets — that give one hope. If you're lucky, the giveaway detail is a little biscuit — amaretto, speculoos, chocolate — placed by your cup. It's a little treat to make the bitter go down and just maybe even help you find yourself on a map. Too sentimental? We're in so deep already, might as well go spot on and bake some espresso biscuits and hope that some things might manage to go overlooked by change and time.

Note: For a fluffier filling, once the chocolate and espresso cream is cooled, whip it until light and airy.

YIELD: ABOUT 25 SMALL SANDWICH COOKIES

For the cookies
· Ingredients for Chocolate Pasta Frolla Dough (p. 219)

For the filling
· 200g (7 ounces) dark chocolate, finely chopped
· 130g (½ cup plus 1 tbsp) heavy whipping cream
· 4 tsp espresso powder

Make your cookies
Follow the recipe for the Chocolate Pasta Frolla Dough to mix your dough (p. 219, A), form the dough into a disk, and chill in the fridge for at least 1 hour or for up to 3 days.

Once the dough is chilled, on a lightly floured work surface, use a rolling pin to break the dough then roll out to about a 2.5mm (¹⁄₁₀ inch) thickness (p. 212). Slide the dough onto a baking tray and chill for 10 minutes in the freezer or 30 minutes in the fridge to make cutting out the cookies easier.

Preheat the oven to 170°C (340°F) (preferably convection setting).

Once the rolled out dough is chilled, use a tiny cookie cutter — I like to use a small heart-shaped cutter — to cut out as many cookies as possible. Reroll and cut any dough scraps. Arrange the cookies, 1–2cm (⅓-¾ inch) apart, on a parchment paper-lined baking tray and bake for 5-7 minutes, or until slightly puffed with firm edges — the short bake keeps the cookies soft rather than crunchy. Let cool completely.

While the cookies cool, make your filling
Put the chopped chocolate in a heat-proof medium bowl.

In a small saucepan, warm the heavy whipping cream and espresso powder over low heat until steaming. Pour over the chopped chocolate and stir to melt the chocolate completely. Chill the mixture in the fridge for about 30 minutes until cool but don't let it harden.

Once the filling is cool, spread it on the flat side of half of the cookies, then top with the remaining cookies to create sandwiches. Store in an airtight container and serve all week.

Spicy Ginger Caramel Shortbread

Once, in a Scottish bakery, I ordered millionaire's shortbread — caramel and chocolate layered onto the country's famously rich shortbread — and presumed I knew what I was in for. But what I didn't expect was a caramel layer buzzing with ginger. It was magnificent. Despite looking for caramel with that same zip ever since, I've never found its equal. Good thing there's no need to search for what you can make at home. This is the recipe I make when the craving strikes. There's enough ginger in this caramel to make your cheeks tingle. Which is the point.

Notes: Dip your shortbreads straight into the caramel for gloss, or spread and fill two cookies to make a sandwich.

For a millionaire's shortbread effect, dip caramel cookies in melted or tempered dark chocolate.

YIELD: ABOUT 20 COOKIES

For the cookies
· Ingredients for Pasta Frolla Dough (p. 218)

For the ginger caramel
· 200g (1 cup) granulated sugar
· 120g (½ cup) water
· 50g (3 ½ tbsp) unsalted butter, room temperature
· 2 tsp ground ginger (for extra zip, do a full tablespoon!)
· 120g (½ cup plus 1 tbsp) heavy whipping cream
· 2 tsp pure vanilla extract
· ½ tsp fleur de sel

Make your cookies
Follow the recipe for Pasta Frolla Dough to mix your dough (p. 218, A), then form the dough into a disk and chill in the fridge for at least 2 hours or for up to 3 days.

Preheat the oven to 170°C (340°F) (preferably convection setting).

Once the dough is chilled, on a lightly floured surface, use a rolling pin to break the dough, then roll out to about a 5mm (⅕ inch) thickness (p. 212). Use a 5cm (2 inch) round cookie cutter to cut about 20 cookies. Arrange the cookies on a parchment paper-lined baking tray and prick each one 3 times with a fork. Bake for 8 minutes, or until just golden. If you like a crispier cookie, bake them as long as 12 minutes. Set aside to cool.

While the cookies are cooling, make your ginger caramel
In a heavy-bottomed medium saucepan, melt the granulated sugar and water over low heat, without stirring, until no more sugar granules are visible. Let come to a gentle boil, then continue gently boiling for 3 minutes. Add the butter and let melt, stirring to incorporate, then stop stirring and let come to a boil. Continue boiling, without stirring, for a few minutes, or until the light yellow syrup darkens to a medium honey color. Add the ginger and give the mixture a quick whisk. Remove from the heat and immediately add the heavy whipping cream, vanilla, and salt. It will splutter and bubble, but just keep stirring until smooth, then set aside to cool and thicken for about 20 minutes.

Once the caramel is a bit cooler, give it a stir to get rid of any skin that might have formed. Dip half of each cookie in the caramel, place on a wire rack set over parchment paper to catch the drips, and let cool completely. Enjoy!

Rye Speculoos

Speculoos is as much a reason as the waffles and fries to wear elastic waist pants when you visit Brussels. It's gingerbread's crunchy Belgian cousin and while these cookies are indeed spiced like gingerbread, most of the flavor and texture comes from Candi sugar, a particular caramelized sugar Belgian beer makers also use in the brewing process. Since Candi sugar can be hard to get a hold of, this recipe uses Demerara sugar and rye flour for a similar snap and flavor. Use a cookie cutter, wooden mold, or knife to shape these.

YIELD: ABOUT 20 COOKIES

For the cookies
· 145g (10 tbsp plus 1 tsp) unsalted butter
· 230g (1 cup plus 2 tsp) Demerara sugar
· 1 large egg
· 225g (2 ¼ cups) light rye flour
· 5g (1 ¼ tsp) baking powder
· ½ tsp fleur de sel
· 1 tsp ground cinnamon
· ½ tsp freshly grated nutmeg
· ¼ tsp ground cloves
· ¼ tsp ground cardamom

For the topping
· Whole or slivered almonds (optional)

In the bowl of a stand mixer fitted with the paddle attachment, combine the butter and Demerara sugar and beat until fluffy. Add the egg and beat until fully combined.

In a medium bowl, whisk together the light rye flour, baking powder, salt, cinnamon, nutmeg, cloves, and cardamom. With the mixer on low, add the flour mixture to the butter mixture in 4 batches. Mix until fully incorporated. Form the dough into a disk, wrap airtight, and chill in the fridge for at least 30 minutes or for up to 3 days.

When ready to bake the cookies, preheat the oven to 170°C (340°F) (preferably convection setting).

On a lightly floured work surface, use a rolling pin to roll out the dough to a 4mm (⅙ inch) thickness. Using 5cm (2 inch) cookie cutters, cookie presses, or a molded rolling pin, cut the dough into cookies. Arrange the cookies, 2cm (¾ inch) apart, on 2 parchment paper-lined baking trays and top with whole or slivered almonds, if using. Bake for 10–12 minutes, or until golden brown. Cool and enjoy. These cookies will stay crisp in a sealed tin or jar for up to a month.

Parisian Flan

Once a baker's bread bake is over, the stones that line a professional oven can radiate heat for days. Flan, a creamy baked custard tarte, is one of the ways French bakers have traditionally harnessed this excess heat. Though you'll find it in just about every boulangerie, there's a lot of mediocre flan out there — bakers often cut corners by using powdered mixes. I've known French bakers to go on rants about these faux flans. But, if you know the difference, you know the passion is justified, as little compares to made-from-scratch flan. If you've never had flan before, fit this recipe into your life in the same place you'd put a great cheesecake. It's so good, I often double the recipe.

Note: The custard filling for this flan is made just like a Pastry Cream (p. 262); the slow room temperature cooling will prevent the surface from cracking so don't cheat!

YIELD: 1 TALL 20CM (8-INCH) FLAN

For the tarte shell
· Ingredients for Basic Tarte Dough (p. 216)

For the custard filling
· 3 large eggs
· 150g (¾ cup) granulated sugar
· 38g (5 tbsp) all-purpose or pastry flour
· 38g (⅓ cup) cornstarch
· 950g (4 cups plus 3 tbsp) whole milk
· Seeds of ½ vanilla bean
· 75g (⅓ cup) unsalted butter, cubed and room temperature
· 1 tsp pure vanilla extract

For the topping
· Simple Syrup (p. 266)

Make your tarte shell
Follow the recipe for the Basic Tarte Dough to mix your dough (p. 216, A) and chill in the fridge for at least 2 hours or for up to 3 days.

Once the dough is chilled, divide it into thirds. On a lightly floured work surface, use a rolling pin to break then roll the first third out to a 3mm (⅛ inch) thickness (p. 212). Use a 20cm (8 inch) nonstick springform pan that is 7cm (2¾ inches) tall to trace and cut a circle of dough. Set this circle in the base of the pan.

Roll the remaining 2 portions of dough into two 32cm (13 inch) long strips, both 8-9cm (3¼-3½ inches) wide — a bit taller than the height of the pan. Trim the sides of each strip to make long rectangles, then press both strips into place to form the sides of the tarte shell. Where these strips meet, trim any overlap and press the dough together to make a seam. Finally, press along the bottom seam where the sides meet the base to seal them together with the fonçage technique (pp. 212-213). Use a knife to trim the top rim so the dough is tidy and level with the pan, then prick holes in the base with a fork and chill in the freezer for at least 15 minutes or until ready to fill.

While the tarte shell is chilling, make your custard filling
In a large bowl, whisk together the eggs, half of the granulated sugar, the all-purpose or pastry flour, and the cornstarch until smooth. Set aside.

In a medium saucepan, warm 755g (3⅓ cup) of the milk, the remaining granulated sugar, and the vanilla bean seeds over low heat until steaming. Remove from the heat. Gradually add the hot milk mixture to the egg mixture in a slow, fine stream, whisking constantly to temper the eggs. Once all the milk is incorporated, return the mixture to the saucepan and place over low heat. Whisking constantly, allow the mixture to bubble and thicken, then add the remaining 195g (¾ cup plus 2 tbsp) of milk and whisk until smooth. Remove from the heat, then add the butter and vanilla extract and stir until the butter is melted.

Set a rack in the middle of the oven and preheat the oven to 175°C (350°F) (preferably convection setting).

Assemble and bake your flan
Pour the custard into the chilled tarte shell, then bake on the middle rack for 12 minutes. Lower the oven temperature to 115°C (240°F) and continue baking for 50 minutes, or until the flan has pretty brown spots on top and still has a strong wiggle. Remove the flan from the oven and gently brush the top with Simple Syrup (p. 266), being careful not to break the surface. Let cool at room temperature for 4-5 hours, then chill in the fridge for at least 1 hour before removing the sides of the springform pan and serving. The flan will keep for up to 5 days in an airtight container in the fridge.

Halva Flan

Nowadays, you'll find flan in every color and flavor under the sun. This is because flan is such an easy recipe to tweak — simply flavor the pastry cream base with extracts, nut butters, jams, liqueurs, or zests (p. 262). Whether you like pistachio, lemon, peanut, or coffee, there are no limits. If it can exist as a pudding, it can exist as a flan. But for all the flans out there, this halva flan is my favorite. It's extra creamy and rich and the addition of tahini lends a smooth sesame halva taste. Top it with crumbled sesame halva after baking or leave it plain for a more classic look. I find the best way to enjoy this flan is directly from the refrigerator, any time after midnight, and preferably standing up with the fridge door open. Share with no one.

YIELD: 1 TALL 20CM (8-INCH) FLAN

For the tarte shell
· Ingredients for Chocolate Pasta Frolla Dough (p. 219), omitting the baking powder

For the halva custard filling
· 3 large eggs
· 133g (⅔ cup) granulated sugar
· 15g (2 tsp) honey
· 38g (5 tbsp) all-purpose or pastry flour
· 38g (⅓ cup) cornstarch
· 950g (4 cups plus 3 tbsp) whole milk
· 150g (½ cup plus 1 tbsp) tahini
· 75g (⅓ cup) unsalted butter, cubed
· 10g (2 tsp) pure vanilla extract

For the topping
· Simple Syrup (p. 266)

Make your tarte shell
Follow the recipe for the Chocolate Pasta Frolla Dough to mix your dough (p. 219, A), omitting the baking powder, and chill in the fridge for at least 2 hours or for up to 3 days.

Once the dough is chilled, divide it into thirds. On a lightly floured work surface, use a rolling pin to break then roll the first third out to a 3mm (⅛ inch) thickness (p. 212). Use a 20cm (8 inch) nonstick springform pan that is 7cm (2 ¾ inches) tall to trace and cut a circle of dough. Set this circle in the base of the pan.

Roll the remaining 2 portions of dough into two 32cm (13 inch) long strips, both 8-9cm (3 ¼-3 ½ inches) wide — a bit taller than the height of the pan. Trim the sides of each strip to make long rectangles, then press both strips into place to form the sides of the tarte shell. Where these strips meet, trim any overlap and press the dough together to make a seam. Finally, press along the bottom seam where the sides meet the base to seal them together with the fonçage technique (pp. 212-213). Use a knife to trim the top rim so the dough is tidy and level with the pan, then prick holes in the base with a fork and chill in the freezer for at least 15 minutes or until ready to fill.

While the tarte shell is chilling, make your custard filling
In a large bowl, whisk together the eggs, half of the granulated sugar, the honey, the all-purpose or pastry flour, and the cornstarch until smooth. Set aside.

In a medium saucepan, warm 755g (3 ⅓ cups) of the milk and the remaining granulated sugar over low heat until steaming. Remove from the heat. Gradually add the hot milk mixture to the egg mixture in a slow, fine stream, whisking constantly to temper the eggs. Once all the milk is incorporated, return the mixture to the saucepan and place over low heat. Whisking constantly, allow the mixture to bubble and thicken, then add the remaining 195g (¾ cup plus 2 tbsp) of milk and whisk until smooth. Remove from the heat, then add the tahini, butter, and vanilla extract and stir until the butter is melted.

Assemble and bake your flan
Set a rack in the middle of the oven and preheat the oven to 175°C (350°F) (preferably convection setting).

Pour the custard into the chilled tarte shell and bake on the middle rack for 12 minutes. Lower the oven temperature to 115°C (240°F) and continue baking for 50 minutes, or until the flan has pretty brown spots on top and still has a strong wiggle. Remove the flan from the oven and gently brush the top with Simple Syrup, being careful not to break the surface. Let cool at room temperature for 4-5 hours, then chill in the fridge for at least 1 hour before removing the sides of the springform pan and serving. The flan will keep for up to 5 days in an airtight container in the fridge.

Crostata Ricotta e Visciole ·
Ricotta and Sour Cherry Pie

Up for a where-have-you-been-all-my-life moment? Try a Crostata Ricotta e Visciole, a specialty of the Jewish bakeries of Rome. It's a creamy ricotta and sour cherry crostata with the texture of a light cheesecake. The foods of Jewish Rome are unique in the European diaspora, and the baked goods are no exception. Even the challahs are often full of glazed fruits and ornamental sugar like so many Italian sweet breads. This crostata, however, is the true gem of these local bakeries. Keep this technicolor and vintage-looking with a lattice and candied cherries on top.

Note: Sour cherries are traditional, but if they're out of season, substitute jam or whatever fruit you have.

YIELD: ONE 28–30CM (11–12 INCH) TARTE

For the tarte shell
· Ingredients for Pasta Frolla Dough (p. 218)

For the sour cherry filling
· 500g (3 ¼ cups) sour cherries, pitted
· 200g (1 cup) granulated sugar
· 10g (1 ½ tbsp) cornstarch
· 2 tsp fresh lemon juice

For the ricotta filling
· 500g (18 ounces) ricotta
· 84g (¾ cup) confectioners' sugar
· 2 large egg yolks
· Zest of ½ lemon
· 2 tsp fresh lemon juice

For the egg wash
· 1 large egg, plus 3 tbsp whole milk, whisked

For the topping
· Pearl sugar
· Fresh or candied cherries

Make your tarte dough
Follow the recipe for Pasta Frolla Dough (p. 218, A), following the instructions for making a lattice. Chill both portions of dough in the fridge for at least 2 hours or for up to 3 days.

While the tarte dough is chilling, make your sour cherry filling
In a medium saucepan, bring the cherries, granulated sugar, and cornstarch to a simmer over low heat. Once the cherries release their liquid and the sugar is melted, add the lemon juice and bring to a low boil. Continue gently boiling until the mixture thickens. Set aside to cool.

Make your ricotta filling
In a large bowl, whisk together the ricotta, confectioners' sugar, egg yolks, lemon zest, and lemon juice until smooth. Set aside.

Assemble and bake your pie
Preheat the oven 170°C (340°F) (preferably convection setting).

On a lightly floured work surface, use a rolling pin to break the larger portion of dough, then roll, cut, and set the tarte shell (p. 218, B–C). When set, brush the bottom of the tarte shell with the egg white, then chill in the freezer for 10 minutes.

To make your lattice, remove the reserved dough from the fridge, roll it out, and chill in the fridge for 10 minutes (p. 218, C *note*).

Once the tarte shell is chilled, spread an even layer of the sour cherry filling in the base, then fill the rest of the way with the ricotta filling. Remove the rolled out dough for the lattice from the fridge, cut it into strips, and crisscross over the top of the ricotta filling (p. 218, D *note*). Brush the lattice with the egg wash, then sprinkle with pearl sugar and bake directly on the oven rack for 45 minutes, or until the lattice is golden, the filling has puffed, and the tarte only has the slightest wiggle. If the lattice starts to brown too much, loosely cover it with aluminum foil and continue baking. Let the tarte cool, then garnish with fresh or candied cherries before removing from the tarte form and serving. The tarte will keep in the fridge for up to 5 days.

Raspberry Oat Slice

The inspiration for this raspberry slice is the Danish bakery treat hindbaersnitter, a classic after-school snack. The original hindbaersnitter is what the Danes call tørkage — literally "dry cake" — but it really tastes something like a cookie. Served in slices and filled with raspberry jam, it's topped with a sugar glaze and sprinkles and looks a little like a Pop Tart. This version features an oat cookie base and skips the sprinkles, so it's a bit grownup. If the sprinkles from the original speak to you, though, please don't let me kill your joy.

Note: Fill with raspberry jam, or go wild with blueberry or fig jam, or even orange marmalade — whatever you have on hand.

YIELD: 14 COOKIES

For the cookie dough
- 400g (3 ⅓ cups) all-purpose or pastry flour
- 220g (2 ½ cups) oat flour
- 10g (2 tsp) baking powder
- 320g (1 ½ cups plus 1 ½ tbsp) unsalted butter, cubed and cold
- 120g (1 ⅓ cups) quick-cooking oats
- 227g (2 cups) confectioners' sugar
- 8g (2 tsp) fleur de sel
- ¾ tsp ground cinnamon
- 2 large eggs, plus 2 large egg yolks, whisked
- 1 tbsp light molasses

For the filling
- 340g (1 cup) Raspberry Jam (p. 260)

For the glaze
- 113g (1 cup) confectioners' sugar
- 2 tsp hot water

Make your cookie dough
In the bowl of a stand mixer fitted with the paddle attachment, combine the all-purpose or pastry flour, the oat flour, the baking powder, and butter and beat on low until sandy. Add the oats, confectioners' sugar, and salt and mix until incorporated. Add the eggs, egg yolks, and molasses and mix until the dough comes together into a sturdy mass. Divide the dough in half, then press into 2 rough rectangles. Wrap airtight and chill in the fridge for 30 minutes.

Once the dough is chilled, line 2 baking trays with parchment paper and lightly dust with flour. Place a rectangle of dough on each baking tray and use a rolling pin to roll out into 2 even rectangles that are about 4mm (1/6 inch) thick and fill the dimensions of the baking tray. Chill in the freezer for 10 minutes or in the fridge for 30 minutes.

Preheat the oven to 170°C (340°F) (preferably convection setting).

Fill and bake your cookies
Once the rolled out dough is chilled, prick each rectangle all over with a fork. Spread jam in an even layer on one of the rectangles, going all the way to the edges. Use the parchment paper to lift and slide the unfilled rectangle onto the jam layer. Make sure the rectangles match, then trim the edges. Bake for 20 minutes, or until the cookie is golden brown. Let cool for 15 minutes.

While the cookies are cooling, make your glaze
In a small bowl, whisk together the confectioners' sugar and hot water until smooth.

Cut the cooled cookies into 14 even rectangles, drizzle with the glaze, and enjoy. These cookies can be stored in an airtight container for about 5 days. If storing, go light on the glaze and allow it to cool and dry before stacking and storing.

Strawberry Cream Rounds

This is a simple dessert with all the crunch and cream of a tarte, but none of the fuss. It's Neapolitan ice cream flavored — strawberry, vanilla, chocolate — which is the best flavor, but if you disagree, sartorialize yours with any flavor of Pastry Cream (p. 262) or any variety of fruit. Serve with whipped cream and a cherry for a nostalgic look.

Note: Both the Pastry Cream and cookie base can be made well in advance, making this an easy dessert to assemble for a dinner party.

YIELD: 12 CREAM ROUNDS

For the cookie base
· Ingredients for Chocolate Tarte Dough (p. 217) or Chocolate Pasta Frolla Dough (p. 219)

For the filling
· Vanilla Pastry Cream (p. 262), chilled

For the whipped cream
· 300g (1 ⅓ cups) heavy whipping cream, cold
· 75g (⅔ cup) confectioners' sugar

For the topping
· 500g (4 cups) small strawberries
· 12 candied, maraschino, or fresh cherries

Make your cookie base
Follow the recipe for the Chocolate Tarte Dough (p. 217, A) or Chocolate Pasta Frolla Dough (219, A) to mix your dough and chill in the fridge for at least 2 hours or for up to 3 days.

While the tarte dough is chilling, make your filling
Follow the recipe for the Vanilla Pastry Cream (p. 262) and chill in the fridge until ready to use.

Preheat the oven to 170°C (340°F) (preferably convection setting).

Once the dough is chilled, on a lightly floured work surface, use a rolling pin to break it, then roll out to a 4mm (⅛ inch) thickness. Use a 10cm (4 inch) round or square cookie cutter to cut the dough into 12 cookie bases. Arrange, 2cm (¾ inch) apart, on a parchment paper-lined baking tray and bake for 10 minutes, or until the cookies have puffed a bit and the edges hold their shape when pressed with a finger. Let cool completely.

When the cookie bases are completely cool, make your whipped cream
In the chilled bowl of a stand mixer fitted with the whisk attachment, whip the heavy whipping cream and confectioners' sugar on high until stiff peaks form.

Assemble your cream rounds
Whisk the chilled Pastry Cream until smooth then spoon or pipe onto each cookie base. Arrange the strawberries on top, then spoon or pipe whipped cream in the middle. Finish each cream round with a cherry and serve.

Pink Grapefruit Curd Linzers

Linzers are nutty Austrian windowpane cookies. I used to live with a poorly-chosen boyfriend in Prague, above a Ukrainian convenience store that got a delivery of linzers once a week — lest we forget that Czechia was a part of the former empire. The linzers were big and heart-shaped and usually so stale and soft that they'd crumble apart at the first bite and fall on the cobblestones. After staring at enough broken hearts on the sidewalk, I decided it was a sign and broke up with the guy. Linzers, on the other hand, are a great cookie — I'd never dump them. Here's my version, made with a bit of toasted walnut and a pretty pink grapefruit curd.

Notes: *For an original jam linzer, use the same cookie recipe and sub the curd for any red jam.*

In place of beet juice, you can use a quarter of a peeled beet instead. Cook the beet with the grapefruit juice and sugar, then remove it before you temper the eggs.

YIELD: 12 COOKIES

For the cookie dough
· 65g (¾ cup) walnut meal
· 220g (1 ¾ cups plus 1 tbsp) all-purpose or pastry flour
· 120g (½ cup plus 1 tbsp) unsalted butter, cubed and cold
· 60g (½ cup plus 1 tbsp) confectioners' sugar, sifted, plus more for dusting
· ½ tsp fleur de sel
· 1 large egg, whisked
· 1 tsp pure vanilla extract

For the curd
· 3 large egg yolks
· 50g (¼ cup) beet juice or ¼ beet, washed and peeled
· 14g (2 tbsp) cornstarch
· 133g (⅔ cup) granulated sugar
· 227g (1 cup) fresh ruby red grapefruit juice
· 28g (2 tbsp) unsalted butter

Make your cookie dough
In a dry frying pan, toast the walnut meal over low heat, stirring occasionally, until aromatic and slightly tanned. Let cool completely.

In a large bowl, toss together the all-purpose or pastry flour and the butter cubes until the butter is coated. Rub the butter and flour together between your thumb and fingers until it has a uniform sandy texture and there are no visible bits of butter. Add the toasted walnut meal, confectioners' sugar, and salt and mix, continuing the rubbing motion with your fingers, until homogenous. Add the egg and vanilla, and mix by hand until just incorporated and there are no dry bits, being careful not to overwork the dough. Form the dough into a flattened disk, wrap airtight, and refrigerate for at least 2 hours or for up to 3 days.

Once the dough is chilled, on a lightly floured work surface, use a rolling pin to break it, then roll out to a 3mm (⅛ inch) thickness (p. 212). Slide the dough onto a parchment paper-lined baking tray and chill in the fridge for 15 minutes to make cutting out the cookies easier.

Preheat the oven to 170°C (340°F) (preferably convection setting).

Once the dough is chilled again, use a 7-10cm (2 ¾-4 inch) round cookie cutter to cut 24 cookies. With a smaller cookie cutter or shot glass, cut small holes or "windows" in half of the cookies. Arrange the cookies, 3cm (1 ¼ inch) apart, on a parchment paper-lined baking tray and bake for 10 minutes, or until the edges just start to tan. Let cool completely. While the cookies cool, bake off the small cut-outs — these are for snacking!.

While the cookies are cooling, make your grapefruit curd
In a heat-proof medium bowl, whisk together the egg yolks, beet juice, cornstarch, and half of the granulated sugar.

In a large saucepan, warm the grapefruit juice and the remaining granulated sugar over low heat until steaming. Gradually pour into the egg mixture in a slow, fine stream, whisking constantly to temper the eggs. Return the mixture to the saucepan and bring to a gentle boil, whisking constantly, over low heat. Continue gently boiling and whisking until the curd starts to thicken. Gently boil and whisk for 2 more minutes, then remove from the heat and immediately stir in the butter. Pour the curd into a jar and let cool completely. Once cool, use immediately or keep in the fridge for up to 10 days.

Dust confectioners' sugar over the cookies with windows. Spoon and smooth some curd onto the whole cookies, then place the window cookies on top to finish.

Mandelbroyt

Twice-baked biscotti-style cookies are not exclusive to Italy. Dried and sliced loaf cookies are found everywhere from the Baltic countries to Provence. Mandelbroyt — literally "almond bread" — is the Eastern European Jewish version. This is my great-grandmother's recipe and what we serve at my bakery. I'm not sure if it's a secret recipe or not, so this might get me into some trouble, but let's take the risk, shall we?

Note: The drying process in the bake means you'll never have to go without — these cookies keep forever.

YIELD: ABOUT 30 COOKIES

- 150g (1 cup) golden raisins or sultanas, soaked overnight
- 360g (3 cups) all-purpose or pastry flour
- 7g (1¾ tsp) baking powder
- 3g (½ tsp) table salt
- 3 large eggs
- 200g (1 cup) granulated sugar
- 100g (½ cup) canola or sunflower oil
- 15g (1 tbsp) fresh orange or lemon juice
- 142g (1 cup) almonds, roughly chopped

For the topping
- Cinnamon sugar
- Slivered almonds

Preheat the oven to 170°C (340°F) (preferably convection setting).

Once the raisins are plump and rehydrated, drain and pat dry on a clean dishcloth.

In a large bowl, whisk together the all-purpose or pastry flour, baking powder, and salt. Set aside.

In the bowl of a stand mixer fitted with the paddle attachment, combine the eggs and granulated sugar and beat on high until fluffy and pale, about 5 minutes. Reduce the speed to low and drizzle in the oil and juice. Continue mixing on low until incorporated, then add the flour mixture a quarter at a time. Mix on low until there are no visible bits of flour, then add the raisins and almonds and gently mix to incorporate. The batter will be loose, very sticky, and moderately fluid. Using a wet spatula to minimize sticking, pour out the batter in 3 long logs onto a parchment paper-lined baking tray, separating each log by 5cm (2 inches). Sprinkle the top of each log with cinnamon sugar and slivered almonds and bake for 35 minutes, or until nicely browned. Remove from the oven and let cool for 20 minutes.

Lower the oven temperature to 115°C (240°F).

After 20 minutes, use a serrated bread knife to slice the logs at a diagonal in 3cm (1¼ inch) intervals to make cookies. Place the cookies, cut-side up, on the same parchment paper–lined baking tray and sprinkle with more cinnamon sugar. Bake for 25 minutes, or until the cookies are dry and crisp. Let cool completely. These cookies will keep in a sealed tin for at least a month.

Franck Perrault

Over a hill of vineyards from the sandy Loire river, there's a smaller offshoot called the Layon that cuts through the shale valley and the village of Saint-Aubin-de-Luigné. The river skirts through back gardens and stone fishing bridges until, at the very end of town, it brushes past a small wood cabin whose chimney puffs smoke even in the heat of summer. The hand-built cabin, with its front porch and rocking chairs, is an unobtrusive anomaly in the French village — it's unfamiliar unless you've been to Quebec. It's a cabane-a-sucre, a sugar shack, though there's no maple syrup cooking here, just bread and pastries turning golden in Franck Perrault's enormous wood-fired oven.

Three times a week, Franck wakes up at 4am to light the fire under the oven, which is loaded with scrap wood. It takes several hours to heat the oven — it's the size of an entire room — to the 350 degrees Celsius (660 degrees Fahrenheit) he needs to bake his bread, but within twenty minutes, the fire is already hot enough to burn the hair off his forearms. The fire builds underneath the baking chamber, funneled through a heavy iron mouth and shot into the main chamber to heat the stone surfaces. He'll load three loaves at a time on a three-meter (nearly nine foot) long bread peel until the oven is full. The oven took an entire summer to build, and a year to fully dry from the construction, but it's

worth it. Even when the day is over and Franck has loaded the oven another two times, it will remain hot. Two days later, he can still roast a chicken in its residual heat.

If you don't know about Franck's fields, his project might just look like a charming bakery with an extraordinary oven. But Franck is a paysan-boulanger, a "farmer baker," and on twelve hectares (about thirty acres) of land in a neighboring village, he grows his own raw materials — he's a one-man show of farm-to-table bread and conservationism. It all started when he and his wife, Céline, found themselves living in North America more than twenty years ago. Over

and very few farms producing good flours were located in the northeast. Nowadays, that's changed, but at the time, it was something for which he would need to return to France, where he would have access to seeds, to land, and to a network of paysans to learn from. So Franck and Céline — and now their two small children — packed up and returned to the Loire Valley.

Back in France, Franck set to work learning from other farmers in the Réseau Semmence Paysannes, a group committed to exchanging information and seeds, and to the preservation of biodiversity and knowledge. Slowly, Franck began to build his project, first baking bread in a lean-to, with a small rotating wood oven resembling an oversized tin can. He had his first harvests from fields that a local organic farmer gave him to use and began to plant experimental patches, multiplying rare grains from single seed stalks.

At first, Franck's bread was all hand mixed, up to thirty-five kilos (about seventy-seven pounds) of dough at a time, and he worked overnight, firing his bread directly, without the use of refrigeration to slow its rise. Eventually he acquired an old GDR sausage mixer whose mixing arm gently mimicked that of his own, and that enormous oven was built. Though Franck was ambivalent about bringing in refrigeration, he did so and it enabled him to push the hydration of his bread — and get a few extra hours of sleep.

When Franck looks around his fournil — where the oven is in the bakery — and the weekend café he's built into the cabin, he can see how far the project has come, but he is quick to talk about the future. As a paysan-boulanger, he sees himself approaching bread primarily through agriculture rather than through the boulangerie profession, and he's often inviting bakers who are interested in his approach. Through this exchange, he learns from their different visions and skills, and everyone benefits.

the course of three years in New York, then four in Quebec — first Montreal, then the Gaspé — they developed a new conscientiousness about food. Franck will laugh and tell you it was the fear of becoming unhealthy on American fast food that pushed them towards organic food stores and farm collectives.

This was in the early two thousands, which was also a moment in the bread revolution. Good bakeries were opening and people were paying attention to raw ingredients, sourcing, and fermentation. At the time, Franck was enrolled in environmental studies at L'Université du Québec à Montréal (UQAM), when he began

building a sourdough starter in their kitchen. After experimenting with bread baking at home, he asked a local baker from their CSA if he could come work for him and, riding his bike through Montreal at 2am one morning, he got his first professional taste of bread baking. Later, when he and Céline moved out to the Gaspé Peninsula, he was baking his own bread weekly.

Around this time, Franck began to hear about and be drawn to the paysan-boulangerie concept — the integration of agriculture and bakery. But there was nothing like this in Quebec at the time. All the grains came from western Canada

Still, to look at Franck's bread, it's hard to think of him as purely a farmer. His mild loaves have arching ears and wide open crumbs. He plays with seeds, olives, and fruits, but his favorite loaves are the ones that let the work of his fields shine: flavorful wheat, metéil — the classic half-wheat-half-rye of France — and einkorn.

These days, Franck is taking another look at agriculture in an effort to head towards what he calls "agriculture de la conservation." If you look at soil holistically, to maintain beneficial bacterias, worms, and microorganisms, a

with few disruptions. He'll forgo overturning the earth, which can often damage the balance of the soil, and plant directly in the earth. "You don't need high tech to do very intensive agriculture," Franck insists. "And you don't need high tech to do high yields. The highest tech is the plants and the soil."

Already, Franck has had success. He's multiplied a handful of grain into three hectares (about seven and a half acres) of timilia, an ancient hard wheat dating back to Greek and Roman times that is now rarely found outside of Sicily. It's a good example of the strength of the

Franck's little cabin, you can again buy pula pasta and biscuits in Anjou.

Though they're serious about ecology and farming practices, Franck and Céline celebrate their community with levity. Every Saturday in their little Québecois bakery, like-minded people, neighbors, and bread enthusiasts come to Cabane à Pain to peek in on the bakery, have a coffee, and take their weekly loaf. Local farmers come to sell their produce and musicians drop in to perform. One farmer might bring thick slabs of salted butter and rounds of Camembert, while another might share a bottle of biodynamic Cabernet Franc from across the river. Children run around the edge of the Layon while their parents chat. To Franck, this is living — in all senses. It's a holistic project that encompasses all facets of life, social and scientific. He hopes for every village to have its own independent bakery and to be part of a network.

> ## " To Franck, it's a holistic project that encompasses all facets of life.

well-balanced, living soil means nutritious, living grains and thus healthier people. "Conventional agriculture," Franck says, "looks at soil like nothing more than a physical support for plants." In his new fields, the earth will be treated like a living organism — made as rich as possible

exchange between French, Italian, and Spanish paysans and seed-savers. His favorite grain, however, is his pula, another hard grain once cultivated in Anjou and Auvergne that was once part of a nineteenth century pasta and biscuit industry now long forgotten. These days, from

"Why go to Mars to look for life," he says, "when we have it here? There's so much to find under our own feet."

Franck Perrault's Pâte aux Prunes

Baker Franck Perrault likes to keep things local, and for him, Pâte aux Prunes is very local. It's a traditional plum pie from the Anjou region of France, and this is his family recipe. It makes use of regional Reine-Claude plums — Greengage plums in English — which are medium-sized and round with green skin and mild but tangy yellow flesh. The plums peak out in round lumps from the pastry for a juicy, early autumn dessert.

YIELD: 1 PIE

For the pastry
· 113g (½ cup) unsalted butter
· 75g (⅓ cup plus 1 tbsp) granulated sugar, plus more as needed
· 120g (½ cup) water
· 10g (heaping ½ tbsp) table salt
· 375g (3 cups plus 2 tbsp) all-purpose or pastry flour

For the filling
· 20 small plums (Greengage or similar)

Make your pastry

In a small saucepan, melt the butter and granulated sugar over low heat. Transfer the mixture to the bowl of a stand mixer fitted with the paddle attachment. Add the water, salt, and half of the all-purpose or pastry flour and mix on low until incorporated. Add the rest of the flour and mix on low until combined. Cover and let rest at room temperature for 1 hour.

Preheat the oven to 170°C (340°F) (preferably convection setting).

After 1 hour, remove a third of the dough. On a lightly floured work surface, use a rolling pin to roll to a 3mm (⅛ inch) thickness, and set aside.

Roll the remaining two-thirds of the dough to a 3mm (⅛ inch) thickness and fit into the base of a 30cm (12 inch) pie plate or tarte pan. Set aside.

Make your filling

Halve and pit each plum, then recombine the halves to keep the globes intact. Tightly pack the recombined plums in the pie plate or tarte pan. If the plums are quite sour, sprinkle with a few teaspoons of granulated sugar, keeping in mind plums are naturally high in sugar.

Cut a small hole in the remaining rolled dough to create a steam vent, then lay it on top of the plums to completely cover. Neatly trim the edges. Bake for about 40 minutes, or until the plums are bubbling through the hole. Dip a small pastry brush in the hole and spread the sweet plum juice across the crust for shine and flavor. Bake for a few more minutes, then serve hot, cold, or anything in between.

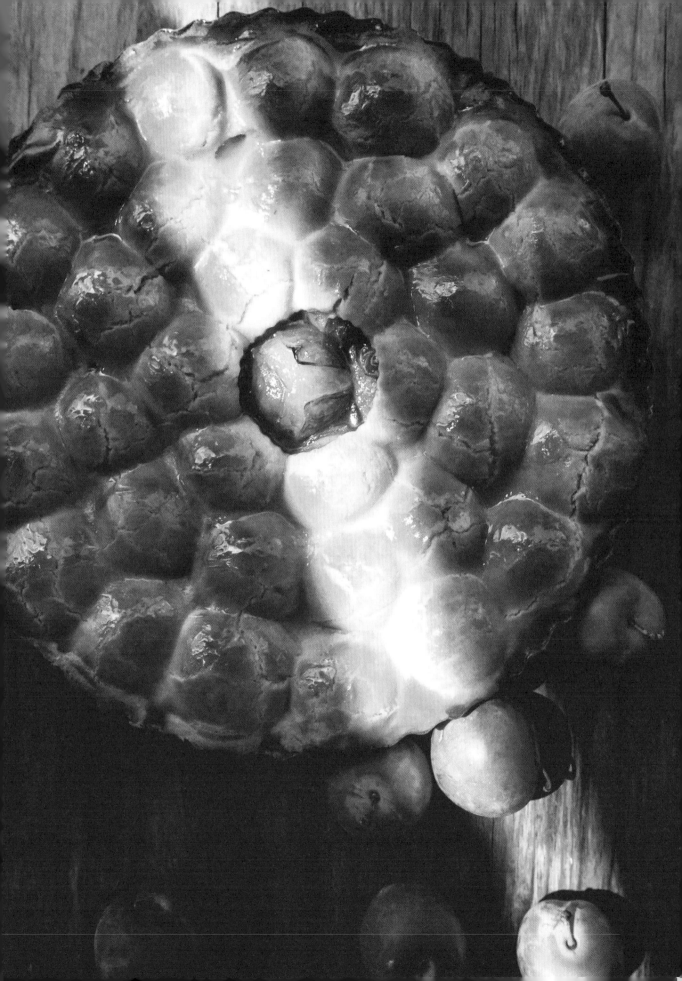

CHAPTER 5

Jams, Fillings, Toppings, and Creams

Jam

Homemade jam, whether canned or refrigerated, is an easy addition to any number of tarts, pastry creams, or cookies in this book. Or heck, just slather it on the breads from Chapter 1. However you use it, here is my super general but consistently successful jam recipe. I use it for raspberries, strawberries, plums, apricots, blueberries, and gooseberries — you name it. For lower pectin fruits like cherries, add an extra squeeze of lemon to help it gel. This recipe uses only fifty percent sugar — believe it or not, that's low for jams — and lets the fruit cook down slowly to thicken. This gives it loads of flavor.

YIELD: 900G (ABOUT 3 CUPS)

· 1 kg (2 ¼ pounds) fruit, halved
· 500g (2 ½ cups) granulated sugar
· 40g (2 tbsp plus 2 tsp) fresh lemon juice (from 1 lemon), plus more as needed

Put a small saucer in the freezer and leave to chill.

In a heavy-bottomed medium saucepan, combine the fruit, granulated sugar, and lemon juice over low heat. Let cook, stirring occasionally, until the sugar is completely melted. When there are no more sugar crystals and the liquid starts to come out of the fruit, turn the heat to medium-low and let it come to a very low boil. The mixture will become quite liquid as the fruit breaks down and a layer of foam will form on top. Skim the foam as it continues to bubble, stirring as needed to prevent the jam from burning. Eventually, the foam will disappear, and the liquid will begin to thicken and reduce. The bubbles will go from small and frothy to large and bursting — watch out for any splatters.

To test the doneness of the jam, remove the cold saucer from the freezer, place a small drop of jam on it, and let cool. Once the jam is cool, push a finger through it. If your finger slides right through and the trail of your finger fills right back in with jam, it isn't ready and you should keep cooking until it is. If the jam wrinkles and resists and the trail of your finger fills in slowly, the jam is ready. Fill jars immediately and either can or refrigerate.

If you want to can your jam for shelf stability, it's not very hard! Because of jam's high sugar and acidity, it's a relatively stable preserve. To can jam, boil jars and lids, then dry them completely in a 200°C (400°F) oven. Fill jars up to 1cm (⅓ inch) below the lid, being careful to wipe away any spills around the rim, and then seal tightly. Place jars in a large pot filled with enough water to cover their lids. Bring the water to a boil, then continue boiling for 20 minutes. Carefully remove the jars from the hot water and let cool at room temperature. Store in a cool dark place until ready to use. Once opened, store jam in the fridge.

Pastry Cream

Pastry cream — or crème pâtissière — is a thick custard that's delicious eaten on its own or used to fill countless brioches, viennoiseries, and tartes. More importantly, it serves as a versatile base for many other fillings.

Note: It's especially helpful to use a high-quality heavy-bottomed saucepan for this recipe. It will help your pastry cream cook evenly without burning.

YIELD: 425G (ABOUT 1¾ CUPS)

- 1 large egg
- 12g (4 tsp) cornstarch
- 12g (4 tsp) all-purpose flour
- 50g (¼ cup) granulated sugar
- 250g (1 cup plus 2 tbsp) whole milk
- 28g (2 tbsp) unsalted butter, cubed and room temperature
- 2 tsp pure vanilla extract
- 1 tbsp fleur d'oranger (orange blossom water; optional)

VARIATIONS:

Vanilla
- Seeds from ¼ vanilla bean

Chocolate
- 75g (2¾ ounces) bittersweet or dark chocolate, finely chopped
- 50g (3 tbsp plus 1 tsp) additional whole milk

Toasted Coconut
- 60g (⅔ cup) finely grated coconut, toasted
- 50g (3 tbsp plus 1 tsp) additional whole milk

Coffee
- 50g (3 tbsp plus 1 tsp) strong coffee or espresso

Citrus
- 2 tsp freshly grated citrus peel
- plus 30g (2 tbsp) fresh citrus juice

Tahini
- 50g (3 tbsp) tahini, added at the end of cooking, at the same time as the butter

Strawberry
- 70g (¼ cup) mashed strawberries or 50g (2 tbsp plus 1 tsp) strawberry jam, added at the end of cooking, right after the butter

In a heat-proof large bowl, whisk together the egg, cornstarch, all-purpose flour, and half of the granulated sugar. Set aside.

In a medium saucepan, warm the milk and the remaining granulated sugar over low heat until steaming. Gradually pour the hot milk into the egg mixture in a slow, fine stream, whisking constantly, to temper the egg. Return the mixture to the saucepan and bring to a gentle boil, whisking constantly, over low heat. As soon as the mixture is thick and pudding-like — this happens rapidly and will be obvious — remove from the heat. Add the butter, vanilla, and fleur d'oranger, if using, and stir until the butter is melted and the pastry cream is smooth. Pour into a bowl, place plastic wrap or parchment paper directly on the surface to prevent a skin from forming, and put in the fridge to cool. When ready to use, remove from the fridge and whisk until smooth.

Variations:
There are nearly endless ways to flavor crème pâtissière. On the left are a few of my favorites. All are added to the milk before heating unless stated otherwise.

Povidla · Plum Butter

Povidla is a thick and sweet but slightly sour fruit butter made from small blue damson plums, the same plums used to make Schnapps and slivovitz. It's typical of Central European and Jewish cuisine, and since it reduces in the oven rather than on the stovetop, it doesn't require all the stirring that jam does. Use in place of poppy seed filling in the Poppy and Sweet Cheese Koláčky (p. 138) for an equally authentic pastry.

YIELD: 600G (ABOUT 2 CUPS)

· 1 kg (2 ¼ pounds) damson plums, diced
· 220g (1 cup plus 1 ½ tbsp) granulated sugar
· 2 tbsp apple cider vinegar
· ½ tsp ground cinnamon
· 3–5 tsp dark rum

Preheat the oven to 110°C (230°F).

In a heavy-bottomed large pot, combine the plums, granulated sugar, apple cider vinegar, and cinnamon over low heat. Let cook, stirring occasionally, until the sugar is completely melted and the plums begin to soften and release their juice. With an immersion blender or food processor, blend until completely smooth. Pour the mixture into a large loaf pan or casserole dish. The plum mixture must be at least 5cm (2 inches) deep, or it can quickly dry out and become fruit leather. Bake, stirring every 30 minutes to prevent a skin from forming, for 3–4 hours, or until dark, thick, and reduced by about half. Remove from the oven, stir until smooth, and pour into clean jars. Put 1 teaspoon of rum on top of the povidla in each jar to help protect it, then seal, and can as you would Jam (p. 260) or simply refrigerate until ready to use.

Lemon Curd

Citrus curds land squarely between jam and pastry cream. They can be sandwiched in cookies, spread on brioche, or poured into a tarte. They can also be made ahead and stored for up to a month in the fridge. This recipe uses lemon juice, but it can be twisted with orange, lime, or grapefruit. And you need not stick with citrus — change the flavor by adding other sour fruits like cranberries, rhubarb, or gooseberries to the citrus-sugar liquid as it cooks, then strain them out before tempering the eggs.

YIELD: 400G (ABOUT 1 ½ CUPS)

· 2 large eggs, plus 2 large egg yolks
· 120g (½ cup plus 1 ½ tbsp) granulated sugar
· 100g (⅓ cup plus 1 tbsp plus 1 tsp) fresh lemon juice
· 90g (6 ½ tbsp) unsalted butter

In a heat-proof medium bowl, whisk the eggs and egg yolks until smooth. Set aside.

In a heavy-bottomed medium saucepan, melt the granulated sugar in the lemon juice over low heat, then bring to a gentle boil. Once bubbling, pour half of the hot liquid into the eggs in a slow, fine stream, whisking constantly, to temper the eggs. Pour the tempered eggs into the saucepan with the rest of the hot liquid and bring to a gentle boil, whisking constantly, over low heat. Continue gently boiling for about 10 minutes, or until the mixture thickens and has a thin pudding-like consistency. Remove from the heat and stir in the butter. Pour the hot curd into a bowl, place plastic wrap or parchment paper directly on the surface to prevent a skin from forming, and let cool completely at room temperature. Once cool, whisk until smooth, then transfer to a sealed jar and store in the fridge for up to 1 month.

Quince Paste

Quince paste is a fantastic accompaniment to bread and cheese but also easy to work into pastry. It takes advantage of the fruit's super high pectin content, which means that when cooked, it will gel and hold its shape in a way most fruits can't. Pretty nifty. I like to add some extra peel for additional pectin and tannins — it's the tannins that turn quince from colorless to ruby red. Use this in the Quince and Melty Cheese Danishes (p. 136) or wherever your fantasy takes you.

YIELD: 750G–1KG (3–4 CUPS)

· 1 kg (2 ¼ pounds) quince
· 500g (2 ½ cups) granulated sugar
· 125g (½ cup plus 1 tsp) water
· 60g (¼ cup) fresh lemon juice
· ½ vanilla bean, sliced lengthwise
  down the middle

Peel the quince, reserving 5 large stips of the peel. Dice the flesh and put in a heavy-bottomed large saucepan. Add the granulated sugar, water, lemon juice, the halved vanilla bean, and the reserved quince peel. Bring to a gentle boil over low heat. Continue gently boiling, stirring occasionally, until the sugar melts, the fruit softens, and the fruit and liquid have darkened to deep pink or red. Stir the mixture occasionally, but be careful not to mash the quince, as that will make it harder to work with as it reduces. This process will take 45 minutes–1 ½ hours, depending on the fruit. Remove the vanilla bean and the quince peels, then pour the mixture into a food processor or blender and blend until smooth and thick like applesauce. Return to the saucepan and cook, stirring constantly, for 15 minutes, or until bubbling.

Pour the paste into a parchment paper–lined loaf pan and chill overnight in the fridge for a softer quince paste — this is my preference. For a more solid, garnet-colored paste, bake in a 90°C (190°F) oven for 2 hours, then chill in the fridge. Quince paste can be kept in the fridge in an airtight container for up to 2 months.

Note: After the final 15 minutes of cooking, you can also pour the quince paste into jars and can as you would Jam (p. 260).

Caramel

This is the basic caramel recipe used in all the recipes in this book. The Salted Caramel Mousse Tarte (p. 228) and Xavier Netry's Pain Café Caramélisé (p. 66) use this exact recipe, while the Spicy Ginger Caramel Shortbread (p. 234), and Tiny Tatins with Tarragon (p. 208) use slightly different ingredients but the same process. Caramel has a reputation for difficulty, but in my experience it isn't — as long as you use your eyes.

YIELD: 450G (ABOUT 2 CUPS)

· 200g (1 cup) granulated sugar
· 110g (⅓ cup plus 2 tbsp cup) water
· 50g (3 ½ tbsp) unsalted butter
· 120g (½ cup plus ½ tbsp) heavy
  whipping cream
· 1 tsp pure vanilla extract
· ½ tsp fleur de sel

In a heavy-bottomed medium saucepan, melt the granulated sugar and water over low heat, stirring occasionally, until no more sugar granules are visible. Let come to a gentle boil, then continue gently boiling for 3 minutes. Add the butter and let melt, stirring to incorporate, then stop stirring and let come to a boil. Continue boiling, without stirring, for a few minutes, or until the light yellow syrup darkens to a medium honey color. Remove from the heat and immediately add the heavy whipping cream, vanilla, and salt. It will splutter and bubble, but just keep stirring until smooth, then set aside to cool and thicken. Once the caramel has cooled for about 10 minutes, it will have a thick but still very fluid consistency. Give it a rapid whisk by hand, then pour into a jar and seal. Caramel can be refrigerated for up to 2 weeks.

Poppy Seed Filling

Thick poppy seed filling is an easy addition to filled doughnuts, hamantashen, enriched doughs, viennoiseries, or rugelach for a nutty, distinctly melt-in-your-mouth flavor. For a very traditional use of poppy seed filling, make the Poppy and Sweet Cheese Koláčky (p. 138).

Note: This filling can be made ahead and kept in the fridge for up to two weeks or frozen for up to two months.

Depending on where you live, ground poppy seeds can be hard to find. If so, use a coffee mill or food processor to grind whole poppy seeds into a rough powder.

YIELD: 450G (ABOUT 2 CUPS)

· 150g (1 ½ cups) ground poppy seeds
· 75g (⅓ cup plus 1 tbsp) granulated sugar
· 210g (¾ cup plus 3 tbsp) whole milk
· 2 tsp unsalted butter
· ½ lemon, juiced
· 2 tbsp honey

In a thick-bottomed medium saucepan, bring the ground poppy seeds, granulated sugar, milk, butter, and lemon juice to a gentle boil over medium heat. Reduce the heat to low and simmer until thickened. Remove from the heat, stir in the honey, and let cool completely before using.

Sweet Cheese Filling

This stuff is so, so good and an absolute staple of Central and Eastern European baking. Maybe the best way to describe it is a baked cheesecake filling. Here I use cream cheese, but you can also use high fat quark, tvaroh (tvarog), or ricotta.

YIELD: 350G (ABOUT 1 ½ CUPS)

· 300g (1 ⅓ cups) cream cheese (or quark or tvaroh)
· 16g (2 tbsp) all-purpose flour
· 16g (2 tbsp plus 2 ½ tsp tsp) confectioners' sugar
· 2 tsp pure vanilla extract
· 1 large egg yolk
· Zest of ¼ orange (optional)

In a medium bowl, combine the cream cheese, all-purpose flour, confectioners' sugar, vanilla, egg yolk, and orange zest, if using, and whisk until smooth. Use immediately or cover airtight and refrigerate for up to 3 days.

Marzipan

Marzipan can be expensive to buy, but easy as anything to make at home. Add to any number of pastries, cookies, or tartes for a layer of sweet, almond flavor. It can also be thinned out with milk and used as a filling for Semla (p. 152).

Note: The recipe calls for a stand mixer, but you can also use a food processor or a wooden spoon.

YIELD: 235G (ABOUT 1 CUP)

· 100g (1 cup plus 3 tbsp) ground almonds
· 100g (¾ cup plus 2 tbsp) confectioners' sugar
· 1 large egg white

In a stand mixer fitted with the paddle attachment, beat the ground almonds, confectioners' sugar, and egg white on medium-high until a thick paste forms, about 2 minutes. Wrap airtight and store in the fridge until ready to use or for up to 2 weeks. Let come to room temperature before molding or rolling.

Simple Syrup

Keep simple syrup on hand and brush it anywhere you need some extra shine or sweetness. Some people use a 1:1 ratio for simple syrup, but I prefer it a little more honey-like, so I increase the sugar in my mixture.

YIELD: 225G (ABOUT 1 CUP)

· 150g (¾ cup) granulated sugar
· 100g (⅓ cup plus 1 tbsp plus 2 tsp) water

In a small saucepan, melt the sugar in the water over low heat. Increase the heat to medium-high and bring to a boil. Continue boiling for about 3 minutes. Let cool, then store in the fridge in an airtight container for up to 1 month.

Streusel

There are very few recipes in this book that would say "no" to a shower of streusel. It's a simple crumble topping that can be baked on any pastry, but it's especially good on those with fruit.

Note: Streusel has to be baked along with your pastry — it shouldn't be eaten raw.

YIELD: 200G (ABOUT 1 CUP)

· 50g (3 ½ tbsp) unsalted butter, cubed and cold
· 50g (¼ cup) granulated sugar
· 100g (¾ cup plus 1 tbsp) all-purpose flour
· ¼ tsp ground cinnamon (optional)

In a small bowl, rub the butter, granulated sugar, all-purpose flour, and cinnamon, if using, between your thumbs and forefingers until it has an even, crumbly texture. Sprinkle onto any pastry after proofing and before baking.

Italian Meringue

Italian meringue is the glossiest and most stable of all meringues, owing to the incorporation of hot sugar syrup. The only trick to making it is a bit of multitasking, but if you read the recipe all the way through and set up your ingredients before you start, it's easier than you might think. Throw it on top of any tarte or dessert to add drama and texture.

Note: It's important to not overbeat the egg whites before you start incorporating the syrup — you want them just past the frothy stage when you start adding the syrup.

YIELD: 250G (ABOUT 6 CUPS)

· 2 large egg whites
· 1 tsp fresh lemon juice
· 100g (½ cup) granulated sugar
· 60g (¼ cup) water

Put the egg whites and lemon juice in the bowl of a stand mixer fitted with the whisk attachment.

In a small saucepan, bring the granulated sugar and water to a gentle boil over medium-low heat. As soon as the mixture starts bubbling, immediately turn the mixer to high to begin whipping the egg whites. Once the egg whites reach soft peaks — just past the frothy stage — slowly drizzle in the hot syrup. Once all the syrup is incorporated, continue whipping until the meringue is stiff and glossy.

Almond Cream and Frangipane

Time to share a secret. The Tart Berry Frangipane Tarte (p. 224) isn't really a frangipane tarte. It's an almond cream tarte. Almond cream is a component of frangipane, but it tends to bake up with a bit more chew and has crispier edges, making it perfect for topping almond croissants or the Twice-Baked Almond Pain Perdu (p. 134). Meanwhile, frangipane — real frangipane — combines almond cream and Pastry Cream (p. 262). It has a bit more stability and holds up better in pastry. Spread in or on any laminated snails, yeasted buns, or fruit tartes you can dream up.

Note: Make these creams with different powdered nuts to create very different flavors. Try walnuts and hazelnuts for an effect more common in Central Europe, or pistachios for all-out decadence.

YIELD: 400G (ABOUT 2 CUPS)

For the almond cream
· 100g (7 tbsp) unsalted butter, room temperature
· 100g (½ cup) granulated sugar
· 100g (1 cup plus 3 tbsp) almond meal
· 2 large eggs, room temperature
· 1 tbsp rum
· 1 tsp pure vanilla extract

In the bowl of a stand mixer fitted with the paddle attachment, beat the butter and granulated sugar on high until fluffy. Reduce the speed to low, add the almond meal, and beat until incorporated. Add the eggs, 1 at a time, followed by the rum and vanilla, and beat until combined. Use immediately or store in an airtight container in the fridge for up to 1 week. If refrigerating, when ready to use, beat in a stand mixer on medium until smooth and spreadable.

YIELD: 667G (ABOUT 3 CUPS)

For the frangipane
· Almond Cream (see above)
· 267g (1 cup plus 2 tbsp) Pastry Cream

In a medium bowl, combine the Almond Cream and Pastry Cream and whisk until smooth. Use immediately or store in an airtight container in the fridge for up to 1 week. If refrigerating, when ready to use, beat in a stand mixer on medium until smooth and spreadable.

Recipes & Ingredients

Methods & Techniques

Page numbers in *italics* indicate illustrations.

For Nana

Acknowledgements

This book wouldn't have come together but for these wonderful people:

Meike Peters, thank you for telling me I had a book to write and then summarily putting all the pieces in motion. A true friend and a true force.

Marlene Melchior, for drinking a bottle of wine and proofreading my proposal, in that order. And thank you for letting me destroy your kitchen in the middle of a pandemic. Your patience is extraordinary.

Holly LaDue, for believing in the project and doggedly growing the seed and finding it a home.

Malgosia Minta, for jumping aboard this epic of planes, trains, and kitchens and making this book beautiful. There's no one with whom I'd rather crash a FIAT in Frosinone.

Franck Perrault, Alessandro Mancini, Xavier Netry, and Julie Bouland — for being the most brilliant folks to ever let me put my hands in their dough.

Michel Darcq, Brian Desgrippes, and Nathan Appelshaeuser of the Lycée professionnel Gustave Eiffel in Reims, for taking a chance on a random American in your incredible and forward-thinking boulangerie program. And thank you to Évelyne Decourt for the introduction!

Luis Filipe Dinis Campos, for always having the time to advise on a temperature or ingredient, all the way from Korea.

Julie Kiefer and Prestel, for taking this on, no matter how big the vision got!

Lauren Salkeld, for your exacting eye, which is a genius unto itself!

Sam A. Harris, for jumping in and taking beautiful photos when the U.K. closed its borders!

Huw Nesbitt, for your views, your edits, and your confidence!

Emily Fine, my very precise mom, for triple-checking my conversions.

Katie Parla, for coming to Frosinone to translate!

Hampus Melin, Emil Goldschmidt, and Sasha Lurje, for advising on recipes Swedish, Danish, Latvian, and otherwise.

Alice Mitev Zuza, Emily Tetz, Tucaiana Lobato, Catherine Geagan, and Jorge Dillas for baking beautifully at Fine Bagels — this book would have been impossible to make without all of you.

And Roman, how did you put up with this, you darling?

© Prestel Verlag, Munich · London · New York, 2022
A member of Penguin Random House Verlagsgruppe GmbH
Neumarkter Strasse 28 · 81673 Munich

Text © Laurel Kratochvila
Photography © Małgosia Minta; except: p. 78 © Monika Walecka; pp. 196–199 © Sam Harris

Library of Congress Control Number is available; a CIP catalogue record for this book is available from the British Library.

In respect to links in the book, the Publisher expressly notes that no illegal content was discernible on the linked sites at the time the links were created. The Publisher has no influence at all over the current and future design, content or authorship of the linked sites. For this reason the Publisher expressly disassociates itself from all content on linked sites that has been altered since the link was created and assumes no liability for such content.

Editorial direction: Julie Kiefer
Copyediting: Lauren Salkeld
Design and layout: Sabine Loos
Production management: Andrea Cobré
Separations: Schnieber Graphik GmbH, Munich
Printing and binding: DZS Grafik d.o.o.

MIX
Paper from responsible sources
FSC® C106600
www.fsc.org

Penguin Random House Verlagsgruppe FSC® N001967

Climate neutral
Print product
ClimatePartner.com/14044-1912-1001

Printed in Slovenia

ISBN 978-3-7913-8839-7

www.prestel.com